P9-BXZ-206

A FUTURE
FOR
TRUTH

A FUTURE
FOR
TRUTH

Evangelical Theology
in a Postmodern World

Henry H. Knight III

ABINGDON PRESS
Nashville

A FUTURE FOR TRUTH:
EVANGELICAL THEOLOGY IN A POSTMODERN WORLD

Copyright © 1997 by Abingdon Press

All rights reserved.

No part of this work may be reproduced or transmitted in any form or by any means, electronic or mechanical, including photocopying and recording, or by any information storage or retrieval system, except as may be expressly permitted by the 1976 Copyright Act or in writing from the publisher. Requests for permission should be addressed in writing to Abingdon Press, 201 Eighth Avenue South, P. O. Box 801, Nashville, TN 37202, U.S.A.

This book is printed on acid-free, recycled paper.

Library of Congress Cataloging-in-Publication Data

Knight, Henry H. III.
  A future for truth : evangelical theology in a postmodern world / Henry H. Knight, III.
        p.   cm.
  Includes bibliographical references.
  ISBN 0-687-00960X (alk. paper)
  1.   2.   I. Title.
  1997

                                                                    CIP

Unless otherwise noted, all scripture quotations are from The New Revised Standard Version Bible, copyright © 1989 by the Division of Christian Education of the National Council of the Churches of Christ in the USA. Used by permission.

96 97 98 99 00 01 02 03 04 05 06 — 10 9 8 7 6 5 4 3 2 1

MANUFACTURED IN THE UNITED STATES OF AMERICA

To Don E. Saliers

teacher, colleague, and friend

CONTENTS

Contents

Part IV
Redemption and the Character of God

ACKNOWLEDGMENTS

Some of the material in this book was originally presented in my courses and seminars in contemporary evangelical theology at both Candler and Saint Paul Schools of Theology. I am grateful for the many conversations with students which have helped me think through the issues and clarify my own position.

I am especially indebted to friends and colleagues who consented to read portions of the manuscript and offer their observations and advice. Among these were Philip E. Thompson, Curtis G. Lindquist, and Charles H. Twombly, who shared their expertise in historical and systematic theology, and Kathryn Simmons Bray, Bruce Bray, and Mike Eighmy, three United Methodist pastors whose practice of ministry is guided by perceptive theological reflection. Two of my colleagues at Saint Paul, Derrel H. Watkins and Tex Sample, graciously and gladly read much of the manuscript and made helpful comments. I greatly appreciate the continued encouragement and insightful observations of Clark H. Pinnock and Steven J. Land as they made their way through complete drafts. I owe special thanks to Don E. Saliers who read the entire manuscript and offered valuable suggestions which manifestly improved the final text. My many conversations over the years with Don Saliers and Steve Land lie behind much of what appears on these pages.

A sabbatical leave granted by the Board of Trustees of Saint Paul School of Theology enabled me to complete this manuscript. I am deeply grateful for their support. Finally, thanks are due to my wife Eloise, not only for typing the manuscript, but for her loving and patient support throughout this entire project.

INTRODUCTION

Truth has fallen on hard times. For most of Western intellectual history, it was assumed there was something called "truth" that was universal—that is, whatever was true was so for all times and places—and could be discovered and understood. The exact nature of this truth was described in many ways, but its existence was never in doubt.

The modern world had its own version. Universal truth would be discovered through human reason; nothing so particular as divine revelation through Israel or in Jesus Christ would be allowed to count unless verified by reason. And so the modern conflict between an increasingly secular philosophy and traditional revealed religion was provoked, mirrored by controversies within Christianity itself by competing "liberal" and "conservative" theologies.

Now, however, the very idea of universal truth has been called into question. The postmodern world which is emerging honors context and particularity, but is suspicious of any claim that purports to be universal. In colloquial terms, while something may be true for you, it may not true for me; to claim something is true for all is at best presumptuous, at worst oppressive.

The good news for Christianity is that the particularity of its claims are no longer an embarrassment. They can no longer be brought before the bar of reason to face a verdict of true or false, for there is no universal reason to make that judgement in a postmodern world. The bad news is that historic Christianity has made universal claims for its particular revelation: Jesus Christ is not just Lord and Savior of the Christian, he is Lord and Savior of the entire world. It is just such a claim that postmodernity finds problematic.

Does Christian truth have a future in this postmodern world? I believe it does and in this book hope to show why. This will not be an apologetic in the classical sense. I will not try to provide rational grounds for faith, which would not be credible in a postmodern world and was not all that effective in convincing the agnostics and atheists of modernity anyway. Rather, I want to explain how it is that Christians believe in a particular revelation that they nonetheless claim is of universal significance—to give an accounting for the hope that is in us (I Peter 3:15) to a postmodern world.

As there are different theories of truth, it is necessary to clarify how I intend to use the word. Correspondence theories of truth hold that truth claims in some fashion reflect reality, they correspond to the facts—this is our everyday, common-sense use of the term. Coherence theories define truth as that which coheres within a body of beliefs. That is, its reference is not to reality itself but to its fittingness within a system of beliefs. Pragmatic theories of truth focus on that which enables us to live or function within the world—what is "true" is what is useful or what works for us. [1]

I will draw upon all of these understandings of truth, but will be especially concerned with the first. This means I will be advancing a realist epistemology, arguing against idealism that we really can know reality external to our minds. It will, however, be a critical realism—truth claims correspond to reality, but often in an indirect or analogical manner. This is especially the case—indeed must be the case—when those claims concern God.

The theology I will present is evangelical. To use such a term requires definition, which I provide at some length in chapter one. A tradition as complex as evangelicalism cannot be described both briefly and well. Because proponents as well as opponents of evangelicalism often construe it more narrowly than it is, I hope this first chapter will be a helpful corrective.

Here, we can simply note that evangelicalism is a kind of Christianity that adheres to historic doctrines, is normally Protestant, and has an emphasis on scriptural authority, conversion and new life. It seeks to be what John Wesley calls "scriptural Christianity." Certainly it is not the only theological stance that honors historic Christianity—many other examples can be found within Eastern Orthodoxy, Roman Catholicism, and Protestantism. But it is one of the most vibrant, with a global presence that shows every sign of continued growth into the next century. My own particular brand of evangelical theology is pietist and Wesleyan—chapter one will make clear the implications of this perspective for the chapters which follow.

In chapters two and three I examine more closely modernism and postmodernism, largely in terms of intellectual traditions rather than cultural change. While the two are intertwined, it is the intellectual that enables me most directly to address the questions of truth and authority that are the concern of this book. My engagement with postmodernism will neither be dismissive nor embracing; I hope instead to listen with care to its concerns and critically examine its proposals. In the process I will identify two different strands of postmodernism, as well as indicate what I take to be the most promising way to engage it as an evangelical.

Chapter four begins my constructive proposal, and is the foundation for the remainder of the book. In it I argue that Christianity rests on the resurrection of the crucified Jesus, and that it is this particular confession of faith that undergirds and indeed enables Christians to understand their world and live faithfully within it. The discussion will show why Christians claim Jesus as a universal Savior and Lord, why this claim in itself is not and cannot be "imperialistic," and how we have come to believe this claim to be true for all.

Scripture is the authoritative and divinely inspired witness to this revelation, and is the subject of the next three chapters. In chapter five I take sides in an intraevangelical debate concerning the nature of scripture. There I describe the central issue not, as is often done, as inerrancy but whether scripture to be true must be propositional. I argue that rational propositionalism provides an inadequate account of the nature of scripture and, in chapter six, offer as an alternative a narrative approach. By way of an examination of postliberal theology I try to show how narrative, metaphor, and other nonpropositional literary forms make authoritative truth claims about God, creation, and redemption.

These two chapters revolve round the issue of reference, that is, how does the scriptural text truthfully refer to the revelatory event. Chapter seven deals with the distance between scripture and our contemporary world: how can texts produced in ancient historical and cultural contexts speak to us today with authority. There I examine scriptural metaphors and how we speak about God, the effect of biblical culture on the message of scripture, and how the gospel is contextualized today in the diverse mosaic of cultures which constitute our contemporary world. The logic of revelation and incarnation is that the universal truth claims of the gospel cannot be expressed in abstract or universal categories but are necessarily conveyed through the particularity of scripture, which is in turn embedded in particular cultural contexts. It is as the implications of the gospel are discovered in each of these contexts that it has its transforming effect.

The final chapters have as their common theme the character and agency of God in redemption. Chapter eight is concerned with what God has done in the incarnation and atonement. I argue that God's character is revealed by God's intentional action in history, and comes to its ultimate focus in the life and death of Jesus Christ. In the process two pervasive Western dualisms—those of mind and body, and time and eternity—are critiqued, especially in their modern forms, and in their place is proposed a more holistic anthropology and an interactive model of God and temporality.

This interactive approach continues in chapter nine, where the focus is on God's present redemptive activity. The mission of God today is identified both with the coming Kingdom of God and the presence of that Kingdom in Jesus Christ. Thus the criterion by which we recognize what God is doing today is the character of God revealed in Christ.

Also in that chapter there is a discussion of how God acts today, examined first by considering the relationship of grace and human freedom. Here we analyze the issues surrounding the evangelical debate over "freewill theism" as an alternative to both classical and process theism. Then we look at the possibilities and limits of divine power, arguing that modernity has placed false constraints on what God could be expected to do. But while affirming a wider possibility for divine action, including "signs and wonders," at the same time it is recognized that all that God does is ultimately in service to God's redemptive purpose and is characterized by the cross of the risen Christ.

Chapter ten considers the intention and action of the people of God in light of God's intention and action through Christ and the Spirit. The themes are forgiveness, holiness of heart and life conceived in terms of affections and other fruits of the Spirit, and empowerment for ministry. Corresponding to this very particular revelation of God in history is a distinctive community which in its life and ministry together gives evidence of being transformed into the image of God. This will mean that in whatever culture a Christian community finds itself, it will face the task of critically evaluating cultural patterns and norms while prayerfully discerning where the Spirit is leading. But it is just such a congregation which through its very life provides persuasive evidence of the truth that the crucified Jesus is the risen Savior and Lord.

Two fundamental purposes have governed the writing of *A Future for Truth*. The primary goal was to offer a constructive proposal for a postmodern evangelical theology that upholds without compromise the truth of the gospel. There will of course be those, evangelical or otherwise, who doubt I have accomplished this. If so, I hope they will nonetheless be provoked to think through the issues for themselves in a new way.

This is in many ways an integrative work, drawing from a wide range of theological insights which I have found helpful and convincing. By showing the linkages between these various ideas, along with some of my own, I hope to offer a fresh vision of revelation and redemption which is at the same time faithful to scripture and the Christian tradition. That such an integrative approach was so used by John Wesley has been a source of encouragement.

The deliberate referencing of a range of evangelical theologians in the service of my own proposal assists the secondary purpose of this book, which is to provide an entry into the thinkers and issues within evangelical theology. While such an introduction is unnecessary for some, it will be very necessary for others. Indeed, for those who are unfamiliar with evangelical theology, some of this material may be quite surprising. I hope it will at least counter some of the stereotypes which abound concerning evangelicalism. In support of this secondary goal, I have provided numerous references and occasional extended discussions in the endnotes, as well as a bibliography of selected works by a wide range of contemporary evangelical theologians.

This is a book in constructive theology. To accomplish its purpose it must necessarily consider a number of philosophical and theological issues, offering possible new insights into the gospel we have received. But I hope it is clear in the pages that follow that my motive for writing is not simply the intellectual pursuit of truth. Rather what is central is a concern to proclaim the truth of the gospel to a postmodern world, for I am convinced that whatever hope we have rests firmly and ultimately in the risen and living Jesus Christ and in the presence and power of the Holy Spirit.

Part I

The Nature of Evangelicalism

CHAPTER 1

The Evangelical Family

Evangelicalism, says William Abraham, is an "essentially contested" tradition.[1] It is common practice, he notes, to define evangelicalism by drawing "up a list of essentials or fundamentals that are the essence or heart of the tradition."[2] This approach is not so much wrong as superficial. It fails to recognize within the evangelical tradition an "intense debate and contest about how best to develop and explain its essential ingredients."[3]

The "evangelical" label encompasses a diverse if not bewildering array of constituents, from conservative Presbyterians to classic Pentecostals to traditional Anglicans to Mennonites. For some, like Donald Dayton, the term is so theologically and historically incoherent it is misleading—he has called for a "moratorium" on its use.[4]

While Abraham continues to find the term useful, he does suggest that a vibrant evangelical theology cannot simply be "evangelical"—it must draw upon a theological model rooted in one of the constituent traditions.[5] More recently, Richard Lints has made a similar case. He describes evangelicalism as a "theological patchwork quilt" in which the various constituent parts have repressed aspects distinctive to their particular traditions. Because it is precisely these deeper traditions—Lutheran, Reformed, Wesleyan, etc.—that can provide the resources for the "construction of a theological framework," Lints urges a pluralism "that could accommodate both a commitment to essentials and a recognition of the theological diversity of the movement."[6] Abraham and Lints offer prolegomena which illustrate their proposals, the former from a Wesleyan perspective and the latter from a Reformed.

Although I agree with Abraham and Lints that we are best served by theologies rooted in our respective traditions, to produce such a theology is not the purpose of this book. Rather, I am attending to the very issues which have led to the modern use of "evangelical" as a term, namely those raised by Western modernity and its postmodern offspring. It was the advent of Enlightenment modernity in the West which gave birth to liberal theology, and led to evangelicalism becoming a contrast term to identify those who resisted a liberal theological approach.

Consequently, I am attracted to Abraham's insight that evangelicals do not have a detailed theological unity but instead share a "family resemblance," providing a unity sufficient "to identify a single evangelical tradition within the Christian tradition as a whole."[7] Likewise, Robert Johnston finds the family metaphor helpful because it implies category boundaries or essential elements which are not rigidly defined but remain fluid or open-ended.[8] If we can conceive of evangelicalism as something like a family, then we can ask what holds this family together and what accounts for its diversity.

Unity in the Evangelical Family

Before presenting my own account of evangelical unity and diversity, it will be helpful to examine several alternative descriptions, if only to begin to indicate more specifically what is meant by the term "evangelical." As Abraham noted, the most common way of defining evangelicalism is by way of a set of beliefs. Alister McGrath, for example, offers a list of "six fundamental convictions":

(1) The supreme authority of Scripture as a source of knowledge of God and a guide to Christian living.
(2) The majesty of Jesus Christ, both as incarnate God and Lord and as the Savior of sinful humanity.
(3) The lordship of the Holy Spirit.
(4) The need for personal conversion.
(5) The priority of evangelism for both individual Christians and the church as a whole.
(6) The importance of Christian community for spiritual nourishment, fellowship and growth.[9]

While helpful, the limitation of such lists is that they tend to be formal statements abstracted from a particular theological tradition. Thus, to know more exactly the content of these evangelical beliefs, one would have to root them in a Reformed or Wesleyan or Anabaptist or similar tradition. Furthermore, they would have to be correlated with other doctrines omitted from these lists—theological anthropology, or eschatology, or a more exact description of God's gracious activity.

The reason they are common emphases, and one factor in the "family resemblance" among evangelicals, is that other more liberal theologies seek to relativize or even deny many of these points. Evangelical theologians see them as absolutely central to Christianity and seek to affirm and communicate these beliefs to the contemporary world.

Stanley Grenz offers an alternative means of describing what evangelicals have in common. Rather than a set of doctrinal distinctives, he argues that "'evangelical' refers first of all to a specific vision of what it means to be Christian," a "distinctive spirituality."[10] It is an attempt to hold in tension piety and activity, the inward and the outward.[11] Central to this spirituality is the desire for scripture to "come alive in personal and communal life." Evangelicals are a "Bible-centered people," convinced that scripture contains within it answers for daily living.[12] Additionally, evangelicals seek a vibrant, personal faith in which Christ is recognized as lord of all areas of life. Indeed, the living Christ is seen as an active participant in the life of each Christian. This sense of the reality of Christ is linked with an emphasis on shared prayer, daily personal devotions, fellowship as an experienced reality, and joyful praise to God through hymns and testimony.[13]

But foundational to all of this is the understanding of being a Christian "in terms of a life narrative." The focus of the evangelical vision is on the sharing of stories. While the stories differ in detail, there is nonetheless a shared format and shared motifs:

> Central to each of our stories is a testimony to the reality of a personal, life-changing transformation. Hence we speak of "sin" and "grace," "alienation" and "reconciliation," "helplessness" and "divine power," "having been lost" but "now being saved." And each story narrates a dividing line between an old and a new life, a line the narrator crossed by means of a religious experience through which he or she encountered the God of the Bible revealed in Jesus of Nazareth.[14]

Whether through a sudden conversion or by way of a longer process, evangelicals testify to a common experience in which the living God is encountered and their lives changed.[15]

Although it must be tested throughout the evangelical family, I suspect most evangelicals will see themselves in Grenz's depiction, be they an Episcopalian at Sunday worship or a participant in a Holiness camp meeting. It certainly is congruent with central concerns in this book.

Diversity Within the Evangelical Family

With this initial look at the beliefs and practices typical of most evangelicals, we can turn to the issue of diversity. Of course, one way of categorizing evangelicals has already been discussed, that is, in terms of historic traditions. Because evangelicals do tend to be conservative in matters theological, they naturally tend to take their own tradition seriously, whether it be Reformed or Wesleyan, Baptist or Pentecostal. As we have seen, this is a strength rather than a weakness.

There have been a range of other typologies proposed, however, which explain the diversity using other criteria. One reason for these typologies has to do with three different historic meanings of the word "evangelical" itself.[16]

The first use is rooted in the Protestant Reformation and is virtually synonymous with "protestant;" it has been used as such on the continent, most especially by Lutherans. In this sense an evangelical is someone who adheres to that which all Protestants hold in common: salvation by grace through faith alone, Christ alone as Savior and Lord, and the unique authority of scripture. The second use centered around the evangelical awakenings of the eighteenth and nineteenth centuries. There the emphasis was on personal conversion (or the "new birth"), holiness of heart and life, personal and mass evangelism, and, in many cases, social reform. The third use refers to a consciously post-fundamentalist movement which emerged in the 1940's, especially in America. Sometimes called "neo-evangelicalism," its proponents disavowed fundamentalist separatism and militancy and called for a renewed intellectual engagement with science and culture and a vigorous, biblically based social concern.

To see the effect of these different usages, we can examine three proposed typologies of evangelicalism. This will not only provide an initial sense of the diversity within the movement, but will demonstrate that whichever of these three definitions one considers primary affects one's construal of evangelicalism.

An early influential typology advanced by Richard Quebedeaux divides evangelicals into five categories: Closed Fundamentalists, Open Fundamentalists, Establishment Evangelicals, New Evangelicals, and Charismatics (which overlaps the evangelical categories).[17] Although Quebedeaux intends to encompass at least the dimensions of the second use of the term, he is clearly looking at evangelicalism through the lens of the third, postfundamentalist use. However, the question of just how fundamentalist you are or how much you have distanced yourself from fundamentalism may not be the most illuminating for the larger evangelical family.

More recently, Gabriel Fackre has proposed a typology consciously based on the second (awakening) meaning of the term, but not so broad as the first; implicitly, it includes the third (postfundamentalist) usage within it. He too has five categories:

(1) Fundamentalist evangelicals: militant, separatist, committed to strict inerrancy of scripture.

(2) Old evangelicals: emphasize a "life of personal piety," a "conversion experience," evangelism, and "disciplined biblical study."

(3) New evangelicals: add to the convictions of old evangelicals "an accent on the rational defense of the faith and seek to relate piety more aggressively to social issues." Both old and new evangelicals may also adhere to biblical inerrancy, but define it more broadly (e.g., authorial intent).

(4) Justice and peace evangelicals: often Anabaptist or high Calvinist (I would add Wesleyan) in origin, they mount a more radical social critique.

(5) Charismatic evangelicals: emphasize the baptism of the Holy Spirit, the gift of tongues, and "a fervent life of prayer, praise, and personal testimony."[18]

Any given individual or group may be found in more than one of these categories.

Now this is a more helpful typology, taking account of a number of distinctively evangelical characteristics which cross denominational traditions. As we shall see, there was perhaps more aggressive social concern among "old evangelicals" than is indicated here, and the idea of "new evangelicals" adding a rational component to the "old" is unsatisfactory. But aside from these historical qualifications, it succeeds as a descriptive account.

A recent typology by Donald Bloesch is more inclusive still, and implicitly draws upon all three of the historic uses of the term "evangelical." His seven categories include (1) Fundamentalists; (2) Confessional orthodoxy, who emphasize "strict adherence to the creeds and confessions of the Reformation;" (3) Evangelical Pietists, including the Holiness movement; (4) Neo-evangelicals, combining "a high view of scriptural authority with the willingness to accept the principle of

historical criticism;" (5) Charismatic evangelicals, including Pentecostals; (6) Neoorthodoxy; and (7) Catholic evangelicalism.[19]

Bloesch's typology expands the boundaries of evangelicalism in
several ways. Confessional orthodoxy includes extremely conservative
groups, some of which (like Missouri Synod Lutherans) are leery of the
evangelical label with its revivalist/conversionist connotations. Even
more striking in his inclusion of Neo-orthodoxy, which despite its
attempt to faithfully reappropriate Reformation theology is not usually
placed under the evangelical label. Catholic evangelicals, who seek to
root evangelicalism in the larger catholic Christian tradition, combines
recognized evangelicals like Bloesch himself with theologians not normally included, like Carl Braaten and Robert Jensen.[20]

Taken together, Fackre and Bloesch provide a comprehensive picture of the diversity within evangelicalism. In spite of their usefulness,
however, these typologies do not show the reasons for such diversity.
Drawing on the three historic uses of the term "evangelical," I will try
to account for this diversity through recounting some of that family
history.

The purpose of this historical sketch is more than descriptive. I hope
to identity a pervasive tension in evangelicalism which has marked it
from after the Protestant Reformation to the present day, and has
significance for evangelical theology in a postmodern world. In the
process, I will indicate my own theological approach within the evangelical family.

Tensions Within the Evangelical Family

"Evangelicalism" as Reformation Protestantism

The roots of modern evangelicalism lie in the theology of the
Protestant Reformation of the sixteenth century, often summarized as
four "alones": grace alone, faith alone, scripture alone, Christ alone.
These emphases constitute something like a platform for the reformation of the church: the "alone" in each case implies the rejection of a
coordinate term which the Roman Catholic church held as equal or
necessary.

"Grace alone" and "faith alone" means salvation is solely through
Jesus Christ's death and resurrection. Faith is received as a gift through
the Holy Spirit, and salvation does not in any way depend on human
works or merit. Justification is by faith alone.

"Scripture alone" emphasizes the unique authority of scripture, which was at one and the same time an account of God's creative and redemptive activity in history and a means through which God speaks the living word to persons today. This countered the Roman Catholic tendency to place tradition and the teaching of the church on the same level of authority as scripture.

By "Christ alone" the Reformers meant there were no other mediators between us and God than Jesus Christ. The grace of Christ is available to all through the Holy Spirit and the preaching of the word, and draws persons into a direct personal relation with Christ. Thus priests and saints as intercessors were unnecessary, and the hierarchical distinctions between spiritual and lay Christians were abolished. There was instead a priesthood of all believers.

For all their differences, the leaders of the Reformation were in general agreement on these beliefs.[21] Their great goal—itself a recuring theme in evangelicalism—was to reform the church. With few exceptions, these Protestant distinctives constitute one layer of the theological inheritance of contemporary evangelicalism.[22]

Scholasticism and Pietism

The theological fragmentation of the Reformation was followed by religious conflict on the European continent and in Great Britain, as Roman Catholic, Lutheran, and Reformed struggled for control of state churches. Although it soon involved political and economic concerns, the Thirty Years War which severely devastated Europe was initially driven and in large measure sustained by religious zeal.

After the war religious conflict was carried on by intellectual rather than military means. Protestant scholasticism, or "orthodoxy," provided a rational defense of Lutheran or Calvinist doctrine and organized theologies of the Reformers into tight, logical systems. What it meant to be a Christian became increasingly to assent to a confession of faith, such as the Augsburg Confession (Lutheran) or Helvetic Confession (Reformed). Perhaps the greatest of the Calvinist scholastics was Francis Turretin, who taught in Geneva a hundred years after the death of Calvin. For Turretin, scripture itself was composed of inerrant propositions which, when rationally arranged, provided a doctrinal system that reflected eternal truth.[23] Turretin was a major influence on some segments of American evangelicalism in the nineteenth century.

The Pietist movement emerged as a strong protest against the rational orthodoxy and nominal religion of the state churches. Beginning within Lutheranism, pietists like Philip Jacob Spener and his disciple, August Hermann Francke, argued that Christianity is more a matter of the heart and life than merely assenting to doctrinal truth.

Spener's *Pia Desideria* (1675) became a manifesto of pietist concerns. Emphasizing personal piety, Spener formed small groups of laity (*collegia pietatis* or "colleges of piety") to both encourage piety in the individual and as a seedbed for reform in the larger church. Thus Spener's pietism is a continuation of the impetus to reform the church which led to the development of Protestantism a century before. To that end, Spener promoted the devotional reading of scripture by laity and the participation of all Christians in ministry. Above all, pietism understood Christianity to be a living faith in Christ which is life-changing in nature.[24]

Another significant seventeenth century movement which has impacted evangelicalism is Puritanism. Largely a Reformed reaction against the Church of England's attempt to find a *via media* between Protestant and Roman Catholic practices, it combined intellectual rigor with spiritual depth.[25] In some ways Puritanism at its best was itself a "middle way" between scholasticism and pietism; like pietism it too was motivated by a desire to reform the church.

Because evangelicalism is informed by both the scholastic and the pietist traditions, it is beset by an internal tension. Apart from simply denying one side of this tension, evangelical theologians have addressed it by one of two ways. The first is a dualism, in which each element is given its own sphere of influence. For evangelical intellectuals this often meant keeping theology as a rational enterprise sealed off from their practice of piety or personal religious experience. The second is an integrative approach, in which theology and piety, reason and experience are interrelated.

"Evangelicalism" and Evangelical Awakenings

The integrative approach was typical of the theology of the eighteenth century evangelical awakenings. Fueled by both pietism and puritanism, the awakenings were in many ways a single, interconnected, trans-Atlantic and transdenominational event. While denominational rivalry and doctrinal conflict would continue in the nineteenth century, it would gradually be displaced by a spirit of cooperation in

24

both evangelism and "benevolent" causes; the roots of that cooperation lay in the eighteenth century awakenings and seventeenth century pietism.

As with the Protestant Reformation, the evangelical awakenings included a diversity of theologies and personalities. Among these were Count Nicolas von Zinzendorf in Germany (whose Moravian Bretheren influenced revival in England and America as well), John and Charles Wesley in England, Howell Harris in Wales, and George Whitefield and Jonathan Edwards in America.[26] What all held in common was an understanding of conversion as a distinct experience of faith, called the "new birth," and a passion for evangelism. Many also exhibited a growing social concern and involvement, emulating their pietist predecessors.[27] The Wesley brothers in particular emphasized sanctification, or holiness of heart and life, which was to become a more widespread evangelical theme. Central to the awakenings was a desire to reform the church in all its denominational variety. All of these concerns had lasting impact on contemporary evangelicalism.

Wesley and Edwards were the chief theologians of the evangelical awakening.[28] Edwards used his considerable theological and philosophical skills to defend the Great Awakening in America from its rationalist critics, denying their sharp dualism between reason and experience. At the same time, he criticized enthusiastic tendencies within the awakening itself. Wesley endorses Edwards' view on this (though not his Calvinism), opposing both rationalism and enthusiasm.[29] Both argued that Christian reasoning presupposes and rests upon faith as a spiritual sense, and the Christian life itself consists of religious affections which are experiential and rational at the same time. These are matters to be discussed in some detail in chapters four and ten.

The Second Great Awakening was an outgrowth of the first. It featured a revivalism that emphasized human free will far more than would be approved by Calvinist Edwards or even Arminian Wesley,[30] seeing that freedom more as a result of nature than grace. Wesley's theme of holiness became a central concern of many across denominational lines. As developed by Methodist Phoebe Palmer and revivalist Charles Finney, the call for holiness became centered on a human act of consecration which elicited an instantaneous, divinely given entire sanctification subsequent to conversion. A more Calvinistic Keswick movement understood holiness as given in conversion on the basis of the cross, but gradually appropriated throughout the Christian life.[31]

The Holiness movement spawned notable efforts toward radical social reform in the early nineteenth century. Exploring the implications of the call to holiness for society, Finney and other leaders of the awakening worked avidly for the abolition of slavery, women's rights, and the improvement of conditions among urban poor.[32]

Of enormous significance to the character and history of Christianity in America is the impact of the awakening upon African-Americans—and their impact upon Christianity. In addition to understanding the gospel from a more African than European perspective, it was being proclaimed and appropriated in a context of enormous suffering and injustice. Here the evangelical awakening was reconfigured into a distinctive spirituality and created opportunities for black leadership and organization elsewhere unavailable in American society.[33]

Reformed Theology at Princeton and Amsterdam

Strongly opposed to revivalism, the Holiness movement, and much of its social reform agenda were the conservative Presbyterians at Princeton. The Princeton theology of the nineteenth century was in many ways an Americanized, post-Enlightenment version of the Reformed scholasticism of Turretin. It countered the experiential Arminianism of the awakening with highly rational and deeply orthodox Calvinism.[34]

It was the theologians of Old Princeton—especially Charles Hodge and Benjamin Warfield—who developed the modern doctrine of the inerrancy of scripture which has become such a controverted issue in contemporary evangelicalism. Buttressed by a commitment to Scottish common-sense philosophy, the Bible was understood to be a book of divinely given facts or propositions, accessible to human reason and understandable to any unbiased reader. The Princeton theologians thus believed scripture to be an accurate representation of external reality, unaffected by the point of view of the authors.[35] Hodge summarizes his method this way:

> If natural science be concerned with facts and laws of nature, theology is concerned with the facts and principles of the Bible. If the object of one be to arrange and systematize the facts of the external world, and to ascertain the laws by which they are determined; the object of the other is to systematize the facts of the Bible, and to ascertain the principles or general truths which these facts involve.[36]

This is theological method modeled on the scientific method of Francis Bacon.

In contrast to the integrative approach of Edwards and Wesley, Hodge and Warfield saw theology as an objective, rational endeavor which must be protected from the more subjective influence of piety or experience. It was not that they lacked piety themselves,[37] rather they feared that Christianity would be seen as a purely subjective enterprise, not grounded in factual truth. The Enlightenment criteria for what counted as "true" pushed them to a rational apologetic which emphasized historical and scientific evidences for the truth of Christianity.

Evangelicals in Europe provided an alternative to the approach at Princeton. Most significant was the Dutch Calvinism of Abraham Kuyper and Herman Bavinck.[38] While they were respected by Warfield and shared Old Princeton's opposition to revivalism (in their case as much due to its individualism as to its conversionism), the Amsterdam theologians had a rather different theology of scripture.

For Kuyper and Bavinck, the authority of scripture is upheld by an internal testimony of the Holy Spirit rather than a reasoned assessment of factual evidence. Unlike the theologians at Princeton, they denied a common human rational capacity. Rather, like Edwards, they believed the human capacity to reason to be fallen and incapable of discerning truth apart from faith, which was a gift of the Holy Spirit. This meant that instead of reason preparing the way for faith (as in the Princeton theology) faith became the ground of reason. Thus grounded, the Christian could then begin to envision all spheres of society—science, culture, and government—under the Lordship of Christ.

The Dutch theology, with its recognition of multiple coherent worldviews and a more flexible approach to scripture was in many ways positioned far better than any of the nineteenth century American evangelical traditions to engage modernity. Common sense realism and Baconian scientific method, whose assumptions had been shared by virtually everyone from Hodge to Finney, were challenged by Kantian idealism and Darwinian science. The new nineteenth century awareness of historical and cultural change was especially troubling, leading as it did to the critical historical method of interpreting scripture.

The Road to Fundamentalism

The defection of intellectuals to more secular ways of thinking, the division of Protestantism into liberal and conservative wings (the former more accommodating to the newer ideas than the latter), and the growth of a large Roman Catholic presence all had the effect of disestablishing evangelical Protestantism as a dominant cultural and intellectual force. The earlier optimism which suffused most wings of evangelicalism was replaced by a more pessimistic attitude toward the future in America.

We can see this most dramatically in the shift in the evangelical commitment to radical social reform. Revivalists in the latter part of the nineteenth century left the social gospel to the liberals, focusing instead on the conversion of individuals. This new attitude—what David Moberg has called the "Great Reversal"[39]—is illustrated well by this pair of quotes selected by Donald Dayton.[40] The first is from Charles Finney:

> Now the great business of the church is to reform the world—to put away every kind of sin. The Church of Christ was originally organized to be a body of reformers. . . . The Christian church was designed to make aggressive movements in every direction . . . to reform individuals, communities, and governments, and never rest until the Kingdom and the greatness of the Kingdom under the whole heaven shall be given to the people of the the the saints of the most high God—until every form of iniquity shall be driven from the face of the earth.[41]

The second, from revivalist D. L. Moody, shows the contrasting viewpoint:

> I look upon this world as a wrecked vessel. God has given me a life-boat, and said to me, 'Moody, save all you can.' God will come in judgement and burn up this world, but the children of God don't belong to this world; they are in it, but not of it, like a ship in the water. The world is getting darker and darker; its ruin is coming nearer and nearer; if you have any friends on this wreck unsaved you had better lose no time in getting them off. . . . No, grace is not a failure, but man is. . . . Man has been a failure everywhere, when he has had his own way and been left to himself. Christ will save his church, but he will save them finally by taking them out of the world.[42]

Even so, it would be wrong to say evangelicals had abandoned social concern. Participants in the Holiness movement were most especially involved in a range of activities on behalf of the poor. What they had largely abandoned were efforts toward political and social change; this may partly be due to their own increasing marginalization from the economic, intellectual, and political centers of power.

This cultural pessimism is also manifested in the popularity of dispensational eschatology. Prior to the Civil War, evangelicals of all types, from Princeton to the Holiness movement, were postmillennial, that is, they believed Christ's thousand year reign on earth predicted in the Book of Revelation would occur through the church, to be followed by Christ's own personal return to earth. Historic premillennialism argued the opposite: Christ would suddenly return at an undetermined time and then personally reign on earth for a thousand years.[43]

Dispensationalism was premillennialism with a difference. Developed by John Nelson Darby in England in midcentury, dispensationalism argued all of history, from creation to eschaton, can be divided into six or seven dispensations, each characterized by a distinctive manner of God's relationship with humanity. Befitting its strict Calvinist origins, dispensationalism saw all history, from creation to eschaton, as predetermined. It believed Old Testament prophecies concerning Israel are not symbolically fulfilled in the church but await a literal fulfillment in history. The founding of the church interrupted the prophetic timetable, but when Christ returns, true Christians will be raptured with Christ into heaven, enabling the prophecies to be fulfilled. There will follow a time of tribulation, after which Christ and the raptured saints will return to earth to reign for a thousand years.

Dispensationalism is as much a hermeneutic as it is an eschatology. To understand any passage of scripture, it must first be asked within which dispensation that passage should be placed. Every passage is correctly understood only when it is interpreted literally in terms of its dispensational context. Thus, the ethic of the Sermon on the Mount is often viewed as an ethic of the coming kingdom, not applicable to our current dispensation.[44]

Popularized at the annual Niagra Bible Conferences which began in 1876, dispensationalism became increasingly favored among conservatives, especially Baptists and Presbyterians—Methodists, suspicious of its Calvinistic flavor, were slower to adopt it. Dispensationalism tended to foster a doctrinal rigidity and separatism which made it initially unattractive to many, but would eventually contribute to the development of fundamentalism. The *Scofield Reference Bible* (1909) did much to enhance its popularity in conservative churches.[45]

Fundamentalism as a term was derived from a series of ten essays published by Amzi Dixon and Reuben Torrey under the title *The Fundamentals: A Testimony to the Truth* (1910). Written by a broadly representative group of conservative theologians (and absent dispensational emphases) these small books provided a doctrinal rallying point in the conflict with theological liberalism.[46] Out of this came the five "Fundamentals of the Faith," a kind of fundamentalist platform:

(1) the verbal inspiration of scripture

(2) the virgin birth of Christ

(3) Christ's substitutionary atonement

(4) Christ's bodily resurrection

(5) Christ's imminent and visible second coming

This was designed to assert the truth of key doctrines which liberals were seen as denying.[47]

As conservatives increasingly lost the fundamentalist—modernist controversy,[48] fundamentalism came to designate the more militant wing of the movement. Ernest Sandeen defined fundamentalism as the union of the Princeton theology's teaching on the inerrancy of scripture with dispensationalism;[49] George Marsden more correctly identifies the "victorious life" branch of the Holiness movement and revivalism in the D. L. Moody tradition as additional constituent elements.[50] Thus, old enemies became joined in a common movement to preserve the gospel from the threat of liberal apostasy.

Fundamentalism in this narrower sense had a number of distinctive characteristics. As has been mentioned, it held to the strict inerrancy of scripture and a premillennial dispensational eschatology. In addition, it tended to view evangelism and social concern as mutually exclusive, endorsing the former while condemning the latter. Although it could be anti-intellectual, it was nonetheless highly rationalistic in its approach to scripture. Fundamentalism tended to be not so much anti-scientific as defending a Newtonian or Baconian view of science against Darwinism and other newer methodologies. Most of all, it was militantly separatist, breaking fellowship with "apostate" Christians who no longer held to doctrinal truth. Unity, the fundamentalists insisted, could never be purchased at the expense of truth.[51] In spite of its revivalism, fundamentalism is in many ways a more populist and militant expression of the scholastic tendency within evangelicalism.

The Pentecostal Awakening

At the same time as fundamentalism was taking shape, a new evangelical tradition was emerging out of the radical wing of the Holiness movement. Pentecostalism is arguably the most significant movement in twentieth century Christianity, having had global impact.[52] While fundamentalism with its concern for rationally established doctrinal truth tended toward the separation of doctrine from experience, Pentecostalism in the tradition of the evangelical awakenings emphasized doctrines as experienced realities. It therefore is a radicalized version of the integrative approach of evangelical pietism.

The heart of Pentecostalism is the belief in and experience of the power of the Holy Spirit, which sanctifies the heart and endues one with power for ministry. The latter is the result of a second or third instantaneous act of grace, subsequent to conversion, which gives the believer gifts of the Holy Spirit for ministry and mission. This "baptism of the Holy Spirit" is evidenced by speaking in tongues.[53] Fundamentalists, believing that miracles of God were for the purpose of authenticating the credentials of the early apostles and had therefore ceased in the present age were among the strongest foes of Pentecostalism, seeing miraculous claims as hoaxes or works of the devil.[54]

Although Pentecostals adopted a modified form of dispensational premillennialism, they were far more optimistic than the fundamentalists. They believed they were seeing beginning of a great new work of God, the outpouring of the "latter rain," in which the gospel would be taken to all the world. Moreover, many also initially hoped that the barriers of race and class would be swept away, as they were to some extent at the Azusa Street Revival (1906); however, a decade later, the racism in American culture began to have an impact on the new movement, leading to increased segregation.

In the 1950's and 1960's, the Pentecostal Spirit-baptism began to be experienced by mainline Protestants such as Episcopalians, Lutherans, Presbyterians, and Methodists. Even more astonishing, Roman Catholics received the experience in the mid 1960's.[55] Although these Charismatics (or Neo-Pentecostals) affirmed the baptism of the Holy Spirit as an experience subsequent to conversion, they reinterpreted it theologically in terms of their own denominational tradition. Most, but not all, denied the Pentecostal teaching that Spirit-baptism is always evidenced by speaking in tongues;[56] nonetheless, the use of a "prayer language" remained a central feature of the movement.

The 1970's brought a new wave of independent charismatics, who were neither Pentecostal nor associated with a traditional denomination. Highly controversial and theologically diverse, their prominence in the charismatic movement has produced numerous defenders and detractors.[57] One strand, the so-called "third wave" of the Spirit, is notable for involving heretofore resistant evangelicals in the "signs and wonders" movement.[58]

"Evangelicalism" as Post-Fundamentalism

While fundamentalism remained doctrinally distant from this massive Pentecostal/charismatic explosion, it suffered from its own internal tensions. In the 1940's a group of fundamentalists mounted a strong critique of their tradition and began a new conservative movement which was then termed "neo-evangelicalism." Besides insisting that dispensationalism was not the only theologically orthodox eschatology, these new evangelicals focused on three concerns they had with fundamentalism.

First, they rejected fundamentalism's separatist mentality and practice of denouncing other Christians as apostate. They sought instead to persuade liberals of the truth of historic Christianity and to cooperate with other Christians in common endeavors. The emergence of evangelist Billy Graham as the public symbol of evangelicalism reinforced this move away from separatism—the Graham crusades pointedly included leadership from mainline as well as conservative churches.

Second, they rejected fundamentalism's anti-intellectualism. In the spirit of Old Princeton, they sought to foster rigorous scholarship and a vigorous engagement with contemporary science and culture. Early theologians such as Carl F. H. Henry, Edward John Carnell, and Bernard Ramm demonstrated this new spirit— Ramm's groundbreaking book on science and Henry's lifelong critique of culture are examples.[59]

Third, they rejected fundamentalism's retreat from social concern. Henry's *The Uneasy Conscience of Modern Fundamentalism* (1947) made a biblical case for evangelical social concern;[60] he exemplified that concern by helping to form World Vision, International, to combat world hunger. Evangelicals were soon found all across the political spectrum.[61] Henry's humane conservatism was complemented by the more transformationist approach of Ronald J. Sider and Evangelicals for Social Action.[62] Even more radical was the countercultural politics of Jim Wallis and the Sojourners community.[63]

One aspect of fundamentalism they did not reject was the authority and inspiration of scripture, with its commitment to inerrancy. The new spirit of intellectual inquiry, however, began to raise questions and offer formulations which many found troubling. Carnell was sharply criticized for admitting there were difficulties in scripture,[64] while Ramm began moving in new directions, drawing on Dutch Reformed and later Barthian insights.[65] By the 1970's arch-conservative Harold Lindsell published *The Battle for the Bible*, accusing evangelicals of abandoning their commitment to scriptural inerrancy.[66] This is an issue that remains unresolved.[67]

The Tension Between Scholasticism and Pietism

In recounting this complex history, I've suggested that the tension between scholasticism and pietism pervades the evangelical movement. The neo-evangelicals leaned heavily in the scholastic direction, understanding theology as a rational discipline to be kept separate from an equally necessary evangelism and life of vital piety. As with their predecessors at Princeton, a reasoned apologetic became central to the entire theological enterprise. In the process, they have tried to define evangelical theology for the entire movement.[68]

This doctrinal presumption is often allied to historical interpretation—a preference, says Dayton, for a "Presbyterian paradigm" rather than a "Pentecostal paradigm" in interpreting the history of evangelicalism.[69] Sometimes this can be remarkably blunt, as when John Gerstner, virtually equating evangelicalism with Old Princeton, then astonishingly asserts that "Finney, the greatest of nineteenth-century evangelists, became the greatest of nineteenth century foes of evangelicalism."[70] More often, it is simply telling the story with Hodge and Warfield at the center while leaving Finney and Palmer safely on the margins. This is evangelicalism very "narrowly conceived" indeed!

Certainly the broad evangelical tradition is otherwise: the awakenings and the Holiness/Pentecostal movements are central to that history and Dayton's "Pentecostal paradigm" is a most appropriate lens through which to interpret it. This is not merely an argument about how to read history, however, for it is the pietist element in the evangelical family—the tradition of the awakenings—which holds the most promise for evangelicalism in a postmodern context.

I will be defending this claim throughout the book, most especially in the final chapter. While drawing on the insights of a wide range of contemporary evangelical theologians, it will be clear, I hope, that my overall approach has especially been inspired and informed by the theologies of John Wesley and Jonathan Edwards.

To say this is at the same time to indicate what this pietist/scholastic tension is not. First of all, it is not a conflict between Calvinism and Arminianism. While revivalism and the Holiness movement in nineteenth century America did become highly Arminianized (in ways that would make Wesley uncomfortable!), the century prior saw ardent

Calvinists like Edwards and Whitefield at the very center of the awakening.

Nor is this a tension between populism and intellectualism. Evangelicalism has been a populist movement, and this has led to a variety of excesses, including shallow thinking.[71] But this has also been its glory, not only in that masses of people have been reached with the gospel across social, economic, and racial lines, but that persons society have written off have been taken seriously as leaders and thinkers, at least within their segment of the movement. It is by no means obvious that the highly educated Hodge, who was opposed to women's rights and believed slavery to be among the *adiaphora*, was a more perceptive interpreter of scripture than the Holiness revivalist or African-American slave preacher who thought otherwise. Even so, the awakening tradition has included many highly educated thinkers—Edwards and Wesley were theologians of the first order, and Finney was no intellectual lightweight.

Dayton sees the fundamental theological difference between Hodge and Finney to be "the relative emphasis they gave to sin and redemption." While Hodge denied God's grace would overcome human sin in this life, Finney looked for God to transform both people and society.[72] Dayton argues that this explains why the Princeton theology was more pessimistic concerning social change, while the Holiness movement more optimistic. It enabled elements of the Princeton theology to be later linked with an even more pessimistic dispensationalism in order to form the fundamentalist coalition.[73]

This is a most helpful insight, to which I offer a few qualifications. It is not their Calvinism per se that led Princeton and the dispensationalists in a pessimistic direction—Calvinism can also have a transformative emphasis, as it does with Dutch Calvinism or with revivalists like Whitefield. Nor does this distinction rest on a doctrine of original sin as total depravity. While Finney had abandoned that view, Wesley upheld it, holding both for the total corruption of the *imago Dei* and its full restoration by grace in this life—in the words of Gordon Rupp, both a "pessimism of nature" and an "optimism of grace."[74] Instead, it is the pietist/awakening tradition which most strongly and consistently upholds the transforming power of God in this life—that is, has a strong doctrine of the Holy Spirit.

Robert K. Johnston distinguishes between those evangelicals most centrally oriented toward a "theology of the Word" from those centered around a "theology of the Spirit." "While one branch of the evangelical family has understood its informing center to be the Christ of Scripture, the other branch has stressed new life in Christ."[75] While the former "tends toward creedal definition and is prone at its worst to a literalism in biblical interpretation and a legalism in regard to experience," the second "tends toward the intuitive and interpersonal and is prone at its worst to a mysticism or a psychologism."[76]

My difficulty with Johnston's analysis is that, even when qualified as a matter of emphasis, this duality of Word and Spirit doesn't faithfully represent large segments of evangelicalism. It rather presupposes a distinction between scripture and experience, wherein to emphasize one is to de-emphasize the other. This bias becomes clear in Johnston's claim that while "one begins with *God's* action in regard to humankind" the other begins "with *humankind's* experience of God in his creation and redemption."[77]

I would frame the distinction this way: both traditions begin with God's action toward humanity; the scholastics emphasize that action as recorded in scripture and expressed in doctrine, while the pietists emphasize that the God who acted redemptively as recorded in scripture continues to do so today. While scholasticism has tended to protect the "objective" truth of scripture and doctrine from contamination by "subjective" experience, the pietists have insisted that Christianity involves more than mere assent to doctrine. Rather than emphasizing experience over doctrine (much less understanding experience as the source of doctrine), the pietist tradition has rejected an objective/subjective dualism and instead sought to integrate scripture and doctrine with heart and life. Scripture itself is a living word which directs and transforms lives, doctrine is meant to be an experiential reality, reason is grounded in faith, and beliefs form and shape the Christian life. There simply can be no new life in Christ apart from a faithful indwelling of scripture.

Part of my task in the pages ahead will be to show how this integration can be understood, as well as its implication for postmodern issues. This will involve among other things tracing the relationship between God's action in Christ and present activity through the Spirit, examining the nature of scripture in relation to the Christian life, and providing a depiction of the church as a distinctive people of God.

To set the stage for this, we must first tell yet another story, that of modernity and postmodernity. Then we can see more clearly how evangelical theology has responded to modernity, and in what ways it can constructively engage the concerns of postmodernity.

Part II

Postmodernity
and the
Truth of the Gospel

CHAPTER 2

Theology in the Midst of Modernity

Theological reflection does not occur in a vacuum. Theologians and churches find themselves, happily or unhappily, as inescapable participants in human culture. While cultural change may be welcomed or resisted by theologians, it cannot be ignored.

In this chapter and the next I will show how evangelical theologians have responded to the massive changes in Western culture designated "modernity" and "postmodernity." I hope this will not only describe various alternative approaches, but make clear the reasons for my own proposal in the remainder of the book. This account of modernity and postmodernity will be brief, simply highlighting central themes and issues. More detailed histories and analyses are readily available.[1] My concern here is primarily with the ways in which theologians have dealt with or are presently dealing with these two cultural movements.

Modernity and the Search for Truth

"Modernity" designates the historical period in Western society which followed the medieval age. The term carries with it connotations of superiority; as Thomas Oden notes, "There is a pretense in modernity that what is not modern is not adequate, is antiquated, therefore to be thrown away."[2] This is indicated by the once prevalent characterization of modernity as a move from the "dark ages" to a new time of "enlightenment"—a characterization that events of the twentieth century have strongly called into question. Although a good case can be made for rooting modernity in the Renaissance,[3] where humanity is placed at the center of cultural and intellectual concern, I shall begin the story a bit later, with the Enlightenment. It is there that what I take to be the salient features of modernity are clearly articulated and defended.

In particular, I will begin with the French philosopher René Descartes (1596–1650) who laid much of the philosophical foundation of modernity. He sought to counter the increasing skepticism toward received authorities such as scripture and tradition by re-establishing Christian truth claims on a more solid foundation. His method was to doubt everything until he found something which was self-evidently true. The one thing he could not doubt was that he himself was doubting. Put positively, his foundation was "I think, therefore I am" (*Cogito ergo sum*); it was upon this basis that he then deduces the existence of God and of external reality. While Descartes' proposal is the culmination of a gradual change in perspective, it is nonetheless radical in its implications. Most important is the shift in how truth claims are verified: the ultimate authority would no longer be God's revelation but human reason. The claims of scripture and tradition would be accepted as true if they were rationally defensible.

Most of the features of modernity are found in the Cartesian approach. Among them are the following:

(1) Individualism—The autonomous individual is free to think for him or herself, released from bondage to community or tradition.

(2) Rationalism—Reason is a universal human capacity; what is reasonable for one person should be reasonable to all.

(3) Methodological doubt—The way to truth was not "faith seeking understanding" (Augustine) but thoroughgoing critical reflection. As Lesslie Newbigin put it, "By relentless skepticism . . . every claim to truth was put was put through the critical sieve in which only the indubitable would be retained."[4]

(4) Dualism—Reality is understood to consist of mind and matter. This undergirds a subject/object dualism as well as a mind/body dualism.

(5) Optimism—Through reason humanity would set itself free from superstition and attain true knowledge. Once unfettered from the past, reason would through science and culture lead to inevitable human progress.

All of this rests on an epistemology through which individuals can come to rational agreement over what is true. Instead, what it precipitates is a profound disagreement over epistemology, albeit one in which all parties share the assumptions enumerated above.

Descartes' particular proposal was a form of rationalism, in which the foundation for certainty is in indubitable first principles grasped intuitively by the mind. One then reasons deductively, as in geometry, establishing further truth on the basis of this foundation.

This approach was at odds with that of the new science championed by Francis Bacon (1561–1626). Baconian method proceeds inductively, from particular data gathered by an objective observer and then combined to form general truths. The scientific knowledge thus gained would enable the increasing control and subordination of nature, eliminating its threats and harnessing it for the benefit of humanity.

This more positive view of experience was championed by the English philosopher John Locke (1632–1704), whose empiricism became the major alternative to Cartesian rationalism. For Locke the mind is a blank table (*tabula rasa*) upon which experience, usually mediated through the senses, makes an impression. This produces simple ideas in the mind, which reason then organizes into more complex ideas. While the knowledge attained did not have the certainty desired by Descartes, it was nonetheless highly reliable, not only for science but in religion and ethics.

Although Locke denies the Cartesian claim of innate ideas in the mind, he shares with Descartes a common understanding of "ideas." As Diogenes Allen notes, "Ideas gain something of a quasi-autonomous reality" in that they are "what we attend to; they are the objects of our thoughts."[5] Ideas are thus distinguished from the external objects they ostensibly represent; the existence of an idea in the mind does not in itself guarantee the existence of a corresponding external reality.

It is this feature of early Enlightenment epistemology which invited a forceful challenge by the Scottish philosopher David Hume (1711–1776). Hume argued that ideas we use to interpret reality, such as "causality" and "substance," are not themselves the result of impressions on the mind derived from experience. Because knowledge is based solely on perceptions we can have no confidence that what we claim to know actually corresponds to reality.

Hume's skepticism was countered by two contrasting approaches, each of which sought to restore confidence in human reason as the avenue to truth. The first was the realism of Thomas Reid (1710–1796), the Scottish "common sense" philosophy mentioned in chapter one. Reid held the error of both rationalism and empiricism to be their conceiving of "ideas" as objects in the mind which are independent of the reality they represent. Instead, Reid argued we know reality directly, as it is, verified as such intuitively rather than by a chain of reasoning. Thus he modifies to some extent the Cartesian dualism of mind and matter, subject and object. Reid's philosophy became widespread in early nineteenth century America in a popularized form, and continued to influence the Princeton theologians in the late nineteenth century and (in a debased form) fundamentalism in the twentieth century.[6]

The second response was the idealism of the German philosopher Immanuel Kant (1724–1804). Unlike Reid, Kant accepts the dualism which posits ideas in the mind which are distinct from external reality. Seeking to restore the epistemological confidence which Hume had undermined, Kant agrees with the empiricists that our senses provide the data for knowledge, but with the rationalists that our understanding of that data is only possible through interpretative categories found universally in the human mind, such as "substance" and "causality." It is these innate categories which make experience possible. As a result, Kant agrees with Hume that we cannot know reality as it is (the *noumena*), but in contrast to Hume insists we have certain knowledge of reality as we experience it (the *phenomena*).

One casualty of Kant's proposal is belief in the external reality of God; God is associated with the noumenal world we cannot know. Thus he finds unconvincing the classical arguments for the existence of God. But while "pure reason," which deals with the objective phenomenal world, can neither prove nor disprove God, "practical reason," which deals with the subjective world of human freedom and ethical obligation, does make room for faith. Religion, then, is removed from the realm of facts, science, and "objective" truth, and placed in the realm of faith, values, and "subjective" belief.

Lesslie Newbigin illustrates the implications of this clearly.

> It is certainly not more than a hundred years since children in Scottish schools learned at an early stage the fact that "Man's chief end is to glorify God and enjoy him for ever." This was as much a fact as the movement of the stars and the Battle of Bannockburn. Today it is not taught as a fact. . . . It is a matter of personal choice, of having "a faith of your own." We do not ask whether the belief is true, but whether the believer is sincere in holding the belief. On the other hand, it does not occur to us to ask whether a person is sincere in his or her beliefs about physics; we ask whether the belief is correct.[7]

It is perhaps not too much of an oversimplification to say liberal theology was quite happy with this apportionment of fact and faith while conservative theology sought to move Christianity back to the realm of "facts."

The Distinctive Approaches
of Liberal and Evangelical Theology

Because the Enlightenment provided new criteria for assessing truth claims, theology was faced with the decision of whether to resist the new epistemology or adopt it and rethink theology accordingly. The liberals chose the latter; the conservative response, as we shall see, was more ambiguous. By first examining how liberals responded to the challenge of the Enlightenment we can more clearly understand the dilemma faced by evangelicals.

The first wave of liberal rethinking was the deism of the early Enlightenment, which sought to remove God as an active agent in the world. While some early deist writings tended toward pantheism, the God of most deists was a transcendent Creator who designed creation to operate according to universal laws of nature, making divine intervention unnecessary. Science could then discover those laws free of the threat that they would be suddenly be overturned by a particular miraculous divine act. Deists reduced Christianity to moral teachings which themselves could be discovered in nature by reason apart from scripture, as illustrated in the title of Matthew Tindal's influential book *Christianity as Old as the Creation: or the Gospel a Republication of the Religion of Nature* (1730). Thus deism denied the incarnation and resurrection, as well as traditional teachings on original sin and atonement.[8]

Although popular among intellectuals in America and Europe, deism ultimately ran afoul of the critiques of Hume and Kant. Modern liberal theology begins in the nineteenth century with the thought of F.D.E. Schleiermacher, and is decidedly post-Kantian in nature. It shares the desire of its deist predecessors to design a theology without an awkwardly interventionist God, but does so through divine immanence rather than radical transcendence. Kenneth Cauthen, paraphrasing Henry Churchill King, argues that this liberal reconstruction of theology was necessary because "new ways of thinking and feeling were permeating the minds of sensitive men in such a way that they gradually became alienated from older modes of thought."[9] Or as Bishop John Shelby Spong put it much more recently, "I am determined to make the Bible make sense to modern men and women without having them park their brains at the door of the church before they come in."[10] Liberal theology has at its heart a profoundly apologetic intent: to enable the gospel to make sense to modern men and women.

Cauthen summarizes well the approach of post-Kantian liberalism in terms of continuity, autonomy, and dynamism. By continuity Cauthen means the liberal tendency to reduce or eliminate distinctions between supernatural and natural, God and creation, humanity and divinity, Christianity and other religions. Key to this is the immanence of God, in which God is understood not apart from the world but as a living force permeating creation, history, and culture. Miracles are therefore de-emphasized and reinterpreted.[11]

If God is immanent in all things, then God can be discovered in all things and known by everyone, not just Christians. Jesus may be the one who was supremely conscious of God's presence or taught and exemplified most clearly God's way of life or, in a few more recent liberals, Jesus may be one of many ways to God. But if God is immanent in humanity, then the traditional distinction between the divine and human in Jesus becomes insignificant. Natural human goodness is emphasized rather than depravity, and salvation is more an awakening to the divine impulses within us than a radical transformation effected from without.[12]

Second, liberal theology saw reality not in static but dynamic categories (in contrast not only to traditional conservatives but to deists as well). God was the immanent source of historical change, cultural evolution, and human progress.[13] This especially reflects the optimism of Western modernity in the nineteenth century, arguing that the progress modernity attributes to enlightened humanity is to the eyes of faith the work of God. As with secular thought, liberal theology has a more sober perspective in the twentieth century, while retaining divine immanence as its central principle.

Third, liberal theology recognized the modern emphasis on the autonomy of human reason and experience, insisting that all religious affirmations either be grounded in or affirmed by reason and/or experience.[14] Here faith is clearly placed on the subjective side of the subject/object dualism. Thus scholarly examination of scripture and tradition can proceed according to modern principles of critical historiography without undermining faith—the denial of the resurrection as an objective event, for example, does not effect the subjective faith of Christians then or now, of which it is an expression.

Here we see a major distinction between how liberal and evangelical theologies have responded to modernity. For liberals, Christian scripture and tradition is an attempt, in particular times and places, to give expression to the experience of God, to put faith into words. It is only natural that in modern times some of those ways of expressing the faith—miracles, incarnation, resurrection—may appear incoherent or outmoded. The assertion "on the third day he arose from the dead" can thus be restated as "the apostles had a religious experience after the crucifixion they associated with Jesus." It is only sound apologetics to be willing to discard forms of expression which are no longer serviceable, in order to remove intellectual barriers to recognizing the experience of the divine.

For evangelicals, God has acted in history from the outside, and the language of scripture and tradition authoritatively attest to that divine activity. The experience of faith does not generate that language but is a response to that to which the language witnesses: a God who has acted and continues to act to redeem humanity and creation. Thus traditional doctrines of incarnation and resurrection are not expendable expressions of faith but the very foundations upon which faith stands.

Two recent dialogues between liberals and evangelicals clearly make this distinction. David Edwards (liberal) suggests to John R. W. Stott (evangelical) "that there are some conservative Evangelical ideas which, whether or not they are valid, are not essential if one is to believe the gospel revealed in the Bible."[15] These ideas—which include such matters as an infallible Bible, the substitutionary atonement, that the miracles reported in scripture all actually occurred, and that the Bible provides detailed ethical teaching—"are widely believed not to belong to the gospel itself, not to Christ's glory and sufficiency, but to a dead or dying culture." Edwards hopes to convince evangelicals that by considering "these as optional (not necessarily as wrong) they will find they can communicate the biblical gospel in terms which are far more intelligible, meaningful and credible."[16]

Predictably, Stott declines Edwards' advice. "Would it not be self-contradictory," he asks, "to sacrifice the evangel for the sake of evangelism?"[17] Stott believes "the truth of the finality of God's revelation and redemption in Christ, and so of the Bible and the cross, does not . . . belong to 'a dead or dying culture' but to the everlasting gospel which, though we struggle to communicate it in modern idiom, we have not liberty to compromise."[18] "We do not see ourselves as offering a new Christianity, but as recalling the church to original Christianity."[19]

Although Edwards and Stott are both Anglicans, and relative moderates within their respective theological camps, the differences in method are evident. The reason Edwards wants to move some "evangelical essentials" to the optional column is that he, as a Christian, can no longer affirm them, believing them to be expressions of the faith produced by a very different culture in the past.

Stott worries that Edwards rejects traditional Christian teaching "not on the ground that you consider it unbiblical, but because of other grounds you find it unacceptable."[20] In contrast,

> the hallmark of Evangelicals is not so much an impeccable set of words as a submissive spirit, namely their a priori resolve to believe and obey whatever Scripture may be shown to teach. They are committed to Scripture in advance, whatever it may later be found to say. They claim no liberty to lay down their own terms for belief and behaviour. They see this humble and obedient stance as an essential implication of Christ's lordship over them.[21]

The same dynamic is found in the dialogue between Delwin Brown (liberal) and Clark H. Pinnock (evangelical)—indeed, the issue of method surfaces again and again throughout the entire book. Brown argues that "the difference between liberals and conservatives" is best seen "in terms of the relative balance each gives to the wisdom of the past versus judgements characteristic of the present age."[22] While admitting liberals have sometimes been too quick to dismiss past teaching,

> Liberalism at its best is more likely to say, "We certainly ought to honor the richness of the Christian past and appreciate the vast contribution it makes to our lives, but finally we must live by our best modern conclusions. The modern consensus should not be absolutized; it too, is always subject to criticism and further revision. But our commitment, however tentative and self-critically maintained, must be to the careful judgements of the present age, even if they differ radically from the dictates of the past."[23]

Pinnock, while admitting evangelicals have sometimes "constructed the authority of the Bible in too authoritarian a way," overlooking its human dimensions, nonetheless insists that "Christian theology rests on divine revelation in history,"[24] and it is scripture alone that gives us "access to the original revelation."[25] Pinnock says

> I try to do my reasoning along with the Scriptures rather than against them, and with the Christian community rather than going off on tangents of my own. I try to subject my thinking to the authority of the Bible and to the judgements of traditional theology. I do not care to follow the novel routes carved out by Enlightenment-dominated reason. I do not want to substitute the authority of a Kant or some other modern luminary for the authority of the Bible in the name of ration-

ality. Reason ought not be allowed to vaunt itself above the claims of revelation.[26]

Nor should experience. Pinnock argues the truth content of Christianity "is not something that rises from our experience; rather, it creates experience."[27]

The Apologetic Strategy of Evangelical Theology

Despite the clear-cut distinctions between liberal and evangelical theologies, evangelical approaches have often evidenced an ambiguous relationship to modernity. While wanting to base theology on the authority of revelation and scripture, many evangelicals sought to re-establish that authority through an appeal to reason, understood as a universal capacity exercised by each individual. That is, they argued for scriptural authority and historic Christian doctrines on terms set by Enlightenment modernity.

The question they faced was something like this: on what basis do you make universal truth claims concerning creation and redemption from historically and culturally situated writings concerning particular historical events? How do you justify the "scandal of particularity" in terms acceptable to the modern (read Western) mind? The liberals didn't try—many were perfectly happy with a Jesus who exemplified and taught a universal religiousness or morality, demonstrable apart from Jesus on the basis of reason or experience. Many evangelicals felt compelled to justify their claims, and did so through demonstrating the truthfulness of scripture or the coherence of Christianity as a system of thought.

This apologetic concern is especially characteristic of the neo-evangelicals who emerged out of fundamentalism in the 1940's. While there are a diversity of approaches, they can be placed within two general categories: evidentialist or presuppositional.

Evidentialist apologetics was used by the Princeton theologians, and passed from them into fundamentalism. The central assumption, encouraged by Scottish common sense realism, was a universal human rational capacity to weigh empirical evidence and draw logical conclusions. What all the variants within evidentialism have in common is their appeal to evidence which supports Christian truth claims.[28] The title of Josh McDowell's popular work, *Evidence That Demands a Verdict*,[29] is emblematic of this approach.

John Warwick Montgomery is one of the leading evidentialists, and can serve to illustrate the method. In *History and Christianity* Montgomery first identifies four errors, two historical and two logical, made by a scholar who questions whether anything reliable can be known about Jesus. In particular Montgomery criticizes the tendency to cite modern authorities from the more radical tradition of biblical scholarship while neglecting the primary source documents them-selves, and to declare New Testament documents unreliable because they report miracles, which are *a priori* deemed impossible.[30]

Next, Montgomery defends the historical accuracy of the docu-ments, not assuming their inspiration but treating them "as we would any other historical materials."[31] He applies three tests: bibliographic, in which he shows these texts to be at least as reliable as any ancient writings; internal evidence, in which he argues they represent reliable eyewitness testimony; and external evidence, in which he shows how other ancient documents verify New Testament claims.[32]

Having demonstrated the reliability of the documents, Montgomery then asks what these documents say. His answer:

> They say unequivocally and consistently that Jesus regarded himself as no less than God in the flesh, and that his disciples, under the pressure of his own words and deeds, came to regard him in this same way.[33]

He buttresses this with a survey of various books in the New Testament, showing they all make this claim.[34]

Finally, if "the New Testament documents portray a divine Christ,"[35] Montgomery asks if this claim is factual. Logically, if Jesus was not divine, then Jesus is either a charlatan or a lunatic, or his followers were charlatans or lunatics. Examining the evidence, Montgomery concludes Jesus rightly claims to be the incarnate Son of God, and his followers were convinced of this by his resurrection, which is also supported by historical evidence.[36] Montgomery concludes with "A Historians Ap-peal," in which, given "the weight of historical probability lies on the side of the claim to be God incarnate," the Savior of humanity and Judge of the world, he urges the reader make a personal commitment to the risen Christ.[37]

In laying out Montgomery's argument, I am not as concerned with a detailed analysis of its logic than with its way of thinking and the assumptions upon which it rests. Clearly, his apologetic presupposes modernity's distinction between objective facts and subjective opinions, and on that basis then attempts to argue that Christian claims are indeed factual. Montgomery makes this clear:

> Now, if you are not inclined in the direction of Christianity, as I was not when I entered university, the most irritating aspect of the line of argument I have taken is probably this: It depends in no sense on theology. It rests solely upon historical method, the kind of method all of us have to use in analyzing historical data, whether Christians, rationalists, agnostics, or Tibetan monks.[38]

Yet Montgomery does not fully embrace the kind of historical method "all of us have to use;" in fact, he must challenge it in order to make his case for the resurrection. Given the modern shift from a Newtonian universe to Einstein's relativity, Montgomery insists "No historian has a right to a closed system of natural causation."[39] Instead,

> The only way we can know whether an event can occur is to see whether in fact it has occurred. The problem of "miracles," then, must be solved in the realm of historical investigation, not in the realm of philosophical speculation. . . . All historical events are unique, and the test of their factual character can be only the accepted documentary approach that we have followed here.[40]

Montgomery (rightly, in my view) is challenging the principle of analogy which has governed most historical inquiry since it was articulated by Ernst Troeltsch. According to this principle, that in the past which is difficult to understand is analyzed in terms of something contemporary to the historian. The effect of this principle is to rule out *a priori* unique events in history.[41] That Montgomery must at some point attend to this assumption is telling, for it implies his own historical method rests on different presuppositions that some of his opponents. This may partially validate Carl F. H. Henry's claim that, while the "evidentialist may be less disposed than his fellow theologian to admit that his mind harbors presuppositions," "evidentialists, no less than other theologians, begin with aprioric assumptions."[42]

It is precisely this claim which underlies presuppositional apologetics. Although there are many variations, the two major presuppositional approaches center around Cornelius Van Til and Gordon Clark. Van Til holds that factual validity and historical meaning is only possible if Christian theism is presupposed while Clark argues that only Christian presuppositions are logically consistent.[43]

Carl F. H. Henry is Clark's most prominent student, and is a leading exponent of his method. Henry places presuppositionalism between evidentialism and fideism. While agreeing with the evidentialist "on the

intrinsic rationality of God and of His created universe" the presuppositionalist denies that proofs or evidences based on "empirical observation from the universe and without any appeal to revelation"[44] are a
necessary foundation for Christian truth claims or, for that matter,
convincing. In contrast to fideism, rational presuppositionalism

> does not sponsor a disjunction of faith and reason. It insists that all
> humanity can comprehend God's revelation and, moreover, can com-
> prehend it prior to regeneration or special illumination by the Holy
> Spirit.[45]

Henry describes his as a "deductive theology,"[46] which acknowledges
that, as in geometry, "theological and philosophical systems . . . have
governing axioms." These axioms "are never deduced or inferred from
other principles, but are simply presupposed." From these controlling
axioms each "system's theorems are subsequently deduced."[47]

There are two "basic axioms of the Christian religion":

> The basic ontological axiom is *the living God*; the basic epistemological
> axiom is *divine revelation*. . . . These axioms imply each other. Without
> the living God there would be no divine revelation. Without intelligible
> self-disclosure we would not know that God exists.[48]

Even though axioms themselves are not based on prior principles or
evidence, they "are testable for the consistency or inconsistency with
which they account for relevant data." Because Christianity is a comprehensive belief system which involves "shareable knowledge," it "does
not disdain the canons of rationality."[49] Logical consistency cannot
validate a truth system, but it can invalidate one; it is thus "a negative
test of truth."[50] Henry's apologetic strategy is thus to demonstrate all
competing systems of truth are logically inconsistent, while Christianity
is both logically consistent and externally verified by scripture.[51]

This is a pre-eminently logical apologetic. Henry contends against
many postmodern thinkers that the laws of logic are universal—they
are unaffected by cultural pluralism or by humanity's Fall into sin. Logic
is at the heart of God who is the "truth and the source of truth" and
remains integral to the *imago Dei* after the Fall.[52] "In a universe where
the *Logos* is the source and support of created existence, logic is the *form*
of reality."[53]

Henry would understand himself to be repudiating the philosophical systems of the Enlightenment for one based on the revelation of God.
Indeed, uncovering hidden presuppositions and exposing internal in-
consistencies can be a helpful and revealing exercise. But Henry's

approach remains one based on a logical appeal to rational individuals. While perhaps criticizing the autonomous authority which modernity gives to individuals, Henry nonetheless presupposes that authority: since virtually everyone has a rational capacity, everyone is capable and responsible to render an intellectual judgement on the validity of Christianity. That Henry is certain a logical judgement can only go one way does not change who it is that makes the judgement.

The rationalist apologetics of both evidentialism and presuppositionalism by no means represents the whole of evangelicalism, even of the postfundamentalist variety. Perhaps the strongest and most persistent critic of this entire approach is Donald G. Bloesch. While the evidentialists "are fascinated by the empirical rationalism of the later Enlightenment, especially as it came to America in the form of Scottish realism," the presuppositionalists tend "to maintain continuity with the idealistic rationalism of the early Enlightenment."[54] The danger of both is that, by tying theology so closely to philosophical method,

> The Word of God becomes a rational formula wholly in control of the theologian, and theology becomes the systematic harmonizing of rational truths rather than an incomplete and open-ended explication of revelational meaning that always stands in need of revision and further elucidation.[55]

The ground of certainty is not in rational argument but "in the inward confirmation of the Spirit concerning the objective validity of the biblical revelation."[56] Clearly Bloesch suspects that in much evangelical apologetics, the philosophical tail is wagging the theological dog; indeed, how can it be otherwise if one seeks to make one's case in terms established by Enlightenment epistemology?

Bloesch calls his own position "a *fideistic revelationalism*, in which the decision of faith is as important as the fact of revelation in giving us certainty of the truth of faith."[57] Theology is thus "grounded not so much in noninferential beliefs as in the living God himself, whose credibility is not guaranteed by foundational presuppositions but by his actually speaking to us day by day in our life and work."[58] The Holy Spirit addresses us through scripture in ways that "can never be fully assimilated by the human mind;" to understand more thoroughly what is revealed we must act in obedience to it.[59]

In Bloesch there is the suspicion that the wedding of modern rationalism with Protestant scholasticism shifts our attention from the living reality of God to written propositions or doctrinal systems. It is a pietist suspicion that the cognitive is being separated from and given priority over living faith. It is also a Barthian suspicion that, while God is either being inductively demonstrated as ultimate or honored as the primary axiom, the freedom of God is subtly but ever so thoroughly being domesticated by human reason.

This is not to say that Bloesch absolutely rejects apologetics or metaphysics. What he objects to is their playing a central or foundational role in theology. Apologetics can be useful, both for those outside and inside the community of faith.[60] Furthermore, the Christian faith "contains a metaphysic of its own that challenges other metaphysical claims;"[61] in its interpretation of reality in light of the "story of faith," theology "will necessarily use philosophical concepts as well as biblical imagery in this task."[62] Thus the truth claims of Christianity have "metaphysical import:"[63]

> Against the temptations to gain support from either antiquity or modernity, Christian faith presents a picture of God that both shocks antiquity and overturns modernity.[64]

It would be inaccurate to describe Bloesch as opposed to conceptual truth. Indeed, in an "era when propositional or conceptual truth is being sacrificed for existential and emotive truth," he intends to "reaffirm the conceptual side of revelation."[65] What he denies is that this truth is "a product of our superior reasoning as Christians" or is something "we claim to have discovered by ourselves." It is rather "a transrational truth" which claims us, "not an abstract, theoretical truth" but "the speech of God enveloped in mystery."[66] But if Bloesch's approach is not rationalism, neither is it pure fideism, for it begins "not with our act of faith but with God's action toward us."[67]

The import of Bloesch's critique can be stated this way: the apologetics of liberal and evangelical theology in the end have more in common than their sharply contrasting conclusions might suggest. Both in good Cartesian fashion posit something like a mind/body dualism, in which reason and/or experience becomes a privileged human capacity. For Henry it is reason: a divine *Logos* whose primary attribute is reason creates a rational universe and communicates to humans in a rational manner. Humans created in the image of this rational God can through reason understand both divine communication and the rationality of the universe. This means that it is the mind—the seat of reason—that is most like God.

It is the linkage of a human capacity with divinity that Bloesch (following Karl Barth) rejects. The problem is not only that Henry tends to discount the effect of the Fall on the reasoning capacity; it is also that it tends to subtly escape the bounds of finitude as well. Henry makes reason universal because he insists the laws of logic are universal. But even if this is granted, it is human beings who actually reason, interpreting their world and applying those laws, and those humans are both fallen and finite.

Neither evidentialism and presuppositionalism would claim to be expressions of modernity—each would root itself in the Thomistic (evidentialist) or Augustinian (presuppositionalist) approaches to the relationship of faith and reason. However, what is modern about both is their distinctive understanding and use of reason to establish the truth of Christianity in a world shaped by the Enlightenment, making their apologetics more reflective of Descartes or Locke than classical theology. In a postmodern context, it puts rational apologetics in the peculiar position of arguing not only for Christianity but for Enlightenment rationality as well, as if the truth of the former depends on that of the latter.

In place of truth as logical certainty (Henry) or empirical probability (Montgomery) Bloesch offers a more chastened approach, marked by a humility that respects the majesty and mystery of God. Bloesch would not want to call his theology postmodern, for the Christian God to which it attests, who "shocks antiquity and overturns modernity," will confound postmodernity as well. Yet his unwavering insistence of the truth of the gospel coupled with a thorough reticence against claiming to know too much provides at least one promising theological direction for engaging postmodernity.

My own theology has more in common with Bloesch than with rational apologetics. While well-intentioned, the apologetic strategies of evangelical theology have conceded too much to modernity at the outset. Their success in convincing those steeped in modernity of the truth of historic Christianity has been marginal, and they have reassured the faithful at the cost of reinforcing the rationalist claims of the Enlightenment which should have been challenged. As a result, they have permitted the autonomous rational human agent, biblical text in hand, to supplant the agency of the Holy Spirit as the interpreter of scripture, who leads us into all truth (John 16:12).

In addressing the issues raised by postmodernity, I therefore have no intention of formulating a revised apologetic which attempts to re-establish the truth of the gospel on postmodern terms. My approach will be to critically evaluate postmodernity from the standpoint of the

Christian faith, with the goal of communicating the gospel in this new context. In the process, I will both challenge and appropriate postmodern insights in order to show how and why the truth claims of historic Christianity can and should be made in this new context.

CHAPTER 3

Theology at the End of Modernity

Modernity, for all its complexity, is the provence of the historian; postmodernity remains the projection of the futurist. The ultimate shape of postmodernity is unclear. What is clear is that we are undergoing a vast intellectual and cultural transformation, rivaling the transition from the medieval world to modernity.

As we shall see, the term "postmodern" does not mean the same to everyone. However, there are several postmodern tendencies which can be identified with some confidence, and this I shall do in section one. Following this, two very distinctive philosophical appropriations of these tendencies will be described. Finally, I will conclude with an assessment of the issues raised by postmodernism for an evangelical theology.

The Collapse of Modern Foundations

We can begin with a preliminary sketch of some distinctive postmodern themes. This will enable us to see what it is about modernity that is collapsing, and in what ways postmodernity is continuous as well as discontinuous with modernity. My approach is to revisit the five characteristics of modernity in chapter two, each of which has become in some way problematic to emerging postmodernity.

(1) *From Individualism to Community.* In postmodernism the autonomous individual of the Enlightenment is being supplanted by a more holistic vision of humanity, emphasizing relationality and cooperation. Instead of the individual being prior to the community, the community is prior to the individual; participation in the community with its network of practices and relationships is what constitutes the personhood of the individual.

That said, there is a tension in postmodern thought concerning the exact relation of person and community. On one hand, individuals are not autonomous minds, as the Enlightenment thought, but think in patterns determined by their socio-cultural context. In the words of Stanley Grenz, "the specific truths we accept" and "even our understanding of truth" itself "are a function of the community in which we participate."[1]

On the other hand, Middleton and Walsh identify a countervailing trend, which abandons the Cartesian search for absolute truth while retaining the Baconian commitment to human autonomy. Here we do not discover the truth but construct it through our language; humanity is thus free to use language to construct a more humane world. "It is," they say, "self-conscious social construction with a vengeance." In this sense, postmodernity is more precisely "late modernity."[2]

(2) *From Rationalist Foundationalism to Nonfoundationalism.* As Roger Olson says, postmodernity

> involves a rejection of epistemological foundationalism and embraces a radically perspectival, pluralistic view of knowledge in which *all* is a form of believing and arises from within a tradition.[3]

That is, there is no common foundation, in either reason or experience, upon which to ground absolute universal truth claims. Richard Lints describes this postmodern epistemology as proceeding "less like building a house" (that is, on a foundation) and more "like engaging in conversation or telling a story."[4] But the implications of this new approach are unclear. Does this mean all truth is relative or that whatever *is* true cannot be expressed apart from a particular believing tradition? Lints warns of the former, terming this a postmodern "epistemic pragmatism" in which "every belief is potentially (and ought to be) revisable." It thus retains the "anthropological foundation" presupposed by modernity, and is only postmodern in that it welcomes "the plurality that comes with it."[5] If all thought is contextual, is there a way to test truth claims that does not depend on universal reason?

(3) *From Methodological Doubt to Traditioned Belief.* In the quote from Olson, we saw that for postmodernism "*all* knowing is a form of believing," inescapably rooted in a particular tradition which makes reasoning possible. Thus one cannot simply reach truth through doubting everything; Descartes himself participated in a tradition of thought whose presuppositions he took for granted, and which made his project thinkable.

However, postmodern thought is not at all clear about what to make of this insight. Does one embrace the underlying beliefs of one's tradition or does one subject those beliefs themselves to a radical critique, exposing their hidden assumptions and the interests they serve?

(4) *From Dualism to Holism.* While modernity sought knowledge through making distinctions and divisions, postmodernity tends toward seeing things holistically. Rather than divide the object of study into its component parts for analysis, the postmodern suspicion is that the whole is greater than the parts, and that both natural and cultural realities are most adequately understood when seen in organic unity.

Secondly, postmodernism denies that knowledge is secured through distancing oneself from the object—what Enlightenment science called "objective analysis." As Grenz puts it, the "world is not simply an objective given that is 'out there,' waiting to be discovered."[6] Rather, knowing is participatory—it requires involvement. One must place oneself actually or empathetically within that which one seeks to understand.

Implied in this is the rejection of the Cartesian mind/body dualism which was presupposed by all subsequent Enlightenment thinkers. The human mind does not exist in some realm of autonomous freedom in distinction from the body, which is securely situated in a world of cause and effect. The person is whole, and it is the whole person who is located within nature and history, inescapably influenced by context yet retaining freedom to think and act.

(5) *From Optimism to Pessimism?* The highly optimistic linkage of knowledge and progress which marked the nineteenth century in the West has been shattered by the uses to which that knowledge has been put in the twentieth century. Furthermore, there is no longer the confidence that humanity can discover an agreed-upon truth for itself. As Grenz notes,

> people are no longer convinced that knowledge is inherently good. In eschewing the Enlightenment myth of inevitable progress, postmodernism replaces the optimism . . . with a gnawing pessimism.[7]

The existentialism of the mid-twentieth century is an early instance of this growing despair.

Yet in some strands of postmodernism, a new optimism in human endeavor has appeared. If reality is really a human construct—the product of culture and tradition—then it opens the way for humanity to construct a better world through reconstructing the cultural lens through which we view reality. In this way we can envision a just society and ecological harmony. Moreover, the recognition of the cultural relativity of truth claims opens the way for diverse cultures to accept and respect one another's differences, and live together in peace.

Here again is the ambiguity which runs through early postmodernism. It on one hand rejects central tenets of modernity. Yet certain strands of postmodernism retain modern emphases, recasting them in the new context. At least two approaches to postmodernity can be discerned. The first, which maintains and radicalizes certain elements of modernity, might be termed "ultra-critical," while the second, more discontinuous approach is appropriately called "post-critical."

The "Ultra-Critical" Approach: The Suspicion of Metanarratives

The roots of this form of postmodernism can be found in the post-Kantian, or "second Enlightenment." The distinction between the two enlightenments is stated succinctly by Walter Lowe:

> The "first Enlightenment," which had as its paradigm Newtonian physics, forced a recognition of *nature* as an autonomous order, to be explored by disciplined investigation. By contrast a second, more praxis-oriented, political Enlightenment . . . may be said to represent a discovery of *history*: i.e., a discovery that existent social structures are not mandated by heaven, but can be refashioned by the collective will of mankind.[8]

In Lowe's analysis, a central concern of both enlightenments was the alleviation of human suffering. While the first discovered that those events of the natural order that cause suffering, such as disease, were not God-ordained but due to natural causation, and therefore could be amenable to potential remedy through science, the second likewise found that suffering due to the social order was amenable to potential remedy through social change.[9]

While the second Enlightenment was able to expose the ideologies of the first, it was unaware of its own. It approached history the way the first approached nature in that it sought some sort of natural order within history. This it did through a kind of narrative, which begins with a primal unity, is followed by a fall into disunity, and culminates in a final and (sometimes) inevitable restoration. The versions of this story were manifold: Hegelianism, Marxism, and social Darwinism are the more obvious examples of such "metanarratives," each one purporting to be universal and true. But the problem with a metanarrative is, in order to attain the greater end, it tends to justify human suffering in the present as part of the necessary means.[10] How then to expose the ideologies of the second Enlightenment?

The resource for such a critique was found within the second Enlightenment itself, in the form of "hermeneutics of suspicion." Ludwig Feuerbach (1804–1872) was the pioneer, arguing that "God" is really a projection of our best human qualities on an infinite screen; theology is anthropology writ large.[11] Karl Marx (1818–1883) followed by showing how social arrangements reflect the hidden interests of the reigning economic class. Sigmund Freud (1856–1940) demonstrated that underlying human behavior were unconscious motivations, some with moral import. And Friedrich Nietzsche (1844–1900) saw behind culture and morality the desire for power.[12]

What unites these diverse thinkers is their desire to unmask what is hidden, to bring to light that which secretly oppresses, in order to set humanity free. They are "protest atheists," who see religion not as benign superstition but as one element in the complex of forces which keep humanity bound—the "opiate of the people" (Marx), an "infantile disorder" (Freud) or a "slave morality" (Nietzsche). Their methods have a common shape: an interpretation which refuses to take appearances for granted, but seeks to expose the interests which actually create, sustain, and defend those ostensible realities.

It is post-structuralists (or deconstructionists) like Jacques Derrida and Michel Foucault and neopragmatists like Richard Rorty who have appropriated this hermeneutic of suspicion and turned it on the overarching metanarratives themselves. In so doing, they give expression to a major shift in Western thought and culture. Middleton and Walsh describe this shift as the suspicion

> that the sure, absolutist claims of modernity are nothing more than historically conditioned conventions, of no more intrinsic worth than the conventions of non-Western or premodern cultures. And this suspicion is bolstered by the growing awareness of the violence inflicted by the modern West . . . not only on colonized and marginalized peoples, including women, but also . . . on the earth itself.[13]

The concern of the ultra-critics is not simply to expose universal claims as culturally conditioned, but to end the violence and suffering perpetrated in the service of those claims.

As Middleton and Walsh put it, this approach insists that "By granting an aura of universal truth to our local conventions, the Western intellectual commitment to realism serves ideologically to legitimate Western conquest and superiority."[14] The heterogeneity of reality is reduced to a simple, intellectually graspable system. What is lost is difference—the rich tapestry of culture, race, gender, and the earth itself is "dissolved or repressed into a totalizing vision of the world." Because such a vision excludes not only that which is different but "those who see things differently" it is "inherently violent" as well.[15]

It is, then, the metanarrative—the overarching explanatory story—which suppresses difference and engenders suffering. It is this the deconstructionists wish to deconstruct. In the oft-quoted words of Jean-Francois Lyotard, "Simplifying in the extreme, I define *postmodern* as incredulity toward metanarratives."[16]

As the Lyotard quote illustrates, for many this "ultra-critical" approach is what they mean by postmodernism. The "postmodern" label is appropriate on one level, for the deconstructionists and their kin are a sustained resistance movement against the tendency of Western modernity to absolutize itself. But in another sense they represent a form of late modernity, in which the logic of methodological doubt is carried to its fullest extent. While denying the autonomous self, they nonetheless retain a sense of collective human autonomy in that old realities can be rejected and new realities socially constructed. If humanity is no longer the arbiter of absolute truth, it remains the determiner of what counts as "true" and useful within a given social context.

Because these thinkers see "truth" as a social construct, relative to innumerable historical and social contexts, they are often charged with relativism.[17] That is certainly a fair reading, but some qualifications should be noted.

Foucault, who is closest to Nietzsche in his thought, understands any claim that something is rational, good, or true to be a form of power on behalf of certain interests to the exclusion of others. He rejects all theoretical language and general descriptions for the particular, and decries all normative judgements as hidden assertions of power. To describe an act as "criminal" or "insane" simply raises the question of who gets to define those terms and who does not. Foucault seems to advocate praxis without theory, and this does entail a relativism.

Derrida argues not only that texts have no external or objective reference but that they have an indeterminate meaning in themselves. Structuralists like Ferdinand de Saussure (1857–1913) had held the former view, but saw meaning as generated by the relations between the different elements of a text. Texts thereby generate their own meaning apart from external reality.

Derrida believes this alleged "structure" is not already in the text to be discovered by the reader but is actually imposed from without, by the interpreter. His thought, in the words of Walter Lowe,

> amounts to a series of strategies for undercutting or "deconstructing" the twofold lure of metaphysical monism (which collapses difference into one) and metaphysical dualism (which dichotomizes difference, creating opposition).[18]

The tendency of our language and thought is to look for certain terms and concepts to give structure to texts. This is done by setting up contrast terms—"inner" and "outer," "spiritual" and "physical," "existence" and "essence"—which make distinctions. Inevitably, these distinctions take on a hierarchical character, with one term considered "higher" or more central than the other. This oppositional dualism leads to a "metaphysics of presence" in which one element becomes self-evidently foundational while the other—the one that is different— is relegated to the margins. Derrida is convinced this feature of our language marks our culture as well. Philosophically, Enlightenment assumptions about the autonomous self functioned as a "presence" which obscured the relational character of our existence.

This is why for Derrida, meaning is never final—such meaning would be a form of "presence" which would exclude that to which it is opposed. His use of the term *différance* is not only meant to remind us of difference, but to continually defer meaning as well.

Derrida's belief in the indeterminacy of meaning makes plausible the charge that he is a relativist. Lowe, however, proposes an alternative reading. Could it be, he asks, that Derrida is "something more than the playful nihilist;"[19] that his "approach finally makes sense within the context of a fundamental struggle for truth . . . ?"[20] If Lowe is correct, then Derrida is not so much saying that all truth is relative as he is intent on not allowing penultimate claims to masquerade as ultimate truth. This would align Derrida more closely with the post-critical strand of postmodernism discussed in section 3.

Rorty, who appropriates Derrida in the service of a neopragmatism, claims to be antifoundationalist but not a relativist. He understands truth not as that which corresponds to objective reality but that which enables us to live in the world. Freed of the illusion of a timeless metaphysical truth, communities are able through discussion and debate to find common consensus around a more pragmatic truth. This communal construction of a contextualized truth is guided by shared standards for intellectual practice. Rorty is thus more optimistic than Derrida or Foucault, who would warn that it is precisely such communal consensus and shared assumptions that marginalizes that which is different.[21]

The difficulty with ultra-critics like Derrida and Foucault is caused by their concern—dare we say their moral passion—to oppose the injustice wrought by metanarratives. On what basis do they determine what constitutes injustice? Do they not, after all, have an implicit set of standards which they take to be "true," not just for them but for all? Are they not, in other words, self-contradictory on their own terms? Or, is part of their strategy to do both at once—to assert a standard of justice and freedom and simultaneously to deny such a standard is possible, and place us squarely in the tension that results?

Whether or not the ultra-critics are absolute relativists, it is evident that evangelical theology has a stake in making just the sort of over-arching truth claims these thinkers fear. Insofar as they move to embrace relativism, I shall not be able to follow.

However, we should not let the specter of relativism distract us from their more helpful insights. Certainly we must recognize that our theology is not and cannot be free of contextual bias, and to presume otherwise is to give our interpretation unwarranted authority. Moreover, they remind us how again and again culturally-based ideologies have claimed absolute status and thereby authorized injustice and human suffering. Christianity has not been exempt from such use. Unless we take this seriously, we may find ourselves advocating a gospel more indebted to our sin and finitude than to Christ and the Kingdom.

The "Post-Critical" Approach: The Critique of Criticism

If the ultra-critics call into question the Enlightenment quest for universal truth by showing all such "truths" to be contextual in origin and imperialistic in effect, the post-critics question the Enlightenment commitment to methodological doubt and the tradition it has spawned from Descartes to Derrida. While the ultra-critics represent the culmination of the hermeneutic of suspicion, post-critics seek to recover something like a hermeneutic of trust or affirmation.[22]

At the same time, they are decidedly *post*-critical (or "meta-critical") rather than pre-critical; they utilize critique without absolutizing it. Paul Ricoeur, one exemplar of this approach, argues that hermeneutics is animated by a double motivation:

> Willingness to suspect, willingness to listen; vow of rigor, vow of obedience. In our time we have not finished doing away with *idols* and we have barely begun to listen to *symbols*.[23]

For Ricoeur, this double motivation finds expression in a certain order: first critique, then listening faith. The faith which results is no longer

> the first faith of the simple soul, but rather the second faith of one who has engaged in hermeneutics, faith that has undergone criticism, post-critical faith. . . . It is a rational faith, for it interprets; but it is a faith because it seeks, through interpretation, a second naïveté.[24]

Besides the use of critique to expose idolatry and purify faith, there is another nuance to the term "post-critical." It refers as well to those who participated in modernity only to come up empty, who pursued the critical quest to its skeptical conclusion and then became skeptical of skepticism. Thus some post-critics will emphasize a retrieval of tradition as an alternative to a modernity that has failed.

For all its diversity, the post-critical strand of postmodernism can be distinguished from the ultra-critical by a far more positive attitude toward narrative, tradition, and community. In addition, many of its adherents have a more confident epistemology, something on the order of a critical realism. It is harder to generalize about post-critics than ultra-critics, so I will proceed by briefly discussing several representative figures. The ones I have chosen—Ludwig Wittgenstein, Alasdair MacIntyre, and Michael Polanyi—together exhibit the central themes of the post-critical strand.

Of enormous significance for the post-critical strand of postmodernism is the work of the "later" Wittgenstein on the philosophy of language.[25] There he decisively undermines the long dominant representation theory which declares the function of language to represent or picture things in the world (realism) or ideas in the mind (idealism). Instead, Wittgenstein argues that language functions in a variety of ways, and its function depends largely on how it is used in ordinary public discourse.

Language, then, is a social activity. We learn how to use language appropriately—we are trained in its rules or "grammar"— as we participate in the rough and tumble of everyday life. That is, as we engage in the practices which constitute a "form of life," we are trained in a common language which enables us to not only communicate but share concepts and experiences. Indeed, it is language which makes possible our having those concepts and experiences.

There are innumerable overlapping communities of discourse, each with its own language and grammar. What counts as "good" or "true" or "mistaken" varies, depending on the nature of the community and how the language is used. While each of these "language games" has its own logic, none are self-contained; persons not only belong to multiple communities, but there are linkages between them through language that is used in roughly the same way. Furthermore, the grammar of each language game is not rigidly fixed, but evolves as practices change over time.

The postmodern character of this proposal can be seen at a number of points. First, communal practices are prior to and enable our experience, undercutting the Enlightenment ideal of the autonomous rational individual and transcending the subject/object dualism which it implies. Second, by emphasizing the embodied character of human existence, Wittgenstein replaces the mind/body dualism of Descartes and Kant with a more holistic anthropology. It is our embodiment which connects us to the world. Third, he denies the Cartesian assumption that the greater the precision of language, the more accurate it is. Language for Wittgenstein is accurate if it accomplishes its task; exacting precision may or may not be required, and could even be a hindrance in particular instances.

Wittgenstein has been claimed as a precursor to the ultra-critical strand of postmodernism; Rorty considers him an influence on his own thought. Accordingly, Wittgenstein has been variously described as a "constructivist," or "anti-realist," holding that truth is relative to the linguistic community to which one belongs. This misreading is due in part to the failure to note how language games are not mutually exclusive but overlap and impinge on one another. Moreover, Wittgenstein is best seen as an opponent of both idealism and an uncritical realism. His point is not that we cannot know reality, but we do not know it in an unmediated way. Rather, our experience of the world is mediated through and made possible by the linguistic communities in which we participate. This is what gives us the language wherein we can ask and discuss whether or not a claim is "true." Thus Wittgenstein opens the way for a more critical, or "non-dualistic" realism.[26]

Finally, Rorty's appropriation of Wittgenstein appears to be selective. Unlike Rorty, Wittgenstein does not talk of a given community reaching a consensus on certain beliefs; rather they have a consensus on the use of language which enables them to discuss with understanding their varying beliefs.

While Wittgenstein developed a postmodern description of linguistic communities, Alasdair MacIntyre has proposed moral communities which transcend the universalist and individualist ethics of the Enlightenment. MacIntyre shows how the "Enlightenment project of justifying morality"—that is, the attempt to develop an "independent rational justification of morality"[27] failed because it sought to derive a universal ethic from human nature. Whether the chosen human element was rationality, emotion, or the will, no credible basis for traditional Western morality could be established. There was no criterion or framework of belief within which the rival accounts of morality could be assessed. The result was emotivism, wherein what is considered moral is understood as simply the expression of the feelings or attitudes of the individual.

Their premodern predecessors, both classical and religious, had grounded ethics very differently. Their accounts of the moral life depended in each case on the contrast between human nature as it is and human nature as it could be, with a means to move from the former to the latter.[28] It was the description of the essence or goal (*telos*) of humanity which provided the criteria for what is moral, not the actual condition of humanity in its present state—that actual condition constituted the problem for which ethics was the answer. By divesting themselves of premodern conceptions of either the creation or goal of humanity, Enlightenment thinkers were left with the impossible task of grounding morality in human nature as it is.

MacIntyre envisions the recovery of moral communities which embody particular moral traditions that provide just such a description of the *telos* of humanity. He defines a living tradition as "an historically extended, socially embodied argument" concerning "the goods which constitute that tradition."[29] Thus the quest for the *telos* is conducted within a tradition of discourse about the object of the quest.

Such a tradition provides an ongoing unity and identity for the lives of the participants in the community by way of a narrative which identifies the *telos* or central good around which all other goods can be ordered. In one sense the *telos* of the narrative is already known as the ethical goal toward which all participants strive; in another sense the *telos* is only fully known as it is sought by way of encountering dangers, temptations, and distractions along the way.[30]

It is the stories of the community which educate the members of the community as to the virtues necessary for the realization of *telos*.[31] These virtues are dispositions which not only enable persons to overcome the dangers along the way but sustain their participation in those communal practices through which the common goods of the tradition are realized.[32]

Like Wittgenstein, MacIntyre questions the modern assumption that the individual is prior to the community. Instead, we become who we are through the cultivation of those virtues which enable us to engage in the practices of a community. That is, our characters are formed and shaped by the stories and tradition of our community. His ethics is marked not by the Enlightenment concern for what the individual should choose but rather by what kind of persons we should be.

Although he draws heavily upon Aristotle, MacIntyre is not simply returning to a premodern ideal. Rather he sees the moral community as he has depicted it as an ever-new possibility, to be manifested in a variety of forms. "What matters at this stage," he concludes, "is the construction of local forms of community within which civility and the intellectual and moral life can be sustained."[33] Thus he does not seek to impose a particular narrative or tradition on everyone, but rather to expose the implicit governing narrative of modernity and describe the conditions under which alternative moral narratives can take root. At the same time, he does not join the ultra-critics in deconstructing all narratives; rather he sees tradition, narrative and community as the essential context within which moral personhood is possible.

Is MacIntyre, then, a relativist? At first glance it might seem that he is, for he makes the very postmodern claim that

> Each tradition can at each stage of its development provide rational justification for its central theses in its own terms, employing the concepts and standards by which it defines itself, but there is no set of independent standards of rational justification by appeal to which the issues between contending traditions can be decided.[34]

Yet this does not entail relativism for two reasons. First MacIntyre specifically advances a carefully crafted version of the correspondence theory of truth, in which a prior belief is held to be false by a tradition when there is a "lack of correspondence, between what the mind then judged and believed and reality as it is now perceived."[35] MacIntyre notes that the judgement that a prior belief is false is a failure of the mind, not of its objects. It is the mind which stands in need of correction. Those realities which mind encounters reveal themselves as they are.[36]

By distinguishing between reality and our knowledge of reality, MacIntyre combines confidence in what one now knows with a continual openness to new knowledge.

Second, like Wittgenstein, MacIntyre does not view the independence of one community's standards of rational justification from another's to mean that the two traditions cannot communicate—"What is said from within one tradition" can be "heard or overheard by those in another."[37] Rather than being isolated, traditions can mutually challenge and inform one another in a variety of ways.

This can be especially significant when a tradition faces an "epistemological crisis," in which unresolved issues begin to accumulate or new inadequacies are discovered which resist solution by inquiry and debate according to the tradition's own standards. Such a crisis demands an "imaginative conceptual innovation" which at one and the same time develops new concepts and theories while maintaining continuity with the "shared beliefs which define the tradition."[38]

One way an epistemological crisis can be provoked is through an encounter with a rival tradition. A community may adopt a new tradition—the word "conversion" comes to mind, although MacIntyre does not use it—if, by the standards of the old, it is found to be "superior in rationality and in respect of its claims to truth than their own." In other words, the new tradition has exposed "a lack of correspondence" between the dominant beliefs of the old and reality.[39]

Michael Polanyi, a scientist turned philosopher, shares many of MacIntyre's concerns. He sees the Enlightenment as culminating in both moral nihilism and totalitarianism which are strikingly at variance from the deeper Greek and Christian intellectual traditions of the West. The result in the twentieth century has been massive suffering and pervasive anxiety. He believes the cause lies in the growing lack of confidence in our capacity to know; the failure of Enlightenment epistemology to understand how we actually come to know something as true.

Polanyi proposes an alternative epistemology based upon two central concepts: "tacit knowledge" and "indwelling." Much as Wittgenstein turned to ordinary language to understand its use, Polanyi examines everyday knowledge for clues to how we know. What he finds is that most of our knowledge is tacit—it is like knowing how to ride a bicycle or use a tool. Initially, it is awkward until one learns the skill, then it becomes unselfconscious and natural. The bicycle rider can focus not on balance but destination, the person with a hammer can focus not on how to hammer but on the nail. Neither could tell you exactly how they ride or hammer, but clearly they have acquired the knowledge enabling them to do so. It is a knowledge that does not depend on logical demonstration from the evidence nor on knowing its scientific explanation.[40]

What Polanyi noticed was that such knowledge involved a kind of Gestalt, in which the various parts become integrated into a whole that makes sense. That is, we attend *from* the particulars and *to* the meaning of the whole. Thus, in the words of Drusilla Scott, the "intuition by which a great scientist sees a new pattern in the facts is only a development of an everyday skill."[41]

How do we develop the epistemological skills involved in tacit knowing, which enable us to make sense out of our world? Polanyi argues that it is through indwelling our own particular culture and tradition. As Scott explains,

> Our whole cultural heritage in which we grow up, the language, the moral values, the artistic standards, the ways of behaving and dressing and looking at the world—all this is gradually taken into ourselves, or we came to dwell in it, and to use it as our means of handling and understanding the world. It is futile to think we could get to any understanding of the world except by starting from the particular inheritance in which we happen to have been brought up.[42]

Like Wittgenstein's language game and MacIntyre's moral community, Polanyi believes that it is the very particular tradition of which we are apart that enables us to reason, know, and speak of reality at all.

Yet while we begin our knowing within our own particularity, we reason with "universal intent"—we make "statements that claim to be accepted by anyone who understands the problem for which they offer an answer."[43] This is entirely appropriate, for what we have to deal with is a common reality, which we seek to truthfully describe in the language available to us. Polanyi is explicit in this:

> We can account for this capacity of ours to know more than we can tell if we believe in the presence of an external reality with which we can make contact. This I do. I declare myself committed to the belief in an external reality gradually accessible to knowing.[44]

This reality, because it is independent of us, draws us ever closer, attracts us with its beauty, depth, and mystery.[45] There is thus no unchanging knowledge for Polanyi—as we seek this reality, we come to know more and sometimes we learn to see this reality in a new way, intuitively viewing the particulars in a new pattern, which we believe more adequately expresses it.[46]

That there is no unchanging knowledge does not mean for Polanyi there is no truth. What we know is true if it shows forth the internal coherence of reality.[47] It is genuine knowledge which does not entail Cartesian certainty and precision, but does evoke confidence and commitment.

Polanyi is "committed to a belief" in this external reality. Underlying his epistemology is a necessary but unprovable faith commitment—necessary because it is the precondition for knowledge, unprovable because there is no universal rational foundation upon which it rests. The Kantian dualism between fact and faith is thus a misunderstanding of both science and religion, for each rests ultimately upon faith that there is a reality which can be known.

This is why knowledge for Polanyi is personal yet objective. It involves creativity and originality, an imaginative insight into the pattern of reality. But knowledge is not a product of a disembodied mind, but of a whole person who lives in the world and is in contact with it. Such knowledge is always accountable to an independent reality encountered not as a construct but as a given.[48]

In this we can see what distinguishes post-critical thinkers like MacIntyre and Polanyi from those who are ultra-critical. The latter argue for a postmodern idealism in which a pattern constructed by our minds is then imposed imperialistically on texts and the world. They are suspicious of the hidden motives behind these constructs and therefore call them into question. The post-critics are postmodern realists for whom the pattern is in reality itself, intuitively grasped by persons who indwell particular communities and traditions. Yet because of this particularity there is for them always a gap between what we know and reality as it is; our knowledge is true yet revisable, and rightly evokes in us humility but not presumption.

Given this, it is no wonder the post-critics are more comfortable with narrative, tradition, and truth claims. Such claims can be made precisely because they *are* revisable, and it is living traditions which enable us who participate in them to know and express the truths with confidence but not finality.

There are rich resources for theology in this post-critical approach. Postliberal theologians like Hans Frei, George Lindbeck, and Stanley Hauerwas have already made creative use of post-critical insights,[49] and evangelicals are beginning to do likewise.[50] The impact of this form of postmodernism on my own thought as well as that of other evangelicals will be clear in the chapters that follow.

The Challenge of Postmodernism

How shall evangelical theology engage postmodernism? We cannot in my judgement permit either strand of postmodernism to establish criteria for what is deemed an acceptable theology—we leave that strategy to the liberals. As I shall argue in the next chapter, an evangelical theology must be grounded in and held accountable to God's revelation in Jesus Christ.

That said, we nonetheless have a responsibility as Christians living in this time in history to critically evaluate postmodern thought, rejecting whatever is inconsistent with that revelation and utilizing in a nonfoundational way whatever enables us to understand more deeply and communicate more effectively the faith we profess. There are at least two ways we can constructively approach postmodernism.

First, we can listen with care to the concerns which motivate postmodern thought, identify those we believe are legitimate, and attempt to address them from the standpoint of evangelical Christianity. For example, the ultra-critics find metanarratives both incredible and imperialistic. We can and should show why we make universal truth claims on behalf of a very particular revelation, as well as how that revelation is neither imperialistic or oppressive. These are, in my judgement, valid concerns, but they can only be addressed appropriately by showing how our truth claims arise out of the internal logic of the revelation itself. This I seek to do in chapter four.

Second, we can utilize postmodern resources when they enable us to more faithfully and effectively understand and communicate that revelation. Here the post-critical strand is especially helpful through providing new insights into the relationship between tradition, narrative, community, and truth. A critical appropriation of post-critical thought may open new ways of thinking—or enable the recovery of old ways of thinking for our day.

There is one further challenge to an evangelical theology, indeed to any theology, which emerges from postmodernism taken as a whole. Put succinctly, it is the question "What difference does all of this really make?" That is, if Christian claims are true, then there should be some evidence in how we form our communities and live our lives in the world. This is the most important concern of them all. It will be directly addressed in the final chapters as the culmination of the theology I am proposing; because of this, it will at the same time be our constant companion as we set forth an evangelical theology for a postmodern world.

CHAPTER 4

The Resurrection of the Crucified Jesus

It was the particularity of Christian claims—that God's act of redemption for the world was in and through a particular person, Jesus of Nazareth—which modernity found so offensive. The problem was not that Christianity claimed to teach universal truth—those claims, after all, could be verified by reason. It was eminently acceptable for Jesus to be a teacher of universal truth, or for his life to exemplify that truth. But to insist a particular person who lived at a particular point in history is the Savior and Lord of the entire world seemed more like muddled thinking than good news to those schooled in Enlightenment assumptions—a "scandal of particularity."

But assumptions they were, the product of the Western intellectual tradition. In contrast to modernity, the postmodern world is happily populated by a host of particular claims, with an accompanying diversity of cultures and beliefs. The particularity of Jesus Christ is in itself not problematic to postmodernity. It is the claim that Jesus is of universal redemptive significance that it finds difficult—a "scandal of universality."

Thus for very different reasons, modernity and postmodernity resist the Christian linkage of the universal with the particular. Why, then, do most Christians not only continue to claim but proclaim Jesus as Savior and Lord of all? How is this theology not simply one more example of an unwarranted and oppressive metanarrative? And how do Christians know what they say they know?

The Resurrection: A Theological Revolution

"Christianity," says Jürgen Moltmann, "stands or falls with the reality of the raising of Jesus from the dead by God."[1] That "this Jesus God raised up" (Acts 2:32)—that Jesus of Nazareth, who lived a particular kind of life and died a particular kind of death has been raised from the dead and is presently alive, to die no more—is the basis for the Christian claims that Jesus is Lord and Savior of all, indeed, that Jesus is the divine Son of God. As Paul wrote the Corinthian church, "if Christ has not been raised, then our proclamation has been in vain and your faith has been in vain. . . . But in fact Christ has been raised from the dead." (I Cor. 15:14, 20).

Some of the Corinthian Christians, like so many others both then and now, sought to incorporate Christian teaching within their pre-existing understanding of God and reality. With this the resurrection simply would not cooperate. As Lesslie Newbigin has said so well, "the simple truth is that the resurrection cannot be accommodated in any way of understanding the world except one of which it is the starting point."[2]

The resurrection, contrary to what some modern theologians seem to think, was not at all plausible to the allegedly primitive people of the first century. They, like we, were very much aware that human beings do not rise from the dead to live forever, certainly not in the midst of history. T. F. Torrance rightly notes that both incarnation and resurrection

> forced themselves upon the minds of Christians from their own empirical and theoretical ground *in sharp antithesis* to what they had believed about God and *in genuine conflict* with the . . . world view of their age.[3]

The impact of Jesus' resurrection led to nothing less than a paradigm shift among the early Christians, in which their vision of God and reality was radically reconfigured and given now meaning. As Torrance says, the resurrection event (as well as the incarnation) "took root within the Church only through a seismic restructuring of religious and intellectual belief;"[4] the shock waves are evident throughout the pages of the New Testament itself. It was a theological revolution.

Describing the resurrection event as provoking a paradigm shift both then and now is in sharp contrast to the views of some liberal theologians, which Peter Carnley aptly terms the "resurrection as non-event." What these liberals hold in common is a belief that "faith is based on the completed life of Jesus" which ended with the crucifixion. The resurrection story is "a way of expressing this faith; it is the product of faith rather than the ground of it."[5] That is, it was not the event of Easter which evoked the disciples' faith, but the event of faith in the disciples which was subsequently expressed by way of the Easter story.

Proponents of this view operate well within the assumptions of modernity. Faced with an event that contradicts modern Western understandings of history and science, they seek an alternative explanation which makes this event unnecessary. Thus they reinterpret the accounts of appearances of the risen Jesus and the empty tomb as ways of expressing a faith or mission which did not die on Good Friday but persisted in the hearts of the disciples.

The difficulties with this approach are well-known.[6] It presumes to know what the New Testament writers *really* mean when they say "Jesus is risen!" Clearly it cannot mean what it seems to say— that the Jesus who was crucified has come back to life to die no more—so it must mean something else, like "My faith in Jesus lives on in spite of his death" or "The work of Jesus continues." The problem is, of course, that this is not what the texts actually say—it is a reading into the texts a meaning that is not there. From the earliest accounts (e.g. Paul in I Corinthians 15) the testimony is that the risen Jesus appeared to the disciples, and that this resurrected Jesus was the same one who had been crucified.

Understanding the resurrection as an event which led to a paradigm shift is also in contrast to the apologetic approach of evangelical evidentialists such as John Warwick Montgomery who make a case for the resurrection as an historical event. The difficulty is not necessarily with the particular arguments used; indeed while not conclusive, many are persuasive. The problem is with what is assumed at the outset, that the resurrection, to be true, must be rationally defensible in terms of a modern Western understanding of history and rationality. This concedes too much to the Western worldview. I agree instead with Newbigin that "We cannot demonstrate the truth of Christianity by reference to something else."[7]

Newbigin's elaboration of this point is important. When Christians are asked on what grounds they base their claim that Jesus is Savior and Lord, "what is really being asked, of course, is that we should show that the gospel is in accordance with the reigning plausibility structure of our society." That, says Newbigin, "is exactly what we cannot and must not do." Instead, Christians offer an entirely "new starting point for thought," God's own revelation in those events to which the Scriptures testify, and whose center is in Jesus Christ.[8]

So: a paradigm shift occurred, indeed occurs today for anyone who comes to believe in Jesus Christ. What are the basic features of this new way of understanding reality which the resurrection makes possible?

> The heart of its meaning is eschatological. As Torrance says, the resurrection of Jesus heralds an entirely new age in which a universal resurrection or transformation of heaven and earth will take place, or rather has already begun to take place, for with the resurrection of Jesus that new world has already broken into the midst of the old.[9]

This is why in the New Testament the resurrection is the decisive turning point which confirms Jesus' life, gives power to his cross, exalts him as eternal Lord, and inaugurates his presence to all through the Holy Spirit. Christology, eschatology and soteriology all come together in the resurrection; through it, the particular person Jesus of Nazareth is given universal significance.

All pre-resurrection reflection on the meaning or identity of Jesus was revised, confirmed or discarded in light of the resurrection. The resurrection did not substitute a "new" Christ of faith for an "old" Jesus of history (as Kantian modernity might suppose) but clarified just who that Jesus was and is.

There are two types of encounters with the risen Jesus: the visible appearances to the early disciples (I Cor. 15:4–7) and his presence through the Holy Spirit, especially in the midst of the community gathered for worship. These experiences of the risen Jesus implied Jesus' ultimate significance, for a resurrection is an eschatological event. While a general resurrection was expected at the end of history by much of Israel, the resurrection of one person in the midst of history was totally unanticipated. Even in the New Testament, where Jesus predicts his own resurrection, the disciples misunderstand and doubt him; indeed, in Matthew 28:17, at the ascension of Jesus some still doubt.

It is in the face of this astonishing encounter with the risen Jesus that the disciples begin to proclaim that Jesus is Lord. The ultimate future—the Kingdom of God—had not only been proclaimed by Jesus but was now seen to be embodied in his life and death, his teachings and miracles, his words and actions. He was Lord of all, and would one day return and bring the Kingdom of God to completion. On the basis of the resurrection, the history of Jesus is read forward to the eschaton, and the life of the coming Kingdom is seen as already present in Jesus.

But the logic of the resurrection requires a backward reading as well. Because he is risen, the particular identity of Jesus reveals the nature of the God who raised him and of the eschatological future he anticipates. Jesus' identity with God in the resurrection is the basis for his identification with God in the incarnation. It is also the basis for the worship in the early church which acknowledges Jesus as God.

The eschatological ultimacy of the resurrection has two aspects. First, it is universal in scope, embracing not just Israel but all of history and creation. This was not of course instantly obvious to the first Christians, but became so as they began (with the Spirit's help) to work out the implications of this event. The second aspect is its finality, that because Jesus reveals the Kingdom of God, Jesus is the final revelation of God.

Ultimacy, then, is given to a person—to his own particular actions and teachings; to his own particular interpretation and embodiment of the Kingdom of God; to his life and especially to the death toward which that life led him. It is Jesus of Nazareth and none other who is Savior and Lord.

The risen Jesus is also a living Lord, who is present and active in the world today. This is perhaps an even more controversial claim than Jesus' eventual return, because while that can be affirmed without immediate evidence, present activity cannot. We shall in later chapters consider the forms this active presence takes; this will include a discussion of the church. For now we can note that it is the living presence of Christ which enables persons to have an ongoing relationship with him, and the active power of the Spirit by which persons are brought to new life in Christ. It is also by the Spirit that the work of Christ is presently manifested in the world at large.

Having seen that the resurrection is the necessary basis for Christianity, and examined central elements of the paradigm shift it evoked, it remains to ask how this Christian truth claim can be articulated in a postmodern world. This is, after all, a claim about reality: it insists that a historical person who died is now alive, never to die again, through "an event of cosmic and unbelievable magnitude."[10] If the basis for the claim is the resurrection itself, can it then be tested?

The ultimate test is eschatological—whether or not Jesus Christ returns to inaugurate a Kingdom whose nature corresponds to that of Jesus. But Lesslie Newbigin, drawing on insights of Michael Polanyi, provides a penultimate approach. Newbigin argues that knowing depends on a prior act of believing, a personal commitment to a particular vision of reality "in the knowledge that others may disagree and that one may be proved wrong." But this vision, which for Christians rests on the resurrection, is not "merely subjective;" it is made with "universal intent" and those whose faith is in Christ seek to persuade others "that it is a true account of reality."[11]

What Newbigin suggests is that, if Christian claims are true, then they will enable persons to make sense of reality in a way that can be communicated to others. This does not provide Cartesian certainty, which today is an increasingly incredible claim, but it does provide a "proper confidence"[12] for faith and practice in a postmodern world.

There is an important corollary to this approach. If the resurrection is true, then there will be Christian communities where its impact will be evident, and persons for whom faith in it will have made a significant difference in how they live their lives. For many in a postmodern world, the existence of such communities and lives will be the only evidence they will seek.

The Cross: The Identity of Jesus Christ

While the resurrection gives Jesus an ultimate significance, it does not determine the content of that significance, except by laying the foundation for the claim that it is the crucified Jesus who is Savior, Lord, and God. The content of this ultimacy cannot be imposed on Jesus from the tradition of Jewish eschatology, and much less from Hellenistic ideas of divinity and lordship. The content of this ultimacy—and hence of the Kingdom of God—can only be based on the identity of the one who was resurrected. It is his life and death that says who this Jesus is.

It is to insure the identity of the risen One as the same Jesus who had lived, suffered and died on a cross that the risen Jesus appeared to his disciples. In Luke, two disciples recognize him as he performs the characteristic act of breaking bread (Luke 24:31). John records Thomas feeling the wounds, and then calling the crucified and risen Jesus both Lord and God (John 20:27–28); seven days earlier the risen Jesus had shown the other disciples his hands and his feet and "they were glad when they saw the Lord" (John 20:20). In Acts, Peter boldly proclaims the identity, stating that "God has made him both Lord and Christ, this Jesus whom you crucified." (Acts 2:36; see also Acts 5:30 and especially 10:36–41). Paul, too, emphasizes the identity of the risen Jesus with the crucified, especially in I Corinthians 1–2 where he seems to be faced with docetic tendencies which would universalize Christ at the expense of his particularity, and thus lead persons to seek and expect a very different form of salvation. Early on the life and death of Jesus operated critically to expose distorted Christologies and alien salvations encouraged by Hellenistic religious pluralism.

We have seen that resurrection makes coherent the Christian claim not simply to be inspired by Jesus as a figure from the past but to have a relationship with a living Jesus in the present. Yet logically one could envision another alternative: the risen Jesus could be understood as ascended and absent rather than ascended yet present. It is the life and death of Jesus, together with the coming of the promised Holy Spirit, which rules out that alternative: Jesus' life and death indicate a solidarity of God with humanity which is essential to who Jesus is. For the risen Jesus to not be present would mean he is not the same as Jesus of Nazareth.

I shall be insisting, especially in the final chapters, that knowing about Jesus is not the same as knowing Jesus—there is a vast difference between having information and having a relationship. But here an equally significant point must be emphasized: there can be no personal relationship without personal content, no presence of Christ without identity. Jesus is not whoever we want him to be; he is who he is by virtue of his own words and actions, which we take to be the words and actions of God as well as a human. Presence without identity invites idolatry.

Some liberal theologians are nonetheless prepared to run this risk. Peter Carnley notes that it's "the sneaking awareness that there is not sufficient evidence to prove the occurrence of the resurrection as an event of the past" that has led these theologians to emphasize instead "a present encounter with his glorified presence." However, this "raised Christ tends to become so elusive as to recede from view and all but disappear."[13] The present experience of the risen Christ cannot be detached so easily from Jesus of Nazareth.

While the life and death of Jesus together constitute his identity, it is the cross that is central. It is to the cross which the life of Jesus moves, and it is in the cross that Jesus reveals the love of God and effects redemption. How this is understood will be the subject of chapter eight; that it is the case is the testimony of the New Testament. The cross is a divine sacrifice given out of love for humanity: "God proves his love for us in that while we were yet sinners Christ died for us" (Romans 5:8); "In this is love, not that we love God but that he loved us and sent his

Son to be the atoning sacrifice for our sins" (I John 4:10). The cross is essentially what we mean when we say, "God is love" (I John 4:16).

It is also the very heart of the Christian "metanarrative." The postmodern ultra-critics find any such overarching understanding of reality intrinsically oppressive; since no metanarrative can be universally true, it amounts to the Christian imposition of one particular view of reality on everyone else. Now it is clear Christianity has a metanarrative of the most comprehensive sort, beginning with creation and fall, culminating in the eschaton, and having at its very center Jesus Christ. As we have seen, the Christian claim for truth of this metanarrative rests on the very particular event of the resurrection of Jesus from the dead. How, then, does this truth claim avoid imperialism?

The answer lies in the nature of the metanarrative itself. While the Christian metanarrative can be used to oppress, it is by no means clear that it is essentially oppressive simply by making universal truth claims. Rather, to faithfully live according to this narrative, one must love in the way God has loved us, in response to God's love for us. Given God's love for us as manifested in the life and above all the death of Jesus Christ, to seek to conquer others in the name of Christ is to misunderstand who the Lord Jesus Christ is.

However, the ultra-critics have more in mind than violence when they oppose metanarratives as imperialistic. They mean as well the subtle manner in which one group of persons define reality for another, such that those who are dominant conceptually enslave those who are not. To only argue that, rightly understood, the Christian metanarrative exercises a relatively more benevolent dictatorship is to have a dictatorship still.

This critique pushes us to fundamental beliefs. Ultimately, the Christian account of the meaning and purpose of creation is based on what God has done, not what we have conceived; it is received more as a divine imposition on us via the resurrection than something we impose on others. Because we believe it to be true and receive it as good news, we are compelled to share this gospel with others. But given the nature of the God who we proclaim, we must take care that our sharing is neither manipulative nor abusive. It must be admitted that such care has not always been taken, and insofar that it has not we have betrayed Jesus Christ.

Is it in our interest to spread this gospel? Yes, in the sense that we are motivated by a love that has been graciously given, and which is ultimately beyond our comprehension. Yes, in that gratitude and praise compels us to share that which we have so wonderfully received. But this is not what is normally meant by something "being in our interest." The cross is not a likely object of human self-interest; rather it contradicts what people count as desirable. Of course, it can and has been construed as offering "cheap grace" (in the words of Dietrich Bonhoeffer), but that this is readily seen as a distortion indicates it is not what the cross is about. Rather, the implications of the cross for those who rely on it is that they will reflect the same love in their own lives. "If any want to become my followers," said Jesus, "let them deny themselves and follow me. For those who want to save their life will lose it, and those who lose their life for my sake and for the sake of the gospel will save it." (Mark 8:34–35) This did not win the disciples' votes at the time, and is not our normal inclination today. But it is the way of God.

This introduces a final point. Jesus is simply not the way we would expect or want God to be. We look for coercive power, hopefully manifested on our behalf; what we get is the power of the cross. We can identify then with Peter's reaction to Jesus' predicted crucifixion, "God forbid it, Lord! This must never happen to you" (Matthew 16:22). But God does not forbid it, God undergoes it. The centurion at the cross was more perceptive: "Truly this man was God's Son!" (Matthew 27:54).

The Christian metanarrative does claim universality, but does not do so imperialistically. Rather it poses a question: "Who do you say that I am?" To answer that Jesus is Savior and Lord, the divine Son of God, is to reconfigure the way one understands the world and one's own life. The Christian believes that it is in this way that one begins to live according to the way things really are in the coming yet already inaugurated Kingdom of God.

The Spirit: An Epistemological Revolution

It should be evident from the foregoing that Christian truth claims cannot be established on the basis of some prior or deeper belief. The resurrection is itself the basic belief, which provides a new perspective on reality and gives a new direction to human thought and life. We've seen how such claims, though ultimately eschatological, are nonetheless testable at least in terms of whether their depiction of reality seems to make sense of the world in which we live.

This does not yet answer the question as to how Christians come to know this truth. Although the first disciples were witnesses to the appearances of the risen Jesus, later Christians are not. "Have you believed because you have seen me?" Jesus said to Thomas, "Blessed are those who have not seen and yet have come to believe" (John 20:29).

Those who had not seen were nonetheless convinced that they had experienced something of the presence of the risen Jesus, and had done so through the Holy Spirit. As Carnley says, they claimed to have "experienced a given, empirical reality in their lives," perceiving and knowing "its active presence" not simply "by description but by acquaintance."[14] This was neither an esoteric experience nor a merely cognitive knowing, rather it was an encounter with a reality outside of themselves in a manner analogous to perceiving any other external reality.

Carnley rightly notes that this experience of the Spirit is ambiguous in nature. Persons are

> free to perceive and claim to know its impact in their lives or are able not to be aware of it at all, primarily because of its own very elusive and transcendent nature and their own inclination either to see and attend or not to see by immersing themselves in the natural and material world.[15]

This raises two epistemological issues. The first is, given our immersion in the natural and material world, how do we become aware of this presence? Second, having become aware, how do we know its the presence of Jesus Christ? In both cases, our answer has to do with the work of the Holy Spirit.

To begin with the first: John Wesley was very much aware of how our immersion in our own culture or activities can prevent our attending to the reality of God. We are, says Wesley, "encompassed on all sides with persons and things that tend to draw us from our centre."[16] Such persons and things are not necessarily evil in themselves; indeed, they may well be part of God's good creation. But whatever their nature, the result is that our hearts become "unhinged from God, their proper centre, and scattered to and fro among the poor, perishing, unsatisfying things of the world."[17] Wesley's term for this was dissipation, which he defines as "the art of forgetting God,"[18] being "habitually inattentive to the presence and will" of our Creator.[19]

It is evident, I hope, that the dissipation Wesley describes is not peculiar to eighteenth century England. This is a perennial issue, faced by those who are Christians as well as those who are not. The role of media such as television as purveyors of cultural values only exacerbates the problem in our day.

The "radical cure of all dissipation" for Wesley is faith,[20] and faith is a gift of God, a work of the Holy Spirit. This faith involves trusting in Jesus Christ for salvation but is much more— it is the means by which we know God, as an experienced reality. Wesley describes it as a "spiritual sense," analogous to our physical senses,

> the demonstrative evidence of things unseen, the supernatural evidence of things invisible, not perceivable by eyes of flesh, or by any of our natural senses or faculties. Faith is that divine evidence whereby the spiritual man discerneth God and the things of God. It is with regard to the spiritual world what sense is with regard to the natural. It is the spiritual sensation of every soul that is born of God.[21]

Wesley is not alone in holding a "spiritual sense" epistemology—Jonathan Edwards developed a remarkably similar view. Both Wesley and Edwards were drawing upon deeply rooted themes in scripture and tradition, creatively recasting them in light of the Lockean empiricism of their century.

For both of them, faith was not a human possibility apart from the grace of God. In answering the question of why not all who want such faith have it immediately, Wesley answers (in words Edwards could endorse),

> No man is able to work it in himself. It is a work of omnipotence. It requires no less power thus to quicken a dead soul than to raise a body that lies in the grave. It is a new creation, and none can create a soul anew but he who at first created the heavens and the earth.[22]

Wesley and Edwards were not in agreement on how this grace worked. For Wesley grace enables a free human response which would otherwise not be possible; for Edwards grace is irresistible. Also, Wesley envisions a gradual work of God prior to new birth through prevenient and convicting grace. Nonetheless, it is clear that for both, faith can only be understood as the result of the action of the Holy Spirit.

This work of the Spirit is not so much to create new faculties of human understanding as it is (in the words of Conrad Cherry) to lay "a new foundation" in which the person "participates and from which the human powers operate."[23] In terms of the argument of this chapter, the new foundation which the Spirit provides is centered in the reality and presence of the risen Jesus.

While by no means identical in their beliefs, contemporary evangelicals like Helmut Thielicke, T. F. Torrance, G. C. Berkouwer, and Donald Bloesch echo the general epistemological approach of Wesley and Edwards. They agree that, apart from God, we are unable to know God at all; liberal approaches which begin with human experience may be attuned to the presuppositions of Enlightenment modernity but are a grievous error in Christian theology. We cannot, says Torrance, "substitute some theory of knowledge for the free activity of the Spirit." Our knowledge of God is inexplicable from the human side, for God "outruns all forms of our understanding";[24] the experience of faith, says Bloesch, "is qualitatively different . . . from ordinary human or even religious experience."[25]

Instead, it is only God who enables us to have this knowledge. Torrance states this with admirable clarity:

> As knowledge of God actually arises . . . we know we cannot attribute it to ourselves and know that we can only say something of how it arises by referring beyond ourselves to God's acts upon us. . . . The epistemological relevance of the Spirit lies in the dynamic and transformational aspects of this knowledge.[26]

There is a two-fold nature to this act of God. First, God offers God's own self as an object of our knowledge through acts of revelation in history. Second, the Holy Spirit enables us to know this revelation and appropriate it experientially.

Exactly what the Spirit does is variously explained. For Bloesch "faith is the work of the Spirit in the interiority of our being,"[27] the "intrusion of the Spirit of God into the human soul awakening us to our predicament and moving us to cleave to Jesus Christ as our only Savior."[28] Torrance describes the Spirit as bringing us into a relationship with God whereby we participate in God's own self-knowledge.

Thielicke, in striking language, calls this work the "death of the old Cartesian self" and a "new creation by the Spirit." In sharp contrast to "Cartesian theology" which begins with humanity's capacity to understand the gospel, and therefore leads to a reconstruction of the gospel to make it relevant to human thought or needs, Thielicke argues that the Spirit "incorporates the self into the salvation event instead of the reverse."[29] In the proclamation of the Word, the creative Spirit brings about a new birth in the hearer. In so doing, "it does not fit into the schemata of the old self nor submit to its conditions. It changes the schemata and implied conditions."[30] Thus the Word through the Spirit appropriates us to the gospel and integrates us into God's activity—there is a divine reconstruction of the human rather than a human reconstruction of the gospel.

Herein lies a central difference between Christianity and the ultracritics. They assume the Christian metanarrative is a cultural construct which we choose to believe—it is *our* narrative, and expression of *our* convictions, which we subsequently impose on others. Christians understand the gospel not as something we construct but as good news we receive; it is imposed on us, from the outside. It requires us to die both to our autonomous selves and our cultural certainties; God and not humanity is the agent of reconstruction.

Not only for Thielicke but for all of these theologians, the new birth and the gift of faith means a death to the Cartesian self—to the autonomous rational individual of modernity. This does not mean our human capacities themselves are negated or replaced; it is rather they function in a new context. Reason rests upon a faith commitment, not faith upon reason; the individual is not autonomous but placed within a history and a community which transforms self-understanding and enables one to see the world from a new perspective. Thus language of relationship, participation, and incorporation mark these theologies.

Moreover, they represent an effort to transcend the subject/object dualism of Descartes and Kant. Hence Bloesch describes his theology as "objective-subjective rather than fundamentally objective (as in evangelical rationalism) or predominantly subjective (as in existentialism and mysticism)."[31] Even Wesley and Edwards, who pre-date Kant, were struggling for a more holistic anthropology than the Enlightenment was offering.

The relational unity of object and subject—by way of the divine object who is at the same time the Subject who makes the relationship possible—enables them to talk of personal experience of God who is truly other. This uses the term "experience" in a way quite different from the nineteenth century, for which it meant something subjective or inward. For Wesley and Edwards, it meant an experiential knowledge of a God who is distinguished from ourselves; something akin to this seems to be affirmed by the contemporary evangelicals we have discussed as well. It undergirds a critical realist epistemology in which the knowledge of God is immediate yet mediated, direct yet necessarily expressed in language that is indirect, and which rests entirely on divine grace rather than human capacities.

The second epistemological issue which we raised at the beginning of this section was this: having become aware of the presence of the risen Jesus, how do we know that this presence is the same as Jesus of Nazareth? Indeed, how is it that the "presence of Jesus" and the "presence of God" can be used somewhat interchangeably, as we have been doing in the discussion so far?

This question is one of identity and its relationship to presence. Carnley, whose goal is to provide an account of the structure of resurrection belief, speaks of "knowing and remembering."[32] This is appropriate language for his purposes, for it reflects elements of human knowing. As an alternative I shall use the language of "identity" and "presence"[33] which has the advantage of directing our attention to God—that is, on *God's* identity and presence, and how we can speak of having a relationship with that God.

We can begin by asking what is necessary for us to have a relationship with another person over time. There are, at least two elements to any such relationship. First, someone must be "present;" that is, we must have access to another such that there can be a relationship. Second, we must be able to "get to know" the other person. This implies that any person has a set of distinctive traits—character, habits, personality, and the like—with which we can gradually become familiar, based in part on that person's unique history, cultural background, and formative relationships. This is that person's "identity."

Unlike a human being, God is spiritually present, with the accompanying "elusiveness" which we noted earlier. How, then, does one "get to know" God? The initial answer is that God has revealed God's identity to us by not only acting in our space/time world, but actually entering it in the form of a human being, Jesus of Nazareth. To know Jesus is to know God. While we may be able to talk of a relationship with a risen Christ who is present through the Holy Spirit, the identity of Jesus seems lodged in the past, in a history that has come and gone. And in one sense that is the case: what Jesus said and did, his life and death, is definitive of the identity of Jesus Christ.

Our experience of the identity of Jesus—if it is a living relationship and not simply recalling a past figure who is no longer present, like Socrates or Wesley—must therefore be indirect, or mediated. Presence and identity are one when we encounter the risen Jesus in the communal, liturgical, and devotional contexts which are at the very heart of the life of the church. That is, through the activity of the Spirit, the identity of the risen Jesus is experienced as we participate in word, sacrament, prayers, hymns, fellowship and other means of grace, and come to know him more deeply over time.

It is here that the logic of Wesley's "spiritual sense" epistemology is especially evident. To faith the identity and presence of God are not two things which we somehow must link, but a single experience as we encounter God in scripture, prayer, or eucharist. Faith is indeed "the evidence of things not seen; that is, of past, future, or spiritual things . . . ";[34] it enables us to experience the past reality of the cross, the present reality of the risen Christ, and the future reality of Christ's return all in the present, all as features of the identity and destiny of Jesus Christ and hence as foundational to our identity and destiny as well.

This is at its heart a trinitarian understanding of how we know God. It is Jesus Christ who reveals the identity of God and who is risen and therefore present; it is the Holy Spirit through whom the risen Jesus is universally present and gives us faith to perceive that presence and identity. The Spirit incorporates us and enables our participation in not only the community but the narrative of salvation, and in not only the narrative but the very life of God.

The truth claim at stake in this is eminently personal. It is, in short, the testimony of Christians that this Jesus who they experience as risen and with whom they have a relationship is Savior, Lord, and God; and likewise the God in whom they believe is revealed most fully and faithfully by Jesus of Nazareth. The claim is not simply that certain things about Jesus are true, but that Jesus *is* the truth, and his future is the future of creation. To live truthful lives requires that we be in relationship with this Jesus, so that through that relationship our lives can be transformed and begin to reflect the love which God has so richly given us in Jesus Christ.

Part III

Revelation
and the
Truth of Scripture

CHAPTER 5

The Inadequacies
of Propositionalism

The authority of scripture for theology has faced increasing criticism in the modern period in the West. Many liberals have ceased to accord scripture the primacy it once enjoyed, and a few have abandoned scriptural authority entirely. Evangelicals who resisted the modern turn to individual reason and experience have found themselves on the defensive, compelled now to provide a defense for what was once taken for granted.

The stakes are high indeed. For evangelical theology, scripture is closely linked to the special revelation of God in Israel and in Jesus Christ; many would insist it *is* revelation in its written form, while others would term it the product of revelation and its divinely authorized interpretation. This linkage of scripture to revelation is by way of the inspiration of the Holy Spirit, and it is this unique inspiration which makes scripture authoritative for theology. To understand scripture (as did many liberals) as a purely human expression of a religious experience rather than the written word of God would be to shift the ultimate authority of theology from God to humanity.

In addition to the general suspicion of received authority and the denial that particular persons or events can serve as a basis of universal truth, modernity raised two significant hermeneutical issues, two questions of "distance." The first is the distance between "text and event": does the account of the event or person given in the text accurately correspond to that event or person, or is there a difference between what the text says and what really happened? The liberal suspicion was, of course, that there is a difference; this has inspired among other things the thrice-repeated "search for the historical Jesus."

The second is the distance between "then and now": how can we, in our culture and place in history, understand a text written in a very different culture and historical era? Can such a text be construed as having relevance for us, much less making truth claims which seek our assent and trust? Although these two hermeneutical issues cannot be neatly separated, the first will be more the focus of this chapter and the next while the second will be that of chapter seven.

This chapter will begin by examining one common evangelical response to this challenge, rational propositionalism. While honoring the propositionalist commitment to scriptural truth, the difficulties with that position will point us instead to a narrative approach. In the next chapter we shall look at the chief non-evangelical proponents of narrative, the postliberals, to see if and how they address the question of truth. This in turn will enable us to see the way narratives do make truth claims.

The Propositionalist Approach to Scripture

Perhaps the most prominent proponent of the propositional view is Carl F. H. Henry. Because he has written on this at great length and depth,[1] he will serve as an excellent example of the position.

For Henry, revelation comes at God's initiative, in which "God steps out of his hiddenness to disclose what would otherwise remain secret and unknown."[2] Thus the purpose of this revelation is to provide information about God; its immediate correlate, says Henry, "is not salvation but knowledge;"[3] salvation or judgement is the consequence of our response to that knowledge. Revelation directly addresses our ignorance, not our sin, and it is only if we accept the truth of that revelation that we can then respond in faith and receive salvation.

Revelation understood in this way is both rational and propositional. It is rational because God is rational. As a divine communication, revelation is trustworthy, logically consistent, and without internal contradiction. It is the basis for the only comprehensive and internally consistent system of truth.

But revelation is also rational because we are rational, created in the image of a rational God. Reason is the central attribute of both God and humanity because it is what allows this divine communication. Thus, "Revelation in the Bible is essentially a mental conception: God's disclosure is rational and intelligible communication."[4] Consequently, revelation can be grasped by the human mind without any special insight or illumination.

The mediating agent of all divine revelation is the divine Logos. The Logos was the preincarnate mediator of creation, the incarnate mediator of redemption, and, now glorified, will mediate the coming Kingdom.[5] For Henry, this unity of general, special, and eschatological revelation means as well that there is only one truth (the Logos) and only one rationality in which all humanity is grounded. The postmodern insistence that reason itself is culturally relative is rejected by Henry in the strongest possible terms.

This view of reason as manifest in both creation and redemption as well as a corresponding human capacity effectively undercuts the force of the hermeneutical problem of the distance between "then and now." While by no means denying historical or cultural differences, Henry places the emphasis on rational speech which ultimately communicates across barriers of time and context.

If revelation is both rational and true, then Henry believes it must also be in the form of propositions. A proposition is "a verbal statement that is either true or false; it is a rational declaration capable of being either believed, doubted, or denied."[6] Thus propositions, and only propositions, can be true; this means for Henry that it is nonsense to speak of revelation as true unless that revelation is in the form of propositions.

It is no surprise, then, that Henry finds the Bible to be essentially composed of propositions; it is, he says, "a propositional revelation of the unchanging truth of God."[7] Of course, not every sentence in the Bible is strictly a proposition—there are commands and exclamations as well. But even with these exceptions, Henry insists the "Scriptures contain a body of divinely given information actually expressed or capable of being expressed in propositions."[8]

James I. Packer, one of the most careful defenders of propositional revelation, agrees that the Bible embodies the Word of God, and conveys to us "real information from God."[9] But this is not to deny the complex literary character of the Bible. For example, scripture

> contains much imaginative matter—poetical, rhetorical, parabolic, visionary—which sets before our minds in a vivid and concrete and suggestive way great general principles, the formal statement of which has often to be sought in other contexts.[10]

As with Henry, the important point is that these various genres can all be restated as "general principles," or propositions, and on that basis can be then defended as true.

Propositional revelation implies verbal inspiration; since propositions consist of words, divine authorship must extend not only to concepts but to the words used by the writers of scripture. Inspiration is defined by Henry as the "supernatural influence upon divinely chosen prophets and apostles whereby the Spirit of God assures the truth and trustworthiness of their oral and written proclamation."[11] Both Henry and Packer reject the idea of inspiration as divine dictation in which the humanity of the writers is negated; at the same time they avoid the idea of a divine/human dual authorship. Rather, they seek to uphold both divine and human agency, but in such a way that scripture is fully and authentically the written word of God. Thus Henry speaks of inspiration as "a special confluence of the divine and human,"[12] while Packer describes it as "God's *concursive operation* in, with, and through the free working" of the human mind.[13]

Verbal inspiration in turn implies the inerrancy of scripture.[14] For Henry, the alternative to an inerrant Bible is an errant one, and an errant text cannot be divinely inspired. It would call into question the truth of scripture as a whole.

Inerrancy, however, must be defined with care. Strictly speaking, it applies only to the original texts of scripture (the autographs); minor errors in copying texts do not undermine the claim of inerrancy. It does not imply that modern standards of accuracy can be expected of biblical writers in reporting statistics, historical data, or matters of science.[15] Nor does inerrancy "imply that only nonmetaphorical or nonsymbolic language can convey religious truth."[16] To "read all Scripture narratives as if they were eye-witness reports in a modern newspaper," says Packer, "and to ignore the poetic and imaginative form in which they are sometimes couched" would be an inappropriate "literalistic" reading rather than a truly "literal" approach.[17] Thus inerrancy does not demand the kind of precision that it is often taken to mean; Benjamin Warfield, a central figure in the development of the inerrancy position at Princeton near the end of the nineteenth century, was at the same time an enthusiastic defender of Darwinian evolution.[18]

However, verbal inerrancy does imply that truth is to be expected in "scientific and historical matters insofar as they are part of the express message of the inspired writings." It also means that "truth inheres in the very words of scripture, that is, in the propositions and sentences of the Bible, and not merely in the concepts and thoughts of the writers."[19]

In spite of these qualifications, inerrancy has been a major source of controversy among evangelicals, and a spectrum of alternatives have been proposed. In the 1970's, some evangelicals like Harold Lindsell were alarmed enough to initiate a "battle for the Bible;"[20] more moderate defenders formed the International Council on Biblical Inerrancy (ICBI) and drafted "The Chicago Statement on Biblical Inerrancy" in 1978, followed by a statement on hermeneutics in 1982.[21] One result, which follows the logic of Henry's exposition, is to make belief in inerrancy a kind of shorthand for whether one believes scripture is true; in some circles (and this is opposed by Henry though not by Lindsell) it has become a litmus test for evangelical orthodoxy.

The Problem with Propositionalism

These efforts have not stilled the controversy over inerrancy, however, and for good reason. The propositionalist approach, while seeking to be faithful to scripture, has been led by its apologetic concern to embrace many of the presuppositions of the Enlightenment. The transition to postmodernism as well as the global interchange among evangelicals is increasingly exposing this as an accommodation to modern Western culture.

It is important to state this because propositionalists often see themselves as the defenders of historic Christianity against the corrosive forces of modernity. Certainly that is their intent. They are apt to see those who question strict inerrancy as capitulating to modern relativism and abandoning objective truth, or at least opening the door to an uncertain subjectivism. While it is clear the critics of inerrancy do take historical and cultural relativity more seriously, they at the same time are suspicious of an overblown rationalism, and in this they, not the propositionalists, are the strongest critics of modernity.

Among the more perceptive critics of a rationalist propositionalism are G. C. Berkouwer, Clark H. Pinnock, Donald G. Bloesch, Thomas F. Torrance, Alister McGrath, William J. Abraham, and Stanley J. Grenz. They are by no means in agreement with each other on a whole range of issues. But none of them advocate abandoning reason nor, as is often alleged, do they try to have it both ways. They are not against reason but rationalism (most or all would be "soft rationalists" in Abraham's terms[22]); they do not oppose propositional truth but propositionalism. While no one of them will necessarily endorse all that I propose in this chapter and the next, I will be using some of their insights in both my critique of propositionalism and provision of an alternative.

To begin with rationalism: the propositional approach assumes a human rational capacity untouched by either sin or cultural context. Henry is explicit on both points. Because "the fall of man has not destroyed man's rationality" he insists "the *imago Dei* . . . includes categories of thought and forms of logic ample to the knowledge and service of God."[23] He argues as well that "All human language depends on a common logic and on identical modes of thought";[24] this he bases on his doctrine of the Logos.

Henry seeks a universal reason which, through testing for logical consistency or contradiction, can uphold the authority of scripture before the criticism of modernity. But there is no transcultural reason; there are only fallible human thinkers whose categories and assumptions are supplied by their own particular cultures, including what counts as contradiction or consistency. This is not the same as saying there is no transcultural truth, but simply recognizes the cultural embeddedness of we who seek to know that truth.

Even more serious is the attempt to exempt reason from the effects of sin. What rationalism does, as McGrath says so well, is make "the truth of divine revelation dependent on the judgement of fallen human reason."[25] As I argued in the previous chapter, what is needed is a work of the Holy Spirit which lays a new foundation for reason through faith in the risen Jesus.

Such rationalism enshrines the Cartesian mind/body dualism within theology, and defines revelation as the mind of God communicating information to the human mind. The essence of the *imago Dei* and presumably of God is rationality, understood as a cognitive and logical capacity. I will argue instead for a more holistic anthropology based on religious affections which integrates emotion and reason and takes account of our embodiedness. Knowing God involves not only the mind but the whole person.

An unfortunate consequence of the rationalist approach is its tendency to equate knowledge with information, so that to know God means to know God conceptually. While quite properly rejecting the conclusion of some neo-orthodox theologians that if revelation is personal it must be non-propositional, to reduce the personal to propositional distorts the meaning of relationship.

This is the point of my language of presence and identity in the previous chapter: a relationship, whether with God or another human being, entails an encounter with a complex of experiential and relational elements which are not somehow brought together subsequently but are really facets of a single whole. Thus Torrance is right to criticize a fundamentalism which identifies "biblical statements about the truth with the truth itself to which they refer."[26] Revelation is ultimately personal, and therefore "must be continually given and received in a living relationship with God."[27]

As we have noted, to speak of revelation as personal by no means eliminates propositional speech. William Abraham has argued cogently for the necessity of speech to any personal revelation; because God lacks embodiment, divine speaking is if anything even more crucial to the revelation of God.[28] It links God's intention with God's action, and provides the divine interpretation of redemptive events. Bloesch is entirely correct in his insistence that revelation involves both "personal encounter and impartation of knowledge."[29]

Rational propositionalism not only misconstrues personal revelation, it also misunderstands the relation of language and truth. It does so because it has uncritically assimilated the Cartesian view that only ideas which are clear and distinct can be true. The insistence that revelation be fully propositional is an attempt to meet this criterion. There is a suspicion of language that is poetic or metaphoric; because it is not clear and distinct, it cannot bear truth without being restated in propositional form. Thus concerning scripture Henry assures us that "Regardless of the parables, allegories, emotive phrases and rhetorical questions used by these writers, their literary devices have a logical point which can be propositionally formulated and is objectively true or false."[30]

It is not surprising, then, that Henry engages in an extended polemic against the classical insistence that all language about God is analogical. "The logical difficulty" with such a theory is "its futile attempt to explore a middle road between univocity and equivocacy." The only "alternative to univocal knowledge of God" for Henry "is equivocation and skepticism."[31]

There is an either/or style of thinking in the thought of propositionalists. Language is either univocal or equivocal, clear or unclear, precise or muddled, inerrant or in error. They rule out by definition narrative, metaphor and poetic discourse as bearers of truth in and of themselves. A great divide, bequeathed by the Enlightenment, is presupposed: on one side is reason, propositional speech, clarity, and fact, with all the terms linked; on the other side is emotion, symbolic or poetical speech, unclarity, and fiction.

Central to the next chapter is the presentation of an alternative to this dichotomy. For the moment, let me simply note that what Henry calls "literary devices" are not as he believes merely ornamental or more emotive ways of saying something that could be stated more clearly otherwise, but are alternative and often preferable ways of communicating truth. In other words, they have certain advantages over propositions in conveying revelation.

I shall likewise argue for a broader understanding of truth. Bloesch comes close to my concern when he says the modern view of truth "is basically correctness, precision and accuracy" but the biblical view "is fundamentally fidelity, integrity and constancy."[32] This is more than a truth we cognitively know, it is a truth which transforms our lives. It corresponds to reality, but the reality to which it corresponds is the living God. It is a truth we affirm, but our affirmation necessarily takes the form of a life lived in conformity with it.

A Dynamic Approach to the Inspiration of Scripture

These problems with rationalist propositionalism manifest themselves in their presentations of inspiration, inerrancy, and interpretation of scripture. With regard to inspiration, the concern to insure that the words of scripture are truly from God leads to de-emphasis on the humanity of scripture. While a dictation theory is avoided in principle, the results of inspiration are virtually the same as those produced by divine dictation. For rational propositionalism this has to be the case, less fallible human error be introduced into the biblical text.

For many evangelicals this view of inspiration, with its corresponding claim for inerrancy, seemed more a theory of how God must have inspired the Bible which is then subsequently imposed on scripture than an understanding of how God actually inspired it based on the phenomena of scripture itself. This has led to a number of proposals, all of which attempt to take seriously the humanity of scripture while retaining an insistence on its divinity.

In preparation for the discussion of narrative in chapter six, I will briefly sketch an alternative account of divine inspiration. To begin, we can note with William Abraham that revelation is "polymorphous"—it is an "activity that is accomplished in, with, and through other acts and activities."[33] While such activities must include speech, it clearly involves actions as well. "Revelational activity," Pinnock notes, "includes . . . a great variety of products, including historical events, verbal communication, the astounding event of incarnation, and the outpouring of the Spirit, and it has generated a scriptural witness."[34]

Inspiration is not a discreet act subsequent to the revelatory event or word; rather God, as Abraham says, "inspires in, with, and through" the revelatory acts themselves, as well as through the "personal guidance of these who wrote and put together the various parts of the Bible."[35] Inspiration is a complex process involving the production over time of an authoritative written account of revelation.

The diversity of kinds of material in scripture reflects the varied forms of divine revelation. Thus to take one aspect of revelation, such as the inspiration of the prophets, and apply it to the whole of scripture is not legitimate without further justification. The "Bible is more than prophecy" says Pinnock, and cannot be construed as if every verse "were an oracle from on high."[36]

The purpose of inspiration, as Bloesch puts it, "is not the production of an errorless book but the regeneration of the seeker after truth."[37] It is a medium of revelation, through which we come to know God through the risen Jesus and are brought into a living relationship with that God. Through scripture we are enabled to know and love God. It fulfills this purpose because it is an authoritative, reliable witness to the revelation of God which produced it, and to which it belongs.

Central to any understanding of inspiration is the relation of divine and human activity. On this Abraham offers an intriguing proposal. He makes an analogy between a teacher inspiring his or her students and God inspiring the writers of scripture. The teacher may inspire the students to produce work which, without the creative activity of the teacher, would not have been produced. The work reflects the inspiration of the teacher while nonetheless remaining the work of the students. Thanks to the teacher, their intelligence and talents were greatly enhanced; nevertheless they are not made infallible.[38] It is, says Abraham, an imperfect analogy. God's revelatory activity involves much more than the intellectual activity of a teacher. Moreover, being omniscient, God is both aware of and intentional in producing the inspiration that results from such activity.

Another attractive proposal is made by Pinnock, who seeks "a dynamic personal model that upholds both the divine initiative and human response."[39] Like Abraham he wants "to allow for a human element in the composition of Scripture," but at the same time insists on "a strong role for the Spirit to ensure that the truth is not distorted by the human receptors." This is "not normally in the mode of control, but in the way of stimulation and guidance."[40]

Compared to Abraham, Pinnock emphasizes more strongly the divine involvement and oversight of the entire inspiration process. This emphasis is clear when he speaks of divine inspiration giving scripture its "content" with the human writers providing its "form." However, central to his argument is that we cannot have the content except as it is mediated through the form.

Bloesch uses the terms "form" and "content" somewhat differently than Pinnock:

> Instead of speaking of Scripture as having a divine ground and human form, it is theologically more appropriate to contend that Scripture has a human content as well as a human form; at the same time, it also has a divine content and a divinely inspired form. The human form and content serve the divine meaning.[41]

This seems to me a more accurate way of describing the Bible we in fact have, although it raises a host of interpretative questions we shall have to address in the chapters to follow. However, very much like Pinnock, Bloesch understands the divine message of scripture to be conveyed through the human component. In other words, the humanity of scripture is not a barrier to but the medium of the Word of God.

It is obvious that an understanding of inspiration as suggested here has no need for a doctrine of strict inerrancy (a point which had often been emphasized by Wesleyan-Holiness evangelicals).[42] In fact, a whole spectrum of views have developed on this issue, which Robert K. Johnston and Gabriel Fackre have organized into helpful typologies.[43]

Some have dispensed with the term inerrancy entirely, finding it both unnecessary and misleading. Others have adopted "infallibility" as an alternative term to designate biblical authority and reliability. While infallibility could mean "incapable of error" and in the nineteenth century was used in tandem with inerrancy, today many evangelicals understand it to primarily mean "trustworthy." Rather than claim scripture contains no error, they instead insist that it does not deceive, but leads us to the truth. Much as a person who one has learned is worthy of trust may nonetheless err but would never intentionally mislead, so scripture can be relied upon to direct us reliably to Jesus Christ. Infallibility understood this way seems to me to be an apt description of scripture.

Yet other evangelicals have undertaken the venerable tradition of retaining inerrancy but redefining it to reflect the actual phenomena of scripture. Thus for Pinnock,

> Inerrancy simply means the Bible can be trusted in what it teaches and affirms. The inerrant truth of a parable is of course parabolic, and the inerrant truth of a fable is fabulous. If Matthew gives us some fictional midrash, then it is inerrant according to the demands of this genre. All this means is inerrancy is relative to the intention of the text.[44]

Pinnock correctly recognizes that truth is not always to be equated with historical fact—this is an Enlightenment bias, not a biblical one. Because different genres require different assessments concerning their truth-fulness, no single abstract theory of propositional truth can do justice to scripture in its entirety. To trust scripture "implies that we will be open to the sort of text God actually gave us and not tend to predetermine according to rationalistic criteria the form it ought to take and then twist it into that form by scholarly devices."[45]

Bloesch is uncomfortable with the term "inerrancy" and believes "infallibility" should not be used without qualification; he prefers "veracity" ("unflagging adherence to the truth") and "trustworthiness" ("complete dependability in bearing witness to the truth").[46] "We must affirm" says Bloesch, "that the writers of the Bible, being human, had a capacity for error. But we must also insist that what the Holy Spirit teaches in and through their words is completely truthful."[47]

The heart of the problem theologians like Bloesch, Pinnock, and Berkouwer have with propositionalism is not claims for inerrancy or infallibility, much less for truth. It is the confusion of the affirmation of the truth of revelation with the truth of a particular theory of revelation. They affirm the former but deny the latter—it is no more necessary to believe only propositions can be true in order to affirm the truth of scripture than to believe in transubstantiation in order to affirm divine presence in the eucharist. What is at stake for them is nothing less than the integrity of scripture itself—our willingness to recognize and attend to the Bible in the actual form God has provided it and to the understanding of truth that implies.

One further observation about the rational propositional approach should be noted: it exalts individual interpretation at the expense of the Holy Spirit and the Christian community. The image is always of an individual using his or her reason to ascertain the truth of propositions in scripture. This is the autonomous individual of the Enlightenment, who is the assumed audience for the rational apologetic of the propositionalist. At the same time, it so identifies revelation with scripture that (in the words of Colin Gunton), "the text in some way or other replaces or renders redundant the mediating work of the Spirit."[48]

We have already seen how for Bloesch scripture is a medium through which the Spirit of God brings us the truth of revelation; his is "a theology of Word and Spirit." Pinnock likewise seeks to recover a more dynamic understanding of the spirit, which he believes both liberals and propositionalist evangelicals have neglected. He proposes a dipolar understanding of scripture and Spirit, in which the Holy Spirit uses scripture to speak to us afresh in our present context.[49] Stanley Grenz calls for a "reorientation of the doctrine of Scripture under the doctrine of the Holy Spirit"[50] and a recovery of the role of the community in interpreting scripture. Similarly, Steven J. Land argues for "Spirit-Word" as a dynamic interaction of text and Spirit in which the "word is alive, quick and powerful, because of the Holy Spirit's ministry."[51]

These are themes which I will pursue in the pages ahead. The propositionalist approach to the problem of text and event simply does not do justice to the role of the Spirit or the humanity of scripture, and distorts the literary character of the Bible. In the end, the activity of the living God in reaching out to humanity through scripture is supplanted by the autonomous rational individual assessing and organizing information. The activity of God is thus replaced by human activity. This loss of receptivity to God's own dynamic use of scripture is the hidden triumph of modernity and perhaps the most tragic consequence of the propositionalist approach.

CHAPTER 6

The Promise of Narrative

Propositionalists sought to solve the hermeneutical problem of the distance between text and event by claiming the biblical text was factually without error, and hence accurately portrays the events it reports. Liberals disagreed with that assessment; faced with a discrepancy between text and event, they gave theological authority instead either to an historical reconstruction of the event (what really happened) or to the existential import of the text (what it means to me now).

But what if the historical question is the wrong question? Hans Frei argues persuasively that the Enlightenment has led both conservatives and liberals astray through its identification of truth with factual accuracy. The meaning of the text became detached from its historical reference, and then was judged as to whether what it means comports with what occurred. Conservatives resorted to a highly rationalistic attempt to reassert scriptural authority by demonstrating historical accuracy; liberals, faced with historical inaccuracy, sought the truth of the text in its ability to illustrate general religious truths. Both were directed away from reading the texts as narrative—in Frei's terms, as "realistic" or "history-like" narrative.[1]

While Frei examined the "eclipse of biblical narrative" in modern theology, Stephen Crites argued for "the narrative quality of experience."[2] In contrast to Frei, Crites developed a general theory of human experience in which he sought to show its narrative shape. Persons characteristically understand their lives in terms of a story; narrativity is at the heart of human nature.

Narrative theologies typically incorporate elements of both of these insights, integrating biblical narrative with personal story. But they do so in strikingly different ways. "There is a liberal sense of using the term, narrative theology," says Frei, "which generally says that to be human is above all to have a story."[3] Thus it begins with human experience and from there moves to scripture. Some take a more pluralist approach, encouraging conversation between many secular and religious stories, or seeking to correlate the biblical story with human stories in order to demonstrate the Bible's relevance.[4]

In contrast to this is the postliberal approach represented by Frei, which begins not with human experience but with the biblical story. It does not seek to understand scripture as an aspect of human history and culture, but to understand human history and culture in light of the biblical narrative. It does not ask if the biblical narrative is relevant to our life story, but invites us to rethink and reinterpret our life story in terms of the biblical story. As such, the postliberal approach merits further examination as a potential resource for evangelical theology.

The Promise of Narrative

Before proceeding to do that, one matter needs clarification. I have been speaking of "the" biblical narrative, but it is obvious that in fact there are many distinct biblical narratives in both testaments, most of which have no direct literary connection to one another. In addition, there is a wide variety of non-narrative material as well: psalms, wisdom literature, prophetic literature, epistles, and apocalypses. So how is it then one can speak of a single biblical story?

One answer, advanced by Gerald Loughlin, is that

> the Church has read its Scriptures as narrating one story, and has had little difficulty in determining what that story is. The Church has found the focus or centre of the biblical narratives in the story of Jesus Christ, the story of his life, death and resurrection.[5]

The reason, says Loughlin, was that the church practiced a "ruled" reading of scripture, learned through catechesis, liturgy, and creed. Indeed scripture and creed mutually implicate one another; each is necessary to understand the other.[6] It is the creed which reminds the reader of scripture of the single story which encompasses the particular biblical narratives as well as the other forms of biblical literature.

Gabriel Fackre, an evangelical, makes a similar point. He distinguishes between "canonical story" (biblical narratives), "life story" (personal narrative) and "community story," the latter having

> an overarching plot reaching from Alpha to Omega, gathering up within its sweep all the particulars of canonical tale, and finding a place as well for the experiences of life story.[7]

The first signs of this community story were "the early baptismal rules of faith," preserved in creedal form, as well as the narrative structure of eucharistic prayer.[8]

While there are certainly theologians who deny any unity to the Bible—a point I will address further in this section—it is at least coherent to speak of a single biblical narrative or story as well as the particular narratives from which it is derived and to which it gives unity. I have of course done this already in chapter four, where I considered whether the Christian "metanarrative" was intrinsically oppressive.

Fackre defines "story" as a form of narrative in which there is "an account of characters and events in a plot moving over time and space through conflict toward resolution."[9] Other narratives also provide an account of characters and events over time, but lack the interpretative vision supplied by plot, conflict, and resolution. That is, "story" provides meaning. I shall use the terms "story" and "narrative" interchangeably, understood in the same way as Fackre does "story."

My central contention in this section is that a narrative approach is truer to scripture and has distinct advantages over a purely propositionalist account. There are a number of things which narrative does well, and these are intrinsically related to the salvific purpose of scripture, that is, to enable us to truly know and love God.

The first advantage is that biblical narrative depicts a world which it claims is the only real world, a universal history which reaches out from the text to interpret the world in which we live. As literary scholar Eric Auerbach puts it, the Bible

> seeks to overcome our reality: we are to fit our own life into its world, feel ourselves to be elements in its structure of universal history. . . . Everything else that happens in the world can only be conceived as an element in this sequence; into it everything that is known about the world . . . must be fitted as an ingredient of the divine plan.[10]

Thus our earlier description of Christianity as a "metanarrative" is biblically appropriate.

Frei argues that it is this feature of biblical narrative which modern interpreters miss when they confuse the literal meaning of the text (its "history-likeness") with history itself. Like history writing and the traditional novel, but unlike myth and allegory, "there is no gap between the representation and what is represented by it."[11] In addition, the biblical narrative is quite close to history-writing in depicting a common public world. However, in clear distinction from history-writing, biblical narratives introduce supernatural causation and miraculous occurrences.[12] Thus to insist on a rational demonstration that these narratives either are or are not historical is necessarily to misread them; it is to fail to read them literally, as narratives.

The reason this is so is that, in order to determine their historical accuracy, the narratives are no longer permitted to interpret our world; rather the criteria of Enlightenment modernity are used instead to evaluate the narratives. Thus Frei concludes,

> It is no exaggeration to say that all across the theological spectrum the great reversal had taken place; interpretation was a matter of fitting the biblical story into another world with another story rather than incorporating that world into the Biblical story.[13]

Frei seeks to recover an ability to read narrative as narrative rather than as history, so that we can attend to scripture's portrayal of the world as it really is. The biblical narratives invite us to understand our world in terms of their narrated reality of God and God's purposes, and to live our lives accordingly.

This last point about God's purposes points to a second advantage: a narrative approach provides a way to bring together the diverse components of scripture into a single story without thereby losing their particularity. It allows a unity which preserves diversity.

The legitimacy of an overall biblical narrative can be inferred by the pervasive assumption which runs through the Bible that the particular narrative, prophecy, psalm, saying, or epistle is itself part of a much larger story of God's dealings with the world. In the first testament it is largely the story of God's relationship with Israel; in the second it is God's action in Jesus Christ and its subsequent impact on the church. In each case there is movement through time, characters and events, conflict and resolution. Certain foci are emphasized as central to the story, most notably Exodus and Easter. These foci in turn become key events which coordinate and unify the various portions of the story.

The canonical shape of the Bible also points to a unifying story. It begins with creation and ends with the eschaton, providing a framework which suggests movement from one to another, and invites interpretation of the whole from the standpoint of both origin and goal.

For Frei this unity is especially expressed through figural interpretation. Auerbach defines it this way:

> Figural interpretation establishes a connection between two events or persons in such a way that the first signifies not only itself but the second, while the second involves or fulfills the first. The two poles of a figure are separated in time, but both, being real events or persons,

are within temporality. They are both contained in the flowing stream which is historical life, and only the comprehension . . . of their inter-dependence is a spiritual act.[14]

The claim that events or persons are historical does not rule out a relationship between them. As Frei says, "the figure itself is real in its own place, and right, and without any detraction from that reality it prefigures the reality that will fulfill it." But figural interpretation involves more than biblical events or persons; if it depicts the real world, then it incorporates us as well. Thus figural interpretation "not only brings into coherent relation events in biblical narration, but also allows the fitting of each present occurrence and experience into a real narrative framework or world."[15] We become part of the biblical story.

A third advantage of narrative is that it has a unique capacity to convey the identity of a person, to render an agent. This is most evident in realistic novels where, through the interaction of character and circumstance, we come to know something of what those characters are like. As Loughlin says,

> Realistic narrative permits a form of representation not otherwise possible: the representation of character as engagement with contingent circumstance. This is not just the idea of character engaging with contingency, but of character constituted in and by such an engagement.[16]

Character is revealed not apart from but in and through its engagement with life; narrative is uniquely able to portray that engagement.

Biblical narratives provide descriptive access to the identity of God. Through the story of God's interaction with Israel and the church over time, we come to know the character and purposes of God. For Christians, God is most fully revealed in Jesus Christ. I argued in chapter four that Jesus is not simply whoever we want him to be, but who he is is revealed by what he says and does. The gospel narratives portray Jesus through his words and actions as he interacts with persons and circumstances.[17]

It is the nature of narrative to involve the reader in its world. These three advantages—the depiction of a world, the telling of one story of God, and the portrayal of God's character— are advantages insofar as one participates in the narrative, that is, enters that world, permits oneself to be incorporated into the story, and comes to know the God who is portrayed.

For postliberal thinkers, this means participation in a community which has itself been shaped by the biblical narrative and understands its own identity through those narratives. George Lindbeck speaks of a "cultural-linguistic" community through whose language and practices we are enabled to experience God. This is in contrast to the usual liberal view, in which our language and practices arise as expressions of a deeper religious experience. For a postliberal like Lindbeck it is the reverse: it is the narratives and practices of the community which makes our experience of God possible and gives that experience its distinctive shape and content.[18]

Similarly, George Stroup argues that the interpretative framework we use to make sense of our lives and give us our personal identity is not an individual possession but a communal reality—it is provided by a social context and rooted in a narrative tradition. For the Christian community, it is the biblical narratives which provides identity and a common hope; it is the community in turn which designates certain aspects of those narratives such as the Christ-event as essential for the interpretation of life in the present.[19]

Stroup describes how the hearing of the Christian story can provoke a crisis—a "collision of narratives." "It is at this point," he says, "that identities, even worlds, may be altered and reality perceived in a radically new way." The issue is whether to continue to understand one's life in terms of the old narrative or to adopt the new. To accept the new narrative would be a conversion in which "the individual will begin the lengthy, difficult process of reinterpreting his or her personal history in light of the narratives and symbols that give the Christian community its identity."[20]

It should be evident from this understanding of narrative and its relationship with community that postliberals have deeply appropriated the insights of the post-critical form of postmodernity. Like Wittgenstein and MacIntyre, they think in terms of communities which share common languages and practices, and which make certain kinds of experiences possible. Also like MacIntyre, they appreciate the role of narrative in providing personal and communal identity.

Thus the postliberal form of narrative theology is an attractive alternative to both liberal and conservative theologies which are rooted in modernity. In contrast to the liberals postliberalism maintains the integrity of the text. The meaning of the biblical text is found in what it says, rather than in either a highly speculative historical reconstruction or some ahistorical existential meaning. The identity of Jesus is not to be found by going behind the text or in abstraction from the text but in the text, within the pattern of word and action in the biblical narrative.

In contrast to the rational propositionalists, they are able to maintain a literal reading of scripture without requiring strict inerrancy; this is because they have refused to identify the meaning of the text (what the text is about) as history. Rather, the point of the text is to depict the world and the God who creates and redeems it, and this is done most adequately by a narrative account with movement, plot and characterization than by propositions.

Alister McGrath expresses well the consequences of a narrative approach in contrast to rational propositionalism:

> Any view of revelation which regards God's self-disclosure as the mere transmission of facts concerning God is seriously deficient. . . . To reduce revelation to principles and concepts is to suppress the element of mystery, holiness and wonder to God's self-disclosure. 'First principles' may enlighten and inform; they do not force us to our knees in reverence and awe.[21]

To come to know the living God—to be forced to our knees in worship—is what scripture is for, and narrative is the most adequate medium through which to have a true and growing relationship with that God.

Attractive as it is, the narrative approach can only be appropriated by evangelical theology if it is compatible with claims for the inspiration of scripture by God as an authoritative and reliable witness to revelation. This means addressing more directly in what sense scripture understood as narrative may be said to be "true."

Postliberalism and the Question of Truth

Narrative theology, even of the postliberal variety, has not been met with open arms throughout evangelicalism. Certain leading evangelical theologians, most notably Pinnock, Grenz, Fackre, and McGrath, have given narrative a central place in their theologies. But even they have joined their less accepting evangelical colleagues in raising serious questions concerning postliberalism.

These questions center on a concern for truth, and in many respects parallel the concerns for relativism in the thought of Wittgenstein and MacIntyre discussed in chapter three. The source of this unease lies in the postliberal understanding of a religious community as involving a language and set of practices which shape the lives of believers. The narrative is the narrative of that community, and meaning is established within the community. As Lindbeck says,

> Meaning is constituted by the uses of a specific language rather than being distinguishable from it. Thus the proper way to determine what "God" signifies, for example, is by examining how the word operates within a religion and thereby shapes reality and experience rather than by first establishing its propositional or experiential meaning. . . . It is in this sense that theological description in the cultural-linguistic mode is intrasemiotic or intratextual.[22]

Thus meaning is not to be determined extratextually but intratextually, not in reference to something outside the cultural-linguistic community but within.

It is generally conceded that postliberals have a coherence understanding of truth; the question is rather one of correspondence. Mark I. Wallace (who calls postliberalism the "New Yale Theology") puts this clearly and succinctly: For these theologians, he asks,

> is the biblical world the sole theological determinant of what reality is, as the Yale theologians sometimes assert, or, as they also seem to indicate, is the biblical world simply one language game (Lindbeck, Holmer) or literary picture (Frei) amidst other games and pictures?[23]

Wallace argues that there is a fundamental ambiguity running through postliberalism as to whether the biblical narratives refer to any reality outside of the text.

Other evangelicals concur. Carl F. H. Henry argues that narrative theology "brackets' historical questions by focusing simply on the text and its articles of faith." To read scripture as narrative "does not automatically settle the question whether it much matters whether its content is fiction or history."[24] Donald Bloesch observes that the emphasis in narrative theology "has shifted from exploring the metaphysical implications of the faith to investigating the story of a people on pilgrimage." "Theology can ill afford to ignore the issue of truth," he warns, "for it is truth that gives narrative its significance."[25]

When two evangelicals as different as Henry and Bloesch have such similar assessments, it is well to take notice. But the critique is wider yet, for Alister McGrath, who unlike Henry and Bloesch is sympathetic to narrative theology, nonetheless finds postliberals like Lindbeck "equivocal over whether his cultural-linguistic approach to doctrine involves the affirmation or setting aside of epistemological realism and a correspondence theory of truth."[26] Evangelicals suspect that postliberals reduce truth to internal consistency; in contrast they insist truth "is firmly understood to be located *outside* the language of Christianity as well as within it."[27]

The central point of these critiques—that Christian truth claims are intended to refer to extratextual reality—must be acknowledged by any theology which calls itself evangelical. I intend to show how narratives make just this sort of truth claim. But first, I want to explore whether this reading of postliberalism is itself fair or accurate. In so doing, we will surface certain postmodern concerns relevant to our discussion.

Lindbeck does not deny epistemological realism or propositional truth; in fact he insists a cultural-linguistic approach must allow for it.[28] Thus

> There is nothing in the cultural-linguistic approach that requires the rejection (or the acceptance) of the epistemological realism and correspondence theory of truth, which . . . is implicit in the conviction of believers that when they rightly use a sentence such as "Christ as Lord" they are uttering a true first-order proposition.[29]

Lindbeck distinguishes between "the 'intrasystematic' and the 'ontological' truth of statements." The former are true when they cohere to the language and practices ("forms of life") of a context—the "total pattern of speaking, thinking, feeling, and acting."[30] The latter correspond to reality external to the context.

Lindbeck argues that a statement "cannot be ontologically true unless it is intrasystematically true, but intrasystematic truth is quite possible without ontological truth."[31] Thus a "system" —a religion for example—can have internal consistency yet not be ontologically true. However, a statement cannot be ontologically true unless it is internally consistent—it cannot correspond externally unless it coheres internally. And such coherence occurs when the statement is being "rightly used."

This is absolutely crucial for Lindbeck. He observes that

> the crusader's battle cry "*Christus est Dominus*" . . . is false when used to authorize cleaving the skull of the infidel (even though the same words in other contexts may be a true utterance).[32]

The use of the language does not cohere with the truth of the narrative, thus the statement in this instance is false.

It is here Wallace issues a strong objection: "*misuse* is independent of the *truth* of the claim made;"[33] the distortion of the phrase by the crusader in no way negates the truth of "*Christus est Dominus*." Lindbeck confuses "notions of truth and reference" with "notions of meaning and use."[34]

But this is to miss Lindbeck's point. As Bruce Marshall has shown, the crusader's cry is untrue precisely because it does not mean what Christian narrative and practice says it means: "Christ is not that kind of Lord."[35] Wallace's claim in fact presupposes a narrative and community which provides definition for those terms, and without which they would mean something quite different.

Lindbeck himself anticipates the sort of objection which Wallace makes;

> Paul and Luther . . . quite clearly believed that Christ's Lordship is objectively real no matter what the faith or unfaith of those who hear and say the words. What they were concerned to assert is that the only way to assert this truth is to do something about it, i.e., to commit oneself to a way of life.[36]

What Lindbeck is saying is not that there is no correspondence of Christian claims to a reality external to text or language, but that it is the biblical narrative and the practices of the Christian community which enable us to know what those claims are. And, to know those claims involves a way of life, a pattern of living, both as a mode of learning the content of Christian claims about reality as its expression.

Lindbeck does not make the straightforward kind of claim about truth that McGrath or Wallace would like because his concern lies elsewhere. In a very postmodern manner, he wants to uphold the priority of the community rather than the individual, a holistic understanding of the self rather than purely cognitive, and the particularity rather the universality of context. Evangelical criticisms are fair insofar as they express a concern that Lindbeck address more directly truth as correspondence, but are in my judgement not accurate when they imply inconsistency or misconstrue his purpose.

There is one further aspect to this debate, perhaps the most important of all: postliberals like Lindbeck and Frei resist not so much epistemological realism as the deriving of criteria to demonstrate truth from somewhere other than scripture. That is, they refuse to give ultimate authority to the presuppositions of modernity.

This can be seen clearly in Frei's response to Henry's critique that narrative theology brackets questions of historical fact:

> If I am asked to use the language of factuality, then I would say, yes, in those terms, I have to speak of an empty tomb. In those terms I have to speak of the literal resurrection. But I think those terms are not privileged, theory-neutral, trans-cultural, an ingredient in the structure of the human mind and of reality always and everywhere for me, as I think they are for Dr. Henry.[37]

It may well be, Frei says, "that even scholars won't be using those particular terms so casually and in so self-evident a fashion for much longer."[38] What "historical fact" means is a function of modern Western culture; as that culture changes, so do the assumptions which give those terms their meaning.

That is one concern: the relativity of the meaning of fact. But even if one accepts the concept of fact as modernity understands it, Frei questions whether Jesus Christ "is a fact like any other?" As a name it refers, but "it does not refer ordinarily; or rather, it refers, ordinarily only by the miracle of grace;" it is, he says, "historical reference (to use our cultural category) but it is not historical reference in the ordinary way."[39] That is the other concern: the reduction of Jesus Christ to merely fact, and the consequent misunderstanding that entails.

Instead of adopting the presuppositions of modernity, postliberals argue that our theological norms arise out of scripture itself and then govern our reading of it. The doctrines of the Incarnation and Trinity serve as premier examples of such scripturally-derived norms: they are implicit within scripture and, when made explicit, then serve to regulate our reading of scripture—they prevent, for example, our misunderstanding of Jesus as only a human or exclusively divine.

Moreover, these scriptural norms are narratively embedded in a range of devotional, liturgical and ethical practices which mark the life of the Christian community. To understand scripture is not simply a rational exercise by the individual but a matter of indwelling scripture by way of these communal practices, which both inform and give expression to that understanding.

How shall we assess this debate? First, the postliberals are surely right in opting for communal and holistic ways of thinking over the individualistic and dualistic categories of modernity (a point which McGrath would endorse as well). Second, I also believe it is proper to link the meaning of a statement such as "Christ is Lord" with its proper "use." This does not place the Lordship of Christ at our disposal, but simply recognizes that what we mean by a statement (and whether thereby *we* are speaking the truth) has to do with how we embody that meaning in our lives.

However, this is not the same as asking whether *scripture* speaks the truth. Evangelicals must and do insist that the true meaning of "Christ is Lord" is found in scripture itself, and when understood in scriptural terms means that Christ is in fact Lord whether or not anyone acknowledges it or understands it.[40] Through living with that scripture over time and engaging in the corresponding practices in the community Christians, it is hoped, are growing in the knowledge and love of God and, as they grow, their lives are being shaped accordingly. I will say more on this in the final chapter.

As for Frei's two concerns, I certainly agree Jesus Christ is not an "ordinary" fact of history and that our method for determining what counts as historical fact is itself a product of the modern era. In chapter eight I will be exploring some of the limitations of that historical method. But like Henry and Bloesch, I do not think the historical question can simply be bracketed; it makes a considerable difference to the meaning and truth of scripture whether Jesus died on a cross or of old age. What is needed is a way to ask historical questions that does not place revelation at the disposal of modernity's criteria for truth.

In the remainder of this chapter I will therefore address two issues: First, the relation of narrative to history, and second, how narrative speaks truthfully about the God who both transcends and enters our history.

How Narrative Makes Truth Claims

Biblical narrative cannot escape questions of historical truth because it make historical claims. The persons and events within scripture are for the most part persons and events which occur within our world of space and time, in our history. The Bible insists that the world it depicts is the same as the world we inhabit. Moreover, as Fackre says, the Christian story cannot exclude history or

> it would cease to be Christian, for its central events presuppose hard empirical claims—Jesus did live, Jesus did die on a cross, and on that elusive boundary between empirical and trans-empirical reality Jesus did rise from the grave.[41]

If these propositions are false, then the story is not true, and Christians are living a lie. On this, narrativist evangelicals are united with the propositionalists.

Yet the Bible is not, indeed cannot be simply history. It makes claims not only about people and events but of the divine significance of those events, and of the character and purposes of God. The God who created our world and transcends our history is at the same time redemptively active in our world and has entered our history. Language of historical fact is necessarily inadequate and misleading when it attempts to account for the character and agency of this God.

Scripture therefore consists of both kinds of language—"the histori-cal and the metahistorical," as Bloesch puts it[42]—and any consideration of the truth of scripture must take this into account. Nor can this be done by categorizing scriptural passages as either historical or metahistorical. God has refused to be a deist kind of deity, and has insisted on acting within our history, thus insuring biblical passages will often be historical and metahistorical at the same time.

Bloesch describes this language as "mythopoetic": it "is essentially neither history nor myth but a historical witness to the dramatic inter-section of time and eternity in Jesus Christ."[43] By "myth" he does not mean untrue, but a figural or poetic rendering of diving purpose and activity.

Similarly Pinnock, (here drawing on J. R. R. Tolkien and C. S. Lewis) calls the gospel "the great eucatastrophe," a "myth made fact."[44] It is at one and the same time historical and mythical, factual and symbolic; it makes a genuine claim about history while containing "all the symbolic wealth" of myth.[45] Thus, as C. S. Lewis says, "To be truly Christian we must both assent to the historical fact and also receive the myth (fact though it has become) with the same imaginative embrace which we accord to all myths."[46] It is this "imaginative embrace" of the "symbolic wealth" of scripture which propositionalism fears, but is necessary for the kind of truth the Bible conveys.

How, then, can we understand an inspired text that is both historical and metahistorical at the same time? To begin with the historical ele-ment, there are certain claims which the gospel makes that are inescap-ably factual, and chief among these is the resurrection of Jesus. The "heart of the Christian story is fact, not myth" (Pinnock);[47] while the message of the gospel "is mediated through narrative forms . . . it is grounded in fact, not narrative." (Bloesch).[48] The concern here is to insist that events like the resurrection are actual occurrences in space and time.

At the same time, not all events recorded in scripture have the same historical importance, nor are they necessarily historical to the same extent. For Pinnock, some "are history like but not likely to be historical;" whether Elisha's axehead floated or Lot's wife turned into a pillar of salt is not on the same level of importance as the Exodus or the resurrec-tion.[49] Likewise, Bloesch holds that Christians are not "obliged to accept everything as recorded as being exactly the way it is described even in the stories about Jesus." Nonetheless, "on events that are integral to the message of faith we must not equivocate."[50]

The determination of what events are integral is found in biblical narrative itself. We must therefore attend to the pattern of biblical narratives as well as that of the Christian story as a whole, which reflects the pattern of revelation. As always, there will be differences in interpretation, but the narrative shape of revelation will be the common reference point for discussing those differences.

If there are certain central events in the Christian story whose historicity is intrinsic to their significance, can we then talk of historical verification? On this there is at first glance a divergence between Pinnock and Bloesch. For Pinnock, the answer is yes: historicity means an event is open to historical verification or falsification; such "is the price any claim must pay for making a serious truth claim about reality."[51] In contrast, Bloesch insists that "events of sacred history cannot be verified by the canons of historical science, but they can be illumined."[52]

But what seems like a divergence on whether events can be verified turns out not to be a difference over what historical investigation can accomplish but on the significance of its results. Pinnock's concern is the absolute importance of historical claims: if Jesus' tomb is shown not to have been empty and the appearances of the risen Christ to have not occurred, it would seriously undermine the Christian claim that Jesus is risen from the dead. Bloesch makes a different and equally important point: even if historians could demonstrate with finality the empty tomb and the appearances, they would as historians still be unable to prove the resurrection or its meaning and significance.

To underscore this last observation, historical method as it is usually practiced is by virtue of its own principles especially unsuited to verify or interpret unique events—of which the resurrection and incarnation would certainly be prime examples. Because the historian is committed to looking for causes of events within the world, divine causality is ruled out in advance of the investigation; furthermore, the principle that events in the past are understood in terms of the present tends to make unique events suspect. The tendency is always to discount the claim for such an event and then look for the "real" explanation within our world of space and time.

More will be said about this in chapters eight and nine, where we discuss divine agency. But given the bias inherent in modern historical methodology, its use to verify Christian historical truth claims is somewhat limited. It can say very little about incarnation and resurrection directly that does not misconstrue their reality and meaning. It can, however, say something about the historical effects of those events.

This is what Torrance means by "empirical correlates." The God who transcends space and time truly enters and acts within our spatiotemporal existence, such that through our normal human experience and reason we actually come to know the eternal God. The ascension and Lordship of Christ "has the effect of sending us back to the historical Jesus;" we empty the resurrection "of any real or final significance when we think or speak" of it "without an empirical correlate in space and time such as the empty tomb."[53]

Historical method, then, can provide some assessment of empirical correlates, the effect or consequence of divine action. However, a satisfactory interpretation of them requires theological reflection, which is governed not by the canon of modern historical science but by attending to the revelation of God on its own terms.

This brings us to the "metahistorical" aspect of scripture: how the words of the Bible serve as a medium through which we truly come to know God. I want here to insist upon two interrelated points: the language of scripture is both necessarily inadequate to its divine object and abundantly rich in its description of God. There is a real correspondence between scripture and God, but it is not and could not be a one-to-one correspondence.

The infinite and eternal God has chosen to enter our history and be revealed through human language, including such literary forms as narrative, metaphor, and analogy. Human language can truthfully refer to God and God's actions, but (in the words of Bloesch) "will always fall short of precise or univocal description."[54]

This very inadequacy of human language serves well the purposes of divine revelation. As Torrance says, it prevents our confusing statements about the truth with the truth itself, which is the temptation of thinking "statements are absolutely adequate to their objects." In contrast,

> For a true statement to serve the truth of being, it must fall short of it, be revisable in the light of it, and not be mistaken for it, since it does not possess its truth in itself but in the reality it serves. Thus a dash of inadequacy is necessary for its precision.[55]

Scripture refers us to a divine reality which is independent of it, and the very humanity of its language insures it cannot be confused with the God to which it points. While the words of scripture themselves are not revisable, our understanding of them continually grows and deepens as we participate in a relationship with God through them. Thus our interpretation of scripture should "not focus myopically, as it were, upon the words and statements themselves, but through them on the truths and realities they indicate beyond themselves."[56]

A relationship with God is essential to the proper interpretation of scripture. Torrance rejects the subject/object dualism of modernity which accords epistemological authority to the autonomous individual, and instead posits a "nondualist or unitary relation" between reality and our knowledge of it, "one in which ontological primacy and control are naturally accorded to reality over all our conceiving and speaking of it."[57]

G. C. Berkouwer echoes many of these postmodern concerns. If anything, he is even more radical in his rejection of an epistemological dualism in which the human is the knowing subject while the Bible is the passive object to be known. Such a dualism sets up a false dilemma, a "competition . . . in which the accent on the divine is subtracted from the fully human writings, and it seems as though where God works and is present the human necessarily begins to fade and disappear."[58] In an attempt to understand this passive Bible, the liberals emphasize the humanity of scripture at the expense of its divinity; in order to protect the Bible's authority a conservative docetism minimizes the human in order to secure the divinity.

Berkouwer rightly rejects this entire way of thinking. Seeking to take seriously that scripture is at one and the same time genuinely human and the word of God, he proposes a more unitive and relational understanding, in which it is not possible to discuss the authority of scripture "apart from a personal relationship of belief in it."[59] By "belief" he does not mean an impersonal intellectual assent in the truth of scripture accompanied by subsequent trust in Christ (another version of an Enlightenment dualism) but a personal relationship of trust in Christ in and through scripture.[60] This "active participation" or "involvement and correlation" is not (as conservative dualists fear) a fall into subjectivism; "On the contrary, the pure correlation of faith is decisively determined by the object of faith, namely, God and his Word."[61] Berkouwer simply refuses to permit Enlightenment dualism to set the parameters for our understanding of scripture, and proposes a unitive participational alternative which we would now call postmodern.

Scripture does not point to itself but witnesses to Jesus Christ. For Berkouwer, to believe scripture "does not mean staring at a holy and mysterious book, but hearing the witness concerning Christ."[62] It is precisely this which leads to a respect for the concrete, human words of scripture, "of the human witness empowered by the Spirit."[63] We cannot have the revelation of Christ except in and through the human, and this does not diminish divinity but simply recognizes and honors the manner in which God chooses to work.

Unlike Torrance, Berkouwer does not speak of the inadequacy of scripture to its object. Instead, he points us toward what I believe is a complementary aspect, the richness of the words of scripture such that they continually transcend and transform our understanding and concepts of God. They are, therefore, admirably suited to be used by the Holy Spirit for that purpose.

Clark Pinnock has especially emphasized the richness of scripture—what he calls the "fecundity of the text."[64] He notes three characteristics of biblical language which contribute to its richness.

First, while the various writings in scripture are diverse, they have been brought together as a single canon, and are read in association with each other. Inspired by the same God, the texts are interrelated—they impinge on one another and mutually interpret one another. Pinnock's understanding fits nicely with my construal of the Bible as a loosely-structured single narrative, consisting of a rich diversity of particular narratives and other literary forms. Because there is one divine Author, evangelical theology is justified in seeking an overarching meaning through this rich interplay of biblical perspectives; at the same time it is not free to neglect any voice within this divinely inspired diversity.

Second, Pinnock notes that scripture contains a wealth of metaphorical and symbolic language which "sets up a range of possible meanings that can scarcely be exhausted."[65] This is an important observation, one we shall examine further in chapter seven. The language of metaphor is both generative of thought and a medium of experience; one can return to it again and again to receive fresh insight.

Luci Shaw, who calls God the "First Poet," argues that God has given "his stamp of approval on the imaginative mode of perceiving truth" through the "constant use of imagery in the Bible." The parables of Jesus; the church imaged as body, bride, building, living stones; Jesus as both Lamb and Lion—none of these are sufficient in themselves, but taken together they provide a rich matrix of mutually informing imagery. The Bible is full of these "truth-revealing metaphors;" in scripture "God exposes himself to us in a thousand images stronger than words that leap into life to embody truth."[66]

On one hand, metaphor cannot be reduced to propositional speech, as if the proposition simply stated the meaning of the metaphor in a clearer and more straightforward way. Propositions can be true to metaphors but not exhaustively so; with metaphors there is always more than can be said. On the other hand, metaphors cannot mean just anything; their potential meaning is circumscribed by the narrative or other literary context within which they are embedded.

This leads to Pinnock's third observation: a biblical text is a piece of literature, and like a work of art contains within itself a "fullness of meaning"—it "is available for fresh interpretation without end."[67] Pinnock's argument here is carefully stated. The text cannot

> mean anything at all, subject to the whims of the readers. For it is still anchored in the original situation and still bears the content intended by the writer. . . . The meaning resides in the words of the text, not in our imagination. Nevertheless, granting these solid parameters of meaning the text lays down, . . . the text cannot be exhausted and can always be seen in new and challenging ways as the angle of vision alters and the Spirit speaks.[68]

The idea that a text can have only one meaning is for Pinnock a modern prejudice. A biblical text opens up a "field of possible meanings;" valid interpretation "must fall within the range of possible meanings the text itself creates."[69]

Pinnock rightly insists that meaning resides in the text itself, and not in the reader. In this he is somewhat like Hans Frei. At the same time, he does not completely set the text loose from its historical moorings; the "field of possible meanings" must be in continuity with the original meaning of the text. Here he retains some of the concern for authorial intention which is held by many evangelicals.

The advantage of this approach is that it takes account of both the humanity and divinity of scripture, as well as its historical and metahistorical character. It properly roots meaning in God's acts in history to which scripture is an authentic witness. At the same time it doesn't limit the meaning to human perceptions at a particular time and place. Joel did not have to have Pentecost pictured in his mind for his prophecy to truly refer to that event. There is a single divine Author whose intentions transcend those within the awareness of the inspired writers; it is the fullness of God's intentions which is to be found within the inspired text.

Scripture truly portrays God's activity within and God's purposes for our world of space and time. Moreover, it provides descriptive access to the character of God, most especially as revealed in Jesus Christ. The biblical narrative does indeed correspond to who God is, and faithfully reflects God's redemptive activity and promises.

But this is not a one-to-one correspondence as in propositionalism. To take seriously the inadequacy and richness of the biblical language means we will not confuse the words of scripture with the reality of God; in this sense they insure that scripture is truly without error in its reference to God. "For now we see in a mirror, dimly" (I Cor. 13:12), but we nonetheless really do see. More importantly, it enables the narrative-rich words of scripture to do more than inform—they invite us into a relationship with the God they portray, indeed they make that relationship possible. We cannot have the book without the God whose story is told therein. Moreover, this God is not at the disposal of our reason, but is the active and living divine reality who both judges and enables all our conceptions and experiences, and empowers our growth in the knowledge and love of God.

This is the reason scripture is the way it is—the divine Author has inspired it in such a way that it enables the Holy Spirit to use it to illumine our hearts and transform our lives. It is no accident that so much of scripture is narrative, metaphor, and the like—God is not simply sending us a memorandum but preparing a medium through which we can have a true relationship with God, one in which we come to know God as God actually is. The Holy Spirit uses the narrativic and metaphoric "field of meaning" to speak God's word ever afresh, to address us where we are now, in our own particular contexts. When we read or hear the words of scripture in faith, it is the living Word we truly meet and come to know, and as we do our lives are themselves increasingly conformed to the truth of God.

CHAPTER 7

The Problem of Context

The introduction of the Holy Spirit as the interpreter of scripture brings us to the hermeneutical problem of the distance between then and now. Thus far most of our discussion has focused on reference: how does scripture truthfully refer to God as revealed in special revelation; that is, how is the text true to the revelatory event? Now we must ask if scripture has a word of truth for us today, or if the cultural and historical differences between the biblical world and our own create insurmountable difficulties for its understanding and relevance.

This is a question of context, both then and now. It is complex because we are not simply trying to coordinate a biblical with a contemporary context; there are in fact a variety of biblical and contemporary contexts. The postmodern recognition of diversity makes the task more difficult, but also more essential.

A comprehensive treatment of the issues is beyond the scope of this chapter. My plan is to explore the relation of scripture to context by focusing on three selected areas. First, we shall look at narratives as a context for metaphor, and explore it by way of the issue of language for God. Second, we will examine how scripture that reflects particular historical and cultural contexts has authority for us today, and will draw upon the insights of evangelical feminists. Third, we will ask how the gospel is communicated and embedded in contemporary culture while remaining the gospel still. The common concern in all of this is for the integrity of the gospel—to preserve the particularity of revelation in the face of modern attempts to redefine it while at the same time attending to its universal claims on all our contemporary contexts.

The Narrative Context and Metaphors for God

The debate over what language is appropriate for speaking about God is one of the most contentious and intractable in contemporary theology. In spite of attempts in some quarters to settle it one way or the other by fiat, the discussion is far from over. It is contentious because it is important. First of all, if theology does nothing else, it should endeavor to speak truthfully about God. But, secondly, our language about God reflects our beliefs—how we "imagine" God, as Garrett Green puts it[1]—and this impacts how we live our lives and understand our world. For persons on both sides, much is at stake.

It is intractible because the conflict is based on irreconcilable theological assumptions. This has to do with where we ultimately get our most normative God-language: is it a product of persons in a culture reflecting on religious experience, or is it intrinsic to God's own self-revelation? Evangelical theologians are among those who hold the second position.

To indicate the source of the language does not in itself say how that language is to be understood and used. If evangelicals are to grant legitimacy to the concerns of feminists and others that God language has been used in abusive or oppressive ways (and many of them do) then it is at the point of understanding and use they will be most able to address those concerns.

To make the issues clearer, I want to compare two approaches: that of Sallie McFague, a feminist theologian, and of Garrett Green, a postliberal. Both have given the matter of God-language careful attention, but come to strikingly different conclusions. Then, based on this discussion, I will offer a proposal.[2]

Let me begin with the unremarkable observation that all language concerning God is necessarily analogical. That is, our language does not literally describe God, who is not directly accessible to us, but pictures God in terms of something else that is accessible. This is an unremarkable claim because it is a position held by the entire Christian tradition. Whatever language was characteristically used to describe God, theologians did not mean God was literally male or female or anything else; God was beyond gender and all other particularities of human experience.

This does not mean it is easy to find appropriate language for God. Garrett Green sees a parallel in microphysics, whose theories are often described as "unpicturable." An example is light, which behaves both as a wave and a particle. Both "wave" and "particle" are drawn from our experience and both are needed to picture light; however, "wave" and "particle" are not properties which are found together in our experience. Two seemingly contradictory images are necessary to analogically describe light. Green believes the doctrine of the Trinity is a similar attempt to analogically describe unpicturable reality: three *hypostases* and one *ousia* combine properties not found together in our experience in order to provide a satisfactory description of God.[3]

If language about God is analogical, it is necessarily metaphorical. Thus scripture is rich in metaphor: "The Lord is my shepherd," "I am the bread of life," "Our Father who is in heaven." This richness has not always been seen as advantageous. Classical views of metaphor tended to be "substitutionary," seeing it as a substitute for more literal language. The implication was that a metaphor was ornamental; perhaps aesthetically pleasing but less true than literal speech.

Theologians like McFague and Green subscribe to a "substantive" or "unsubstitutable" view of metaphor. Because metaphors involve rich analogies between two things, they are not reducible to more literal forms of speech. Metaphors are fruitful in that they continue to suggest new meaning; while a propositional statement may be true to the metaphor, it cannot state the meaning in such a way that the metaphor can be discarded.

It is in the description of how a metaphor works that we begin to see the differences that have theological import. Max Black, in his "interactive" theory, argues that a metaphor has two subjects, one primary and one secondary. The metaphor is about *both* subjects—that is, it is bidirectional. For example, "war is a chess game" tells us something about the nature of war, but also something of the nature of chess. Both, says McFague, "undergo change by being thought of in relationship to the other." The theological implications of this are clear: "human images that are chosen as metaphors for God gain in stature and take on divine qualities by being placed in an interactive relationship with the divine."[4] McFague thus adopts this bidirectional approach.

The interactive view of Black has been strongly criticized by Janet Martin Soskice. She argues it is "clearly untrue" that there are two distinct subjects in a metaphor, as it does not account for such acknowledged metaphors as "writhing script." The claim "that both subjects are modified in the interaction" is for Soskice "a puzzling notion," inconsistent with other claims Black wishes to make.[5]

Soskice prefers the "interanimative" approach of I. A. Richards, for whom a metaphor has one subject, or "tenor," and a "vehicle" by which it is presented.[6] She defines metaphor unidirectionally as speaking "about one thing in terms which are seen to be suggestive of another."[7] Thus "man is a wolf" is about "man," not "wolf"; "war is a chess game" would likewise be about "war," not "chess." The theological implication is that human images for God tell us something about God, but nothing about humanity. Green endorses this approach[8] (and so do I).

What we have, then, are two conflicting theories of metaphor, with correspondingly different theological consequences. If metaphor is bidirectional as McFague insists, then to call God "Father" inescapably infers godlike qualities to males. If metaphor is unidirectional as Soskice and Green argue, then to call God "Father" implies nothing at all about males or fathers. This does not mean that no one would ascribe godlike qualities to males, only that it would be both a misunderstanding of the metaphor and a deviation from the way metaphors work in normal speech.

Sallie McFague links the bidirectional theory of metaphor with a distinctively liberal and feminist theology. Arguing that God is not directly knowable, she understands metaphor as "a construct of the human imagination to give expression to our experience" of God. Christianity is deeply metaphorical, and this is especially exemplified by the parables of Jesus. These do what good metaphors do, "they shock and disturb; they upset conventions and expectations and in so doing have revolutionary potential."[9] Indeed, Jesus' own life can be seen as a parable or a "metaphor of God."[10]

The parables, and Jesus as a parable, are clues to the fundamental root-metaphor of Christianity, the reign of God as "a way of being in the world" in tension with conventional ways. It points to a "new quality of relationship" toward God and others, "a mode of personal relationship . . . distinguished by trust in God's impossible way of love in contrast to the loveless ways of the world."[11] This means that personal, relational images are central for imaging God, as they are best able to convey this new relationship.[12]

While metaphoric speech is essential to the faithful expression of the Christian experience of God, literalism is for McFague idolatry. It most often occurs when metaphors "die"—that is, lose their tensive or "is not" quality.[13] Such idolatry encourages us to think of God as literally "father."[14] Living metaphors and parables are valuable in opposing this literalism. While the "is" of the metaphor affirms something real about God, the "is not" decisively undercuts literally equating language with God.[15]

It is not enough, however, to counter literalism and the absolutizing of dead metaphors. The range of metaphors we employ for God must themselves reflect the plurality of human experiences of God. As social, cultural, and historical beings we have a plurality of perspectives. Class, race, sex, education, family, interests, prejudices, concerns all affect the language we choose to describe our experiences of God. Scriptural language is itself the result of such human choices.[16]Thus to absolutize one single set of images for God is to make one set of experiences normative. Traditional language not only can become idolatrous, it can exclude persons unable to relate to it in terms of their own experiences.[17]

By linking a bidirectional view of metaphor with a liberal theology, McFague is able to argue that God-language reflects the human experience of God and is expressed in the language of particular cultures. Since scripture and tradition are produced by males whose ways of thinking are shaped by patriarchal culture, they do not reflect the experiences of women and are at least in part oppressive.

These assumptions about metaphor, scripture, and tradition then set the stage for a three-part feminist critique of God-language. First, "whoever names the world owns the world." Language is not so much a tool we use but a world we inhabit; to change our language is to change our world. Because traditional God-language excludes women, such language must become more inclusive. Resistance to such changes is seen by feminists as resistance to changing one's world[18] (and losing male power).

Second, the problem is not with particular words or phrases but that "the entire structure of divine-human and human-human relationships is under a patriarchal framework" in Western religion.[19] This she seeks to replace with less hierarchical and more relational images.

Third, "religious language is . . . not only about God but also about us." We name ourselves as we name God, the language we choose for God "influences the way we feel about ourselves."[20] Thus, new models of God are required. McFague believes "God the Father," which is the most prominent metaphor in Christian tradition, has been so literalized and absolutized it has become an idol. As alternative metaphors, she suggests God as Mother, liberator, lover, and friend.[21]

Garrett Green would agree with McFague that language is more a house we inhabit than a tool we use. His position is in fact more thoroughgoing: our religious language is not, as McFague assumes, the "articulation of prior religious experience"; it is instead the context which enables us to have that experience.[22] Thus for Green classic texts like scripture do "not express experience so much as they produce it by embodying the community's paradigms."[23] Scripture enables the community "to imagine God, and hence to imagine the world in its essential relation to God."[24] The heart of the Christian paradigm is Jesus Christ, who embodies the image of God.

Green summarizes his central theses succinctly, using the everyday notion of "making an impression on someone":

> Revelation is the impression God makes on us. . . . God has impressed his image, embodied in Jesus Christ, on the original witnesses, who have in turn ex-pressed that image in certain texts; these writings, which we therefore call sacred, once more im-press their form on us, the modern hearers, reshaping us in the image of God.[25]

Scripture, then, is not simply the product of persons struggling to find words for their experience of God. More fundamentally, it is a witness to the revelation of God in Jesus Christ, and embodies the authoritative Christian paradigm precisely because it is the witness to that very particular revelation.

Metaphors for God are to be understood in terms of their role in the biblical narrative. Metaphors are not "independent units of thought, each containing an intrinsic meaning"; their meaning is governed by how they are used in scripture. Thus,

> When Christians call God "Father," it is always shorthand for "the Father of our Lord Jesus Christ." In other words, Christians are not referring generally to God as a father but rather are addressing him in solidarity with Jesus as "*our* Father." The meaning of the metaphor is accordingly to be sought in the story of the one whom Jesus calls Father.[26]

To "tinker with the pronouns or alter the metaphors of such a narrative is to risk losing or seriously distorting its meaning."[27] Instead of treating metaphors as abstractions, we need to re-immerse them "in the concrete text of Scripture in all its bewildering and liberating particularity."[28] What we find when we do is not an authoritarian patriarch but an ironic reversal of power, in which "the Creator of all nature and Lord of all history" chooses "the scattered tribes of Israel to be his people" and "the Lord of life" is obedient unto death.[29] To change the language is to alter the meaning of the story of God.

When we compare the position of Green to that of McFague, what is striking is their utter irreconcilability. By this I do not mean they have nothing to learn from each other. I mean something deeper, having to do with their fundamental assumptions and inner logic.

Both for example agree that our experience is shaped by language. But McFague understands religious language to be most fundamentally an expression of primordial religious experience, calling on it to become inclusive of the experience of women as well as men; Green under-stands such language as a witness to revelation, reflecting the particu-larities of the culture within which the revelation occurred. Thus for McFague new metaphors are necessary and warranted in our modern context, while for Green they are misleading and destructive if not embedded in the story of God in scripture.

Both see issues of overriding importance in this debate. For McFague it is nothing less than whether Christianity can be relevant to the experience of contemporary women or, by absolutizing tradition, finally exclude them from the Christian faith and become an increas-ingly irrelevant relic of a patriarchal past. For Green, the stakes are equally high: it is whether Christianity can remain faithful to the reve-lation of God in Jesus Christ in all its particularity, enabling us to truly experience God, think Christianly about our world, and act accordingly, or whether religious language will be so abstracted from its scriptural context that Christianity will in fact become a new religion, witnessing to a very different God.

Given what I've said thus far about the resurrection, revelation, and scripture, it is no surprise that I find Green's position the most compel-ling. While McFague and Green both appropriate postmodern themes of cultural diversity, community, and relationship, McFague retains something of the modern sense of autonomous agents recreating their world through language. In this she has some kinship with the ultra-critics. Green instead emphasizes the givenness of revelation, occurring at God's initiative, not ours; metaphors for God thus find their meaning not primarily in any cultural context, then or now, but in the narrative of what God has done in Israel and Jesus Christ. He thus has much in common with the post-critics.

For me at least this does not mean we cannot use extrabiblical God-language, even less that we cannot appropriate the rich feminine and genderless imagery for God in scripture itself.[30] It does, however, give a normative status to traditional trinitarian language[31] and require that new imagery not supplant biblical language but be faithful to scripture. The central question of any language, traditional or otherwise, is this: does this language descriptively refer to the God of the Bible or some other god? Even traditional words can be abstracted from the narrative and given a content contrary to that revealed therein.

This last point has been made with great clarity by Elouise Rennich Fraser, an evangelical theologian. She shows why, in the end, we cannot simply rely "on nouns or titles alone to convey the character of God":

The biblical witness to Jesus Christ is not a list of correct titles but a collection of carefully chosen Gospel narratives surrounded on each side by related narrative and non-narrative writings. The ambiguity of titles and nouns used of God is resolved only when they are related to their appropriate story contexts. It is one thing to name God as father or mother. It is quite another to describe God's character by retelling what we hear in the story of Jesus speaking publicly with the Samaritan woman, or of Jesus feeding the five thousand or touching the leper. In the first case, we are left wondering what it means that God is father or mother; or worse, we assume we already know what it means. In the second case, by fixing our attention on the activity of Jesus, we can see the character of God revealed, along with our own character as human beings created in the image of God.[32]

Fraser directs us to the heart of the gospel: God's own action in Jesus Christ, through which we come to know who God is. Because this is related to us in scripture, I have a preference for biblical language that continually refers us back to the story of God.

As an example, consider one of the earliest confessions of faith, "Jesus is Lord." Some might object to the term "Lord" as hierarchical, depicting Jesus (and thereby God) as a male authority figure. This is taking a cultural definition of "Lord" and defining Jesus accordingly.

This, it seems to me, is moving in the wrong direction. Instead, we need to begin with Jesus and ask who this Jesus is in terms of the biblical narrative. There we find a baby born to a poor family far from the centers of power. The news was given not to Caesar or Herod but to shepherds who did not rank high on the social scale of that day. As an adult he went around conversing with people he wasn't supposed to talk with, and having fellowship with those he was supposed to shun. He washed his disciples' feet. When faced with competition for authority among his disciples, he said

> You know that the rulers of the Gentiles lord it over them, and their great ones are tyrants over them. It will not be so among you; but whoever wishes to be great among you must be your servant. (Mt. 20:25–26)

Paul, quoting a hymn of the early church, says of Christ Jesus

> Who, though he was in the form of God,
>   did not regard equality with God
>   as something to be exploited,
> but emptied himself,
>   taking the form of a slave,

being born in human likeness.
And being found in human form,
   he humbled himself
   and became obedient to the
      point of death—
  even death on a cross. (Phil. 2:6–8)

When we say "Jesus is Lord" it is *this* Jesus to whom we are referring. And if *this* Jesus is Lord, then all that is contrary to Jesus—including all that supports injustice, oppression, indignity, and abuse—is not "Lord"—in fact, it is passing away. To fail to claim "Jesus is Lord" is to fail to affirm in the face of sin, evil, and death what Christians know to be true: Jesus Christ is risen from the dead! God's love will triumph over all that is contrary to God's rule and injurious to God's creation.

The metaphor "Lord" does tell us something about Jesus that is true, while "Jesus" does not (unfortunately, in this case) tell us anything about lords. But "Lord" as a cultural term does not define Jesus—it is the biblical narrative that tells us who Jesus is, and provides the proper context for understanding the metaphor.

Historical Context and the Message of Scripture

We have seen that biblical metaphor if it is to be properly understood must have its primary reference in the biblical narrative and only secondarily in the culture of that day. The meaning of the metaphor has its source not in human culture but in God's revelation in and through history and culture. This is true not only for metaphor, however, but for biblical texts in general. While revelation is not the product of culture, it is inextricably embedded in culture.

The theological foundation for this claim is the historical nature of revelation, and most especially of the incarnation. As René Padilla has said, "God contextualized himself in Jesus Christ." It is due to the "very nature of the gospel" that "we know it only as a message contextualized in culture."[33]

What I want to do in this section is explore further the implications of this contextualization for interpreting scripture. This will be far from a technical treatment of biblical hermeneutics, but it will lift up several issues involved in hearing the message of scripture which truthfully witnesses to a revelation in space and time.

It was in the nineteenth century that differing historical and cultural contexts were given methodological prominence. Postmodernity takes these differences further, raising the question of whether truth claims themselves are the products of particular cultures. I have argued revealed truth has its source not in human culture but in God, but that we do not have this truth apart from culturally-given language and ways of thought. Given the full inspiration and authority of scripture, evangelicals are not free to simply dismiss certain passages as captive to an earlier or less enlightened culture; given the humanity of scripture they also are not free to ignore the original historical and cultural context. The hermeneutical task is thus understood as the discerning of transcultural norms within the culture-specific language of scripture. In no area has the results of that search proved more controversial for evangelicals than in the discussion concerning the role of women in church and home.

The differences have proven so intractible and their implications for Christian practice so important that they have spawned two competing interdenominational organizations, both founded in 1987. The Council for Biblical Manhood and Womanhood represents the views of traditionalists or, as they prefer to be called, complementarians. Their central contention is that God created men and women equal as persons and in value, but has given them different roles in church and home. They believe scripture teaches male leadership in both of these spheres, and are alarmed that some evangelicals seem willing to abandon this divine order for a modern cultural alternative amenable to feminist and Enlightenment definitions of equality.[34]

Christians for Biblical Equality was formed to advance the views of biblical feminists, or as many prefer to be called, egalitarians. They argue that the inequality and role distinctions among men and women in human cultures is a result not of creation but the fall. The gospel message of forgiveness of sins and new life in Christ clearly implies equality of the sexes as an aspect of God's overall redemptive purpose. Thus scripture teaches the full equality and partnership of men and women in church and home. They lament that the allegiance of some evangelicals to traditional culture blinds them to the egalitarian message of scripture.[35]

It would be a mistake to think CBMW and CBE divide evangelical scholars along the along the same lines as the issue over inerrancy. There are strong proponents of strict inerrancy in *both* groups,[36] and some who dissent from strict inerrancy at the same time question the egalitarian view. Kenneth Kantzer quite straightforwardly expressed his position when he entitled his address to a CBE conference "The Inerrant Word is Egalitarian."[37]

The dispute has produced a flurry of books, articles, papers, and replies thereto. One area of controversy concerns a number of hard to define Greek words. Does "head" in I Cor. 11:3 ("Christ is the head of every man, and the husband is the head of the wife,") mean "have authority over" (like the head of an organization) or "source" or "origin" (like the head of a river)? Does "authority" in I Tim. 2:12 ("I permit no woman to teach or to have authority over a man,") mean "have authority over" or something like "usurp authority"?—the word only is used here in the New Testament and its extrabiblical meaning in Paul's day probably tended toward the latter definition.

More important for our purposes, much of the debate revolves around the cultural context of particular passages and the relation of those passages to the larger scriptural context. On these points it seems to me the egalitarians make a far stronger case. They also have the more interesting position because—in opposition to evangelical complementarians, liberal Christian feminists, and post-Christian feminists[38]—they hold that scripture fully teaches gender equality.

In dealing with culture in scripture, Robert K. Johnston in an early survey of traditionalist and egalitarian books (all written prior to the formation of CBMW and CBE) noted two distinct interpretative errors. The first was the traditionalist tendency to "spiritualize" culture by minimizing the difference between then and now. In so doing they made certain first century practices universally normative, but not all; most of these writers do not suggest a return to theocracy, the reinstitution of slavery, or greeting one another with holy kisses.[39] Since they recognize these practices as culturally relative, why not conclude the same for those practices concerning men and women?

Early egalitarian writing tended in the opposite direction: instead of conflating culture with the universal message they sharply distinguished them. Thus Robert K. Jewett functionally discards passages where he believes Paul made culturally relative practices normative, and endorses those where Paul is teaching transcendent norms. Johnston rightly doubts whether such a clear distinction can be made between what is human or divine in scripture, or what is cultural or universal—scripture appears to be wholly both at the same time.[40] He asks,

> Is it not true that Paul's "purely" theological insights are, on closer inspection, responses to the cultural crises and life situations of young churches facing concrete problems, and that his "purely" practical advice has within it a theological dimension?[41]

It is because subsequent egalitarian arguments have taken cultural particularity seriously that they have now succeeded in placing the burden of proof on their complementarian opponents.[42] Their central strategy has been to discern transcultural norms within the cultural particularities of scripture.

The most significant reason for their success is that they have focused evangelical attention on the whole of scripture, including its narrative and descriptive parts, instead of on just a handful of passages. Complementarians tend to begin with those particular passages which they see as offering specific and direct teaching on the role of men and women, then, given the consistency of scripture, they proceed to make all else fit their interpretation. Rebecca Merrill Groothuis states the contrasting egalitarian position well:

> It is important to maintain interpretive consistency with the rest of a biblical author's writings as well as the whole of Scripture. Toward this end, unclear and/or isolated passages are not to be used as doctrinal cornerstones, but are to be interpreted in light of clear passages which reflect overall biblical themes. This hermeneutical principle prohibits building a doctrine of female subordination on I Corinthians 11:3–16 and 14:34–35 and I Timothy 2:11–15, for these texts are rife with exegetical difficulties.[43]

The entirety of scripture is the context within which particular, problematic passages are to be understood.

Ranging throughout the New Testament, egalitarians have made a strong case from the gospels that Jesus, in sharp contrast to his own culture, treated women with respect and dignity, that the gospel writers themselves reflect that view, and that the early church as depicted in Acts and in the epistles seemed extraordinarily open to women in leadership roles. One third of the persons named by Paul at the end of his epistles are women. Against the backdrop of first century Palestinian and Greco-Roman culture, early Christianity is astonishingly egalitarian. This underscores another of Groothuis' hermeneutical principles:

> Events recorded in the Bible should also be understood in light of the culture of that time. For example, a woman leader in a highly patriarchal culture would have more significance than a woman in leadership today.[44]

If this picture of New Testament Christianity is close to accurate, what then do we make of those specific passages favored by complementarian exegetes? Egalitarians have shown that the meaning of these passages is far from obvious. Part of the problem has to do with accurate translation; as I have already noted some key words are especially difficult to translate. Moreover, all of these passages have to do with particular situations the nature of which is unclear. Egalitarians have offered potential historical reconstructions to account for these passages that are at least as plausible as those of the complementarians. For example, perhaps wives in the Corinthian church who were either uneducated or recent converts were disrupting worship through asking their husbands questions, something they could do just as well at home. In this case the meaning of I Cor. 14:34–35 relevant to us would not be that women cannot speak or lead in worship, but that our speaking should be orderly and appropriate to the worship of God. It could even be seen as a problem engendered by the more egalitarian practice of the early church.

While I agree with Groothuis (and Millard Erickson, whom she cites) that "texts couched in a context of culturally-specific instructions are not to be taken *a priori* as normative for the present day,"[45] I have a word of caution about extracting the "biblical principle" therein which would then be considered authoritative. While I do believe these texts speak to our situation indirectly, and hence we do need to discern a transcultural norm within culturally-specific instructions, we should not confuse or equate the principle we discern with the text. We can always be corrected by the text, and the passage may yet have more to teach us.

Egalitarians have also shown that the import of the message of scripture tends to unfold over time, what Johnston calls the "continuing actualization" of the implications of scripture.[46] The issue here is not God's progressive revelation but our progressive understanding; the abolition of slavery is an example of this process. What are the implications of scripture for the equality of women in our culture and time in history?

Egalitarians have also successfully rooted themselves within historic evangelicalism, most especially in the awakenings of the eighteenth and nineteenth centuries, where a strong concern for the equality of women emerged and a defense of the ordination of women was advanced.[47] While critically appropriating some contemporary feminist insights, their foundation is biblical—they look to scripture, not "women's experience," as their final authority, and understand the problem of sexism in terms of the larger issue of sin and redemption.[48]

Finally, they have placed the entire question of the cultural role of women and men within the larger scriptural narrative, from creation to eschaton. Here we see one central reason for the divergent complementarian and egalitarian readings of the same passage. As complementarians tell the story, God ordained distinctive roles for men and women in creation, which was disrupted by sin; redemption involves the restoration of those roles in which for the male involves leadership in home and church. Egalitarians believe that men and women were created as equal partners; sin led to the emergence of male dominance and female passivity, in which both no longer fulfill the divine intent. Salvation through Christ has as one of its effects the restoration of that partnership and equality of service, especially in the church and in the Christian home.

In addition to this, Wesleyan, Holiness, and Pentecostal egalitarians have advanced a pentecostal and eschatological argument. Pentecost is understood to have begun a new era in which "your sons and your daughters shall prophesy" (Acts 2:17, NRSV); women as well as men are thus baptized by the Spirit and called equally into all areas of service, inaugurating in the present the life of the coming Kingdom of God.

It is these different ways of telling the Christian story which underlies the debate between complementarians and egalitarians and makes their differences so hard to resolve. But the egalitarians have offered a plausible and in my view compelling scriptural framework within which particular descriptive and prescriptive passages can be seen as both intelligible and consistent.

This also indicates the growing significance of an authentically evangelical feminism for postmodern theology. With the waning of the Enlightenment the presuppositions which undergird the historical-critical method are no longer seen as universally self-evident. While on one hand there will likely be an intensification of interest in the cultural diversity in scripture itself, there will also be more openness to particular claims for divine revelation within history. The argument that scripture has an overarching unity which is manifested in and through a wide range of historical and cultural diversity will not be ruled out in advance. Thus the biblical feminist claim that scripture has a coherent and consistent message of equality for women and men will at least receive a hearing even outside evangelicalism.

This could be the basis for a fruitful exchange between evangelical feminists and those on the more moderate side of nonevangelical Christian feminism. So far, this discussion has not taken place. The reason is that evangelical feminists have focused on their debate with complementarians, and in the face of this challenge have had to emphasize their distinction from more liberal feminists. At the same time, liberal Christian feminists have been concerned to answer post-Christian claims that one cannot be both Christian and feminist; this has in my view led to an unfortunate rejection of scriptural authority and a revision of Christian essentials which is unnecessary. It is time to explore the evangelical case for a scriptural feminism which is rooted unapologetically in scripture and the central truth claims of the faith.[49]

Elaine Storkey has made an important beginning. She notes that secular feminism—whether liberal, Marxist, or radical—has been deeply influenced by the Enlightenment ideal of freedom as individual autonomy, with its concomitant abandonment of the Christian idea of sin. The feminist goal is then to set women free from the shackles of patriarchy. But Storkey warns that to simply enlist Christianity as an ally for this agenda not only distorts Christianity but is self-defeating. Sexism is not the whole of sin, and patriarchy is not the root problem.[50]

Instead, she and other biblical feminists "do not take their cue from the autonomy of the Enlightenment but from a Christian view of people-under-God." Such a perspective understands patriarchy and sexism as cultural manifestations of a deeper problem of sin, and forgiveness by God as the way to freedom.[51] Salvation through Christ necessitates a simultaneous dying to autonomy and inequality and living a new life of equal servanthood under Christ and mutual respect for one another. Thus Storkey not only shows us a feminism determined by the gospel of Jesus Christ as revealed in scripture, she raises the issue of how feminists so deeply indebted to modernity will fare in a postmodern context.

True and False Contextualization

The recognition of a cultural diversity within which no single human culture can claim superiority is characteristic of postmodern thought. It has the effect of dethroning Western culture, although not negating it—the Greco-Roman and Enlightenment traditions remain as participants in a global marketplace of ideas. Accompanying this is a concern for religious pluralism, a topic I will touch on in chapter ten. But for now, I want to consider how the distinctively Christian gospel finds a home in this diversity of cultures. This will not be a full scale contextual hermeneutic. My goal is far more modest: I seek to name several essential theological concerns regarding contextualizing the gospel in light of the argument so far.

The first of these is the most important: true contextualization begins with the biblical narrative, which has been produced by and truthfully presents God's revelation in history. That is, it is above all concerned to maintain the integrity of the gospel. As Lesslie Newbigin says, "What comes home to the heart of the hearer must really be the gospel, and not a product shaped by the mind of the hearer."[52]

This is not a new issue. Paul is often cited as a premier example of contextualizing the gospel:

> For though I am free with respect to all, I have made myself a slave to all, so that I might win more of them. To the Jews I became as a Jew, in order to win Jews. To those under the law I became as one under the law (though I myself am not under the law) so that I might win those under the law. To those outside the law I became as one outside the law (though I am not free from God's law but am under Christ's law) so that I might win those outside the law. To the weak I became weak, so that I might win the weak. I have become all things to all people, that I might by all means save some. (I Cor. 9:19–23)

This serves as a kind of charter for the contextualization of the gospel. Yet in this same letter, whether it be sexual immorality, food offered to idols, abuses at the Lord's table, or the nature of the resurrection, Paul challenges the rather creative contextualization of the gospel by the Corinthian church. Clearly for him, there is a way to truly contextualize the gospel in which the gospel transforms the context, and a false contextualization in which the context fatally alters the gospel.

Helmut Thielicke in this regard helpfully distinguishes between "accommodation" and "actualization" of the gospel. As he defines it, accommodation is characteristic of Cartesian theology, in which the message of scripture is accommodated to the ability of the recipient to understand it. The message inevitably is regulated by a previously determined theory of what is understandable or relevant. In contrast, actualization is the restatement of the message in such a way that it reaches its hearers. While accommodation involves a human reconstruction of the gospel to fit the contemporary context, actualization invites a divine reconstruction of the human context in light of the gospel.[53]

In order for actualization to occur, current terms shed their old meanings—they must die and rise with new meaning. Thielicke calls this the "de-ideologization of terms." As an example, he takes the classic term Logos. When the gospel was communicated to Greek society, Jesus Christ was identified with the Logos. Accommodation occurred when "Jesus" took on characteristics of the Logos as understood by Greek philosophy; actualization was when the meaning of "Logos" was transformed by its new association with the identity of Jesus Christ.[54]

The problem with much that goes under the name of contextual theology today is the approach is more accommodation than actualization. This is a generalization and should be treated accordingly; nonetheless it is a generalization that reflects a common characteristic of otherwise quite diverse approaches to contextual theology.[55]

Consider for example the theologies of liberation from Latin America. They typically begin not with scripture but with a social analysis of their context, and conclude the central feature of that context is oppression of the poor. Subsequent biblical interpretation and theological reflection is then seen as governed by the interests with whom one identifies, either the oppressed or the oppressor. Christian biblical and theological reflection begins on the side of the poor; indeed the "epistemological privilege of the poor" means that only the perspective of the poor can provide an authoritative Christian interpretation. It is no wonder that socio-political liberation is understood as the central if not the sole message of the gospel.

Certain qualifications are in order here. I emphatically do not wish to discount the insights of Christians from among the poor of Latin America nor of liberation theology—in a moment I will try to show why those insights are absolutely essential. What does concern me is the tendency to begin somewhere other than scripture and to lodge absolute hermeneutical authority in a specific class or group. Such a move inevitably leads to either a partial or distorted gospel, and accommodation to humanly perceived needs rather than an actualization of the full gospel. What Steven J. Land says of Pentecostal theology applies here as well: "to do theology is not to make experience the norm, but it is to recognize the epistemological priority of the Holy Spirit in prayerful receptivity."[56] Epistemological privilege belongs to the Holy Spirit as the one who guides us into all the truth (Jn. 16:13).

There is, however, an equally problematic approach to contextualization. This is the imagining that there is some abstract supracultural gospel which can be communicated across cultural barriers. Often this is described as a process of first extracting or decoding the gospel message from its cultural home, and then translating it into a new culture. As we have already seen, such a neat separation of form and content cannot be made. As Dean Fleming insists,

> We cannot minimize the historical nature of the Christian faith. A "supracultural" gospel may exist, but we do not have access to it apart from some human cultural and linguistic formulation; i.e., we cannot know is *supraculturally*. Cultural form and supracultural meaning cannot easily be separated like oil and water.[57]

A gospel free of culture is not a human possibility.

The failure to recognize this has led to an unacknowledged syncretism in Western Christianity in which cultural assumptions have been uncritically permitted to determine the content of the gospel.[58] Most notorious is the impact of Western individualism on biblical interpretation and theological reflection. It becomes natural to read the "you" addressed by Paul in his letters not as the community of believers but as the autonomous individual. Moreover, as René Padilla has said, "the individualism that characterizes Western Culture has clouded the social dimension of the gospel in the eyes of the majority of Christians in the Western World."[59]

How then to maintain the integrity of the gospel while avoiding accommodation to the culture? Here evangelicals from the third world may have much to teach us. Orlando Costas, for example, speaks of three missiological implications of the incarnation. The first is that Jesus Christ has not only suffered "*for* humanity but *with* humanity in the lowest and most horrible form of death." He has fully and completely identified with the poor, oppressed, and marginalized, and is found today "with the outcast and oppressed of the earth."[60] Thus the Spirit of Christ is found in the very experience of oppression.

This experience however cannot have primacy of authority; it must be evaluated in light of the history of Jesus. This is the second missiological implication of the incarnation. Costa insists that

> the true identity of Jesus Christ is not determined by our cultural reality. . . . The true identity of Christ is . . . defined by the life, ministry, and death of Jesus Christ as witnessed to by the New Testament. . . . Any other basis for the identity of Christ is simply illusory and unsustainable.[61]

Dean Fleming makes a similar claim in his critique of a supracultural gospel. Instead of what is sometimes called a "gospel core" of timeless doctrines he proposes a "gospel center" which is found in God's redemptive activity in Jesus Christ within history. This affirms the truthfulness of revelation without denying its contextualized expression within scripture.[62]

Thus the history of Jesus in scripture determines who Jesus is and what the gospel is about, over against theologies which on one hand give context primacy or those on the other that abstract timelesss doctrines from their scriptural and historical context.

Each culture, then, must hear the redemptive story and work out its implications within its own particular context. William Dyrness rightly argues that the authority of scripture in practice emerges

> only from a serious interaction between Scripture and cultural realities. The truth of Scripture has to be worked down into the fabric of our lived worlds, and this takes place only through struggle and interaction with the actual problems of life.[63]

It is not a set of abstract doctrines but scripture itself that is transcultural; "it is through Scripture—as this is read, taught, or preached—that God's presence is manifest in a given culture or people."[64]

Costas' third missiological implication of the incarnation goes to the heart of the truthfulness of the gospel: the experience of Christ must be verified not only by scripture but in the transformation of the situation of the oppressed.[65] I wish to affirm and expand this point—if the gospel is true, it will have a transforming effect on any culture and on the persons within it. Padilla correctly insists that

> to contextualize the gospel is so to translate it that the Lordship of Jesus Christ is not an abstract principle or mere doctrine but the determining factor of life in all its dimensions and the basic criterion in relation to which all the cultural values that form the substance of human life are evaluated.[66]

The gospel, when received in faith, leaves no person unchanged and no society unchallenged.

In my view the initial effect is more personal than social. The goal of the gospel is soteriological, resulting in the gift of new life. But that new life has an immediate social impact. As persons find themselves citizens of the Kingdom of God and disciples of Jesus Christ, they struggle to look with new eyes upon their neighbors and their culture. This propels them into social action to more fully enable God's will to be done on earth as it is in heaven.

It is not simply that the biblical narrative is being read and heard within that culture. It is that the culture itself is being taken up into the narrative, analyzed and evaluated in light of the Kingdom; those who are Christian are thereby enabled to see not only their own lives but their culture in the light of the gospel. "Successful contextualization," says Fleming, "involves an interaction between gospel and context, in which the gospel transforms the context, while the context brings to light deeper levels of meaning from the gospel."[67]

This two way interaction in which primacy is always accorded to scripture occurs only where there is a body of believers who engage in worship and discipleship. True contextualization is not the translation of abstract principles into a new language but the emergence of a new community which (in Newbigin's words) "remembers, rehearses, and lives by the story which the Bible tells"; this occurs "through the continual reading of and reflection on the Bible and the continual repetition of the sacraments of baptism and the eucharist," as well as the living out of this new life concretely as it seeks to be faithful in its particular situation.[68]

The gospel both challenges and affirms aspects of any given culture, but the recognition of those challenges and affirmations do not occur instantly. Christians everywhere have the experience of finding cultural assumptions they once took for granted to now be problematic in light of new insight from scripture. It is often the case that a Christian from another culture can see with clarity what one is unaware of in one's own culture. Christians from Africa may illumine how Americans have compromised the gospel with individualism, or perhaps those from India may expose an uncritical acceptance of materialism in the form of possessions.

Such transcultural sharing is God's great gift to the postmodern church. Padilla is right when he affirms

> that every culture makes possible a certain approach to the gospel that brings to light certain of its aspects that in other cultures may remain less visible or even hidden. Seen from this perspective, the same cultural differences that hinder intercultural communications turn out to be an asset to the understanding of the many-sided wisdom of God.[69]

As Millard Erickson reminds us, this "need not lead to a relativistic or subjective understanding of the truth." Rather, it is persons looking "at that one truth from varying perspectives." Each will see some things which are there but have been missed by others. The result will not be contradictory but complementary.[70]

The hope is that through such global sharing among evangelicals and other Christians a transcultural theology will emerge that is more faithful to scripture, and thereby more reflective of the truth of God's revelation. We are therefore called to witness to the truth of this revelation not only in our own culture but in others as well. We do this not only to share the wonderfully transforming good news which we have received, but in order to hear that gospel afresh from our brothers and sisters within different contexts. We need to receive missionaries as much as we need to be missionaries. As Newbigin says,

> We have to name the name and tell the story. But we do not yet know all that it means to say that Jesus is Lord. . . . We are missionaries, but we are also learners, only beginners. We do not have all the truth, but we know the way along which truth is to be sought and found. We have to call all people to come this way with us, for we shall not know the full glory of Jesus until the day when every tongue shall confess him.[71]

Part IV

Redemption
and the
Character of God

CHAPTER 8

The Love of God

Thus far I have argued that a postmodern evangelical theology must be securely anchored in the resurrection of Jesus Christ which gives a universal and ultimate significance to the particular life and death of Jesus. This action of God in Christ is the heart of a larger pattern of divine activity stretching from creation to the eschaton, and most especially evident in the history of Israel and in the early church.

Scripture was then described as the uniquely authoritative and inspired witness to this revelation, conveying its truth through narrative, metaphor, and other literary genres. What is conveyed is not in the first instance formal doctrines but an overarching story of God which enables us to truly know God and to see the world rightly. Through the Holy Spirit we die to our autonomous selves and are given new eyes to see and new ears to hear; we are incorporated into the biblical narrative which becomes the governing frame of reference for our lives.

We must now say more about the agency and character of God, both of which were seriously questioned by modernity. We have already seen how the supernatural agency of God is replaced in liberal theology by an immanence that is continuous with nature and history, dispensing with awkward claims for miracles or divine interventions which run counter to the predictable laws of science. Modernity also raised to a new urgency the perennial problem of suffering and evil: if God is good and all-powerful, why is there evil? One seemed compelled to choose between atheism and the existence of a God of questionable character.

Postmodernity reopens these issues. In this chapter I want to examine how we might speak of the agency of God, with a focus on what God has done in incarnation and atonement. The thesis is that it is the pattern of God's activity that reveals God's character. In chapter nine which focuses on God's agency in the present, I reverse the argument, claiming that it is on the basis of the character God has revealed that we identify God's actions today. Finally, in chapter ten, there will be a discussion of our agency and character as a response to what God has done in Christ.

The Personal Agency of God

Revelation is an act of God in history. This is the fundamental claim of any evangelical theology without which little or nothing could be said about God or God's purposes. The supreme act of revelation and redemption is the resurrection of Jesus Christ, but this is itself the culmination and confirmation of a much larger pattern of divine revelation.

The God who is revealed—the biblical God—is shown to be both independent from and yet deeply and lovingly involved with creation. Scripture tells the story of this God, utilizing narrative as its dominant literary form; moreover scripture as a whole is canonically arranged as a kind of loosely connected, overarching narrative. As was shown in chapter six, one strength of narrative is its capacity to render the character of an agent. It is through the concrete interaction of person and circumstance that character and purpose are revealed. Thus the Bible as both historically based and narratively constructed is the premier literary medium to enable us to truly know a God who acts in history.

The biblical God is personal, by which I mean is an agent who acts according to chosen aims or purposes. How we can speak of God as personal agent is a central concern of Thomas F. Tracy, whose work I shall utilize in this section.[1] Tracy not only provides an account of divine agency which is congruent with my own description of scriptural revelation, but (without using the term) takes a distinctively postmodern approach which is at the same time faithful to historic Christianity.

Tracy argues that if we are to talk of God or humans as distinctive persons, we must attend to "characteristic patterns of action and emotion."[2] The identity of a person is described in terms of traits of character, and these are expressed and thereby revealed through intentional action.[3] In other words, character requires agency.

By "intentional action" Tracy means that an agent both intends a particular behavior and brings it about.[4] This implies that an agent has at least some freedom over his or her actions, such that the agent can accomplish or at least attempt what he or she has determined to do. Furthermore, what one says is as crucial as what one does, for intentions

140

are often expressed verbally. It is the correspondence of intentions expressed with actions undertaken as a life is lived out over time that gives integrity to a person's character.

Thus it is not isolated acts but the pattern of intentional action over time which most reveals character. This is why, when we are asked what someone is like, we often respond with a story. The "actions narrated in the story display the person's characteristic energy or ambition or wisdom or avarice or the like."[5]

While this brief summary does not do justice to Tracy's careful and thorough argument, it is sufficient to show the linkages of his proposal with my own. When we apply this to God, it shows that the identity or character of God is best revealed through a narrative account of what God has said and done. Because this narrative is found in scripture, the inspiration of the Holy Spirit insures that it faithfully reflects both God's intentions and actions.

Having made a case for divine and human agency as intentional action, Tracy then considers alternative ways that agency might be conceived. He rejects the dominant approach of modernity, which was to describe the human as a duality of mind and body.[6] Originating in the philosophy of Descartes, it sharply distinguished between mind as a thinking substance unextended in space and the body as matter, an unthinking substance extended in space. The advantage of this Cartesian dualism was that it honored both the Enlightenment concern for human rational autonomy (given to the mind) and the scientific assumption that matter operated according to discoverable laws (applied to the body). The notorious disadvantage of this anthropology was there is no convincing way to link mind to body such that one could speak of the person or self as a single, unified whole. The tendency was to resolve this by emphasizing one side of the dualism or the other; behaviorism, for example, sought to fully account for human behavior scientifically, without recourse to human freedom.

Because of this and related difficulties, mind/body dualism has fallen on philosophical hard times. As we saw in chapter three, postmodernity has a decided preference for holistic anthropologies whose subject is not essentially mind or (with behaviorism) body but is a person. Moreover, while the body was secondary to the mind in most modern thought, postmodernity considers embodiment essential to agency. Tracy endorses this approach, describing the person as a "psychophysical" agent and demonstrating how bodily life both limits and enables a person's activity.[7] That is, as biological organisms our actions are necessarily limited and to some extent directed by bodily limitations and needs; within these limits an agent patterns his or her activity not only to meet bodily needs but to fulfill interests that transcend biological utility.[8] At the same time the body is the medium for intentional action, in that it is essential to our accomplishing the actions which we intend.

Let me offer some examples. I might decide to prepare a meal. This is certainly directed to a bodily need and cannot be accomplished without the use of my body. Yet what I choose and how I prepare it is well within the range of choice, and may even say something about the kind of person I am. Later, I might decide to read a book. This is not directed to a bodily need, but it too cannot be accomplished without the use of my body. The fact I chose to read rather than watch television, and the type of book selected, may also reveal something of my character, particularly if this is not an isolated occurrence but a repeated pattern of behavior.

But if embodiment is essential to human personal agency, how can we conceptualize divine agency, when God goes not have a body? This was not a problem for mind/body dualism, where God was simply conceived as a Divine Mind who related to material creation somewhat analogously to the way our minds relate to our bodies. We encountered this modern anthropology in chapter five, where we saw rational propositionalism describing God as a Divine Mind who rationally conveys information to human minds.[9] The demise of mind/body dualism makes this approach problematic, for if "mind" is no longer seen as a distinct entity, then it is no longer a helpful category for describing God as a distinct entity.

Tracy makes clear that the loss of mind/body dualism does not entail the abandonment of theism. What was once meant by "mind" is a set of predicates, including character traits, which can be ascribed to any personal agent.[10] The theologian, says Tracy, can "recast his talk of 'Divine Mind' in terms of a 'Divine Agent' without loss, and have a richer and more versatile way of thinking about God as a result."[11]

But now the question of embodiment must be addressed. Some liberal theologies, such as Charles Hartshorne's version of process theology, have attempted to meet this deficiency by supplying God with a body. The world is God's body, they argue; God and creation are seen as a psychophysical unit. As Tracy shows, such proposals come at the cost of positing an essentially finite God, and its drive to unite God and creation into a single whole may compromise the agency of the creaturely subunits as well.[12]

Rejecting this approach, Tracy argues instead that divine agency not only does not require embodiment but is perfected precisely because it is a nonbodily agency. As to the first point, he says,

> We can refer to this agent as long as we can provide a context in which the agent can be uniquely identified. And we can give a concrete content to the life of this agent as long as we can ascribe intentional actions to him that allow us to characterize his distinctive identity as an agent.[13]

I have argued that such unique identification of God as an agent in history is made in scripture.

As to the second point, Tracy argues that God is not limited by bodily needs nor does God need a body to enact intentions. All of God's activity is thus intentional action, unlimited by external necessity and unrestricted in scope. This does not preclude a self-limitation on the part of God, only that such limitation would come from God's own initiative to fulfil God's own purposes. We shall take up this theme again later in this chapter as well as in the next.

With Tracy's help I have now advanced a formal description of God as a personal agent, and argued that it is God's intentional action as presented in scripture which reveals the character or identity of God. If we then turn to scripture and examine God's intentions and actions, what character is then revealed? A complete answer to that question is outside the scope of this book, but would clearly involve a range of qualities including faithfulness, wisdom, righteousness, and the like. It might as well deal with certain more traditional attributes like omnipotence and omniscience, but these would be defined not by philosophical speculation concerning the nature of divinity but by the biblical revelation of the actual character of God. In fact, all descriptive terms would have as their defining reference the concrete intentions and actions of God in scripture.

Instead of a full and rich descriptive account, let me move instead to the very heart of God's character, and suggest the one element of who God is that governs all the rest. On this I strongly agree with John Wesley when, commenting on I Jn. 4:8, he says,

> God is often styled holy, righteous, wise; but not holiness, righteousness, or wisdom in the abstract, as he is said to be love; intimating that this is . . . his reigning attribute, the attribute that sheds an amiable glory on all his other perfections.[14]

This is the central scriptural claim about God, and while biblical accounts of God's loving intention and action abound, the culmination and the depth of God's love is revealed in Jesus Christ. It is to the revelation of God in Christ I now turn, first with a consideration of the incarnation followed by a discussion of atonement. It is here more than anywhere else that we not only find that God is love, but come to know the particular nature of that love as it was manifested in Jesus Christ.

God as Jesus Christ

Our focus now shifts from God acting in history to the one particular act by which God enters history. It is the incarnation which more than any other divine action reveals the essential character of God, for it is an act which initiates a unified pattern of intentional action in the life and death of Jesus of Nazareth. Here Colin E. Gunton will be a most helpful guide through the relevant issues.[15]

We can note at the beginning that Gunton shares a number of the central concerns of my argument. In particular, he insists that because of the resurrection Jesus is not simply a figure of the past but of the present and future, and it is this perspective which governs the portrayals in the New Testament.[16] Furthermore, the diverse christologies in the New Testament find their unity in the single theme that Christ is the "one in whom the work and presence of God are given through the medium of a human being."[17]

Gunton's target is the understanding of time and eternity as opposites or contradictions, a dualism which dominates Western intellectual history.[18] In its Neoplatonic form, it is this dualism that proved to be such a challenge to early Christian theologians who sought to deal with the nature of Jesus. The early heresies tended simply to opt for one side or the other of the time/eternity divide: docetism for the eternal, adoptionism for the temporal. The later more nuanced heresies of Nestorius and Apollonarius attempted to account for both sides of the dualism while still operating within its framework, leading either to a radical minimizing of the temporal (Apollonarius) or an affirmation of both at the cost of internal disunity (Nestorius).

The problem was the framework itself. Gunton argues that the fundamental New Testament insight is "a view of history in which time and eternity are, so to speak, given together." In a variety of ways the New Testament writers "intermingle time and eternity,"[19] and in so doing are in continuity with their Old Testament predecessors. Indeed it is the interweaving of the eternal and temporal in the history of Israel which is the essential lens through which the claims about Jesus are best understood.[20] Orthodox writers such as Athanasius were orthodox precisely because they remained faithful to this scriptural perspective, refusing to acknowledge dualist presuppositions. Instead of viewing them as opposites, they affirmed an interacting duality of God and creation, an interaction which dualism defines as impossible. Thus for orthodoxy, Jesus really is fully human and divine without compromising his humanity, divinity, or personal unity. As Gunton says of Athanasius, "because of what he believes *to have happened* in time and history" he "is unmoved by mere logical counters. The logic of words must give way before the logic of facts."[21]

It is Gunton's contention—and one I fully endorse—that the dualism of time and eternity is as much a modern presupposition as it was for classical thought. Such a fundamental continuity between premodern and modern perspectives is at first glance a puzzling claim, for the usual reading is that the Platonic tradition was heavily biased toward the eternal while the Kantian grants reality to the temporal. Gunton does not dispute this, but pushes deeper to expose the common dualistic assumption underlying both views.[22]

We have already surveyed this territory in chapter two, and what we said there confirms Gunton's thesis. The deists certainly had a radical dualism of time and eternity, safely moving God out of the temporal order so as not to be in the way of the discoveries of natural law by human reason. Post-Kantian liberals made God immanent within the temporal order and thus avoided the awkward issue of how a transcendent agent could be involved in the world and yet remain transcendent. Jesus became a very human figure who uniquely exemplified a Godly way of life or distinctively possessed a perfect consciousness of God. Gunton, in his own analysis, perceptively notes how Schleiermacher's christology attempts to skirt the ontological issue raised by the earlier orthodoxy through Jesus' experience of god-consciousness, a quality so distinctive that Jesus is at once neither divine nor human but suprahuman; "Jesus' very religiousness takes him out of our class."[23]

The other liberal option, that of Jesus as exemplary, solves the problem by making the historical Jesus the only real Jesus and shifting the locus of our worship from Jesus as divine to the God who Jesus worships. Here again, the troublesome issue of linking the temporal and eternal realms is avoided, with the added bonus that Jesus of Nazareth becomes a candidate for historical reconstruction uncomplicated by considerations of an incarnation.

The most notorious contemporary manifestation of this second liberal option is the "Jesus Seminar," consisting of a handful of New Testament scholars who vote on the authenticity of the sayings and actions of Jesus in the gospels. Objecting to the traditional portrayal of Jesus as divine, their goal is to make available to the public the "real" historical Jesus rather than the mythic Jesus of church dogma. Given this goal and their *a priori* suspicion of the historical reliability of the New Testament gospels, it is no surprise that they find very little that Jesus reportedly said and did to be authentic.

While the Jesus Seminar does not represent mainstream liberal scholarship, much less that of evangelicals, it is a rather flamboyant version of one tendency within New Testament studies. The methodology of the Jesus Seminar and related proposals, both academic and popular, had been thoroughly analyzed.[24] I want to highlight here certain aspects of that critique which illustrate dualist assumptions, drawing on the insights of Luke Timothy Johnson, a widely respected Roman Catholic who represents more mainstream biblical scholarship. Central is their assumption, rooted in the Enlightenment, that the only significant category of truth is history.[25] We saw in chapter two that just such an assumption has governed the theological scholarship of modern conservatives and liberals alike. Here it works to call into question the gospel accounts due to their evident theological bias and to validate the reconstruction of an alternative and presumably more authentic Jesus.

Johnson challenges this assumption on two levels. First, he shows how tentative is any reconstruction of an historical figure, especially when faced with quite limited evidence.[26] That is, the Jesus Seminar participants and others of like mind simply cannot deliver an "objective" or "scientific" result even on the basis of their own assumptions.

But more importantly, those assumptions are themselves highly questionable and heavily indebted to the Enlightenment. In an important statement dealing with the resurrection Johnson insightfully gets to the heart of the problem:

> Insistence on reducing the resurrection to something "historical" amounts to a form of epistemological imperialism, an effort to deny a realm of reality beyond the critics' control. . . . It is . . . an ideological commitment to a view of the world that insists on material explanations being the only reasonable explanations, that reduces everything to a flat plane where not even genius, much less the divine, can be taken into account.[27]

Here we see a clear instance of the "metaphysics of presence" against which Derrida protests. Consisting of a dualism in which one element gains ascendancy over the other, one modern manifestation is the exclusion of the eternal through giving ultimate reality to the temporal. Modernity has not so much abandoned Platonic dualism as it has turned it on its head, and those in the Jesus Seminar are among the least subtle proponents of adjusting Christianity to this modern view of reality.

It is not, however, the Christian view of reality. Johnson argues that the "Christian faith (then and now) is based on religious claims concerning the present power of Jesus" and not on historical reconstructions.[28] The historical Jesus is none other than the risen Jesus, and because of that the postresurrection perspective of the gospel writers, which is treated with such suspicion by the Jesus Seminar, is precisely what enables them to provide access to the "real Jesus."[29]

We have already seen that a similar view is at the heart of Gunton's proposal as well. Jesus is not simply a figure of the past but of the present; "There can only be serious Christology at all if there is a present Christ in the light of which the past Jesus can be considered."[30] Gunton argues that the fundamental error was the equating of "eternity" with "timelessness," and proposes a more eschatological approach in which eternity does not mean removal from time but relationship to all time. Jesus is eternal, and therefore divine, in that he is related to past, present, and future.[31]

Gunton's proposal is both a corrective to the earlier orthodoxy and an implicit response to Derrida's concerns. It is an explicit corrective to an orthodoxy which, especially since Augustine, has simply assumed eternity means God is outside of time. While orthodox Christology was "not the slave but the critic of Hellenistic philosophy,"[32] insisting correctly on the juxtaposition of humanity and divinity in the one Jesus, it nonetheless at times lost the humanity of Jesus in its attempt to link him with a timeless eternity. Donald Bloesch has made a similar point, noting with approval Karl Barth's attempt to place "the philosophical concept of eternity into the service of biblical revelation." The result was to decisively alter the concept, "for an absolute dichotomy between eternity and time is not found in the Bible."[33] For both Bloesch and Gunton, it is essential for a faithful biblical orthodoxy to maintain the distinction between eternity and time while upholding their God initiated relationship.

Gunton provides an implicit response to Derrida's concern (although perhaps not one acceptable to Derrida) at this point of relationship. What is proposed is a duality which is interrelated rather than a dualism that is oppositional. The relational dynamic is exactly the reverse of dualism, for the eternal God does not negate but rather upholds the temporal world; the divine is not aloof from creation but actively and intimately involved. At the same time, the duality prevents a confusing or blurring of the distinction between God and creation as occurs, for example, in process theology.

We can summarize Gunton's constructive proposal in two steps. First, he shows how the Christian claim that the eternal is found within the temporal as a human being can be conceived as "co-presence" in space and time. Our problem with this stems from our preference for visual metaphors, leading us to think of visible substances somehow occupying the same space or point in time. Instead, Gunton proposes an analogy with music, in which different notes are co-present in space and time. This may help us understand patristic incarnational and trinitarian language of interpenetration (or perichoresis), in which discrete realities, much like fields of forces, interpenetrate and interact with one another within the same space.[34] In terms of time, it reinforces T. F. Torrance's claim for a "contingent rationality" in which both science and theology assume that the temporal contains within it a discoverable order that is revelatory of ultimate reality.[35] Thus the temporal life of Jesus has within it an intrinsic pattern which Gunton calls "the logic of divine love," in which "Jesus is God's love taking place in our time and history."[36]

Second, he argues that christological language uniquely attempts to speak of time and eternity together, but, like all language about reality, does so indirectly. Rejecting the modern quest for language that exactly mirrors reality, Gunton utilizes the philosophy of Michael Polanyi to claim that christological language emerges not from objective but participatory knowing, or "indwelling." Christians indwell Christ as they participate in scripture, worship, and community through the Holy Spirit. Traditional christological language is like a model or map, truthful not in exactly replicating the reality of Jesus Christ but in providing a guide to that reality. Its task was to "ensure what we say about Jesus of Nazareth remains true to what he *was* and *is*: the temporal locus of God's love for his creation."[37]

In this way Gunton has provided a postmodern rendering of the incarnation which remains faithful to scriptural revelation. It remains to say briefly how it is, if the eternal can be thought of as appearing within the temporal as a human, that Jesus of Nazareth is the one human uniquely so identified. To put the question this way is of course to put matters in reverse order—it is precisely because Jesus was and is understood as both divine and human that the dualism of time and eternity was questioned in the first place, a patristic anticipation of a postmodern concern.

We provided the primary answer in chapter four: Jesus is identified as the unique incarnation because he is risen from the dead. This is the foundation of the christological claims of the first Christians as well as for us. Moreover, there is in addition the witness of the Holy Spirit which enables us to know the Jesus portrayed in scripture as a living presence in our lives. But more than this can be said. There is the further claim that the intentions and actions of Jesus in the biblical narratives are such that he could not be other than God incarnate.

William Abraham has argued that scripture depicts Jesus as acting "in ways which match the acts that are used to identify God."[38] This could be illustrated from any of the four gospels; let me simply select a few examples from Mark. Jesus astounds the synagogue at Capernaum by teaching not as the scribes but "as one having authority;" even more they are amazed when he casts out a demon simply by commanding it to come out. "What is this?" they ask one another, "A new teaching—with authority! He commands even the unclean spirits, and they obey him." (1:21–28).In like manner he heals Simon's mother-in-law (1:29–31); these are only the first of many exorcisms and healings. He not only heals a paralytic but first pronounces his sins forgiven, leading the unhappy scribes to correctly ask "Who can forgive sins but God alone?" (2:1–12). His teaching authority extends to what is lawful on the sabbath, challenging the Pharisees by claiming that "the Son of Man is lord even of the sabbath." (2:23–28) He stills the storm, leading his awe-struck disciples to exclaim, "Who then is this, that even the wind and the sea obey him?" (4:35–41). Most astonishing of all, he restores to life the deceased daughter of Jairus (5:35–43).

Who indeed is this one who is lord of creation, whose very word can forgive sins, heal the sick, cast out demons, and bring the dead back to life? In the Old Testament, there is only One who is identified by this pattern of action and authority; Jesus is troubling to so many because he fits so well that description.

If this is the case, then Jesus is God manifested as a human being—the eternal has indeed entered the temporal. And this in turn means that Jesus' intentions and actions are themselves revelatory of God. As Abraham puts it, "the incarnation of God in Jesus is allowed to enrich the criteria for divine action already in use"; indeed that revelation "may be qualified and corrected" or at least reinterpreted "in light of the new revelation."[39] To suggest some ways the incarnation enriches our conception of God is the goal of section three.

Jesus Christ as God

To know who Jesus is—to know his character through his intentions and actions as portrayed in the biblical narrative—is to know the character of God. Jesus reveals God as One whose will is life, not death, and who is characterized by a love which willingly accepts humility and suffering. This pattern of divine love is shown in Jesus' teaching, ministry, and death.

In his teaching he proclaimed the coming Kingdom of God, not only as judgement but as grace for sinners. He was consistent with the prophets' twin emphases on loving God (versus idolatry) and loving others (versus injustice), but at the same time extends these by offering forgiveness to sinners and love to enemies. However, Jesus also expressed anger—divine anger—toward injustice, oppression, and hardness of heart. Most importantly, he expanded traditional teaching to reveal God's concern not only for what one does, but also for the content of one's heart or character.

Jesus' ministry was consistent with his teaching. His healing ministry and exorcisms not only demonstrated divine authority but divine opposition to the sickness, suffering, death, and evil which rob humanity of life. He was a friend to lepers, tax-gatherers, women, children, and others who were oppressed, outcast, or degraded by society. He combined his opposition to sin with freely offered forgiveness. By living a life for others, he reveals God as a God for others.

To live such a life, and to claim that it is in conformity to God's own will and to the Kingdom of God, is to invite conflict with powers and authorities, both spiritual and temporal. The religious leaders, while not totally disagreeing, had an essentially different idea of God. The Roman political authorities would be alarmed at any ultimate claims in the name of a Kingdom which so clearly relativized the authority of the emperor. Along with these temporal authorities, the spiritual presence of Satan impinged on the life of Jesus, from the temptations in the wilderness to the Garden of Gethsemene, and kept before him the way of power and authority, and of escape from suffering and death. Jesus took instead the road to Jerusalem, and the cross is in many ways the logical outcome of a life totally devoted to the love of others in the name of God.

Thus Jesus' death is not only the result of opposition to his life and ministry, something that happened to him; it is also a freely undertaken choice, an act of sacrificial love, given on behalf of others. It is an act of God in Christ. God is revealed as the One who serves and suffers in humility, out of love for sinners and in identification with the victims of sin, and is known as the One who brings life out of suffering and death. It is in this way that Jesus' intentions and actions enrich our understanding and experience of the character of God.

All of this points to the centrality of the cross. It is in the cross of Jesus Christ that the identity of God is shown most clearly and the love of God most powerfully. Yet it is such a scandal that except for the resurrection it would have discounted completely any claim for incarnation; even with the resurrection the tendency for Christians is to avoid its implications for belief and practice.

Paul is faced with a Corinthian church who seems to want a risen Lord without a cross. Such a "Lord" can be defined as they wish, but such a "Lord" is not *the* Lord. For *the* Lord is none other than Jesus of Nazareth who was crucified and then was raised from the dead. This may be "foolishness to those who are perishing, but to us who are being saved it is the power of God" (I Cor. 1:18). The cross—"God's weakness"—is the power of God which gives life; thus Paul "decided to know nothing among you except Jesus Christ and him crucified" (I Cor. 2:2).

The cross is the weakness and power of God—but how is it that the cross is *God's* weakness, and in what way does it give life? The difficulty with the first of these questions is this: if God enters into history, can God then be said to be subject to history? Can someone who is subject to history be rightly called divine? Is this perhaps why the cross was "a stumbling block to the Jews and foolishness to Gentiles?" (I Cor. 1:23).

Patristic theologians struggled with this issue, developing the concept of God's impassibility. Their concern was theologically appropriate: they sought a way to say that God is not swept to and fro by suffering and change, but remains faithful to promises and firm in the resolve to save. For them it meant life rather than death was the basic structure of reality, that God (in contrast to humanity) had no "passions" which were the result of death and led to sin, and God's love was eternally reliable and unchanging. At the same time, they in no way wanted to diminish the divinity of Jesus Christ who suffered and died on a cross. Arguing in terms of a communication of properties, they could affirm that divinity did in fact participate in suffering and death, but by way of the humanity of Jesus.[40]

In spite of their intentions, the doctrine of impassibility has historically invited a less than biblical picture of God. Ultimately, it tends toward a God unaffected by creaturely suffering, raising serious questions about God's capacity to love. Moreover, it undermines the personal unity of Jesus himself, encouraging a somewhat Nestorian christology.

The Bible, unencumbered by the Platonic linkage of suffering and change, has no difficulty in portraying God as entering into human suffering while remaining unchangeable in character. The Old Testament abounds with the "pathos" of God, most especially in the prophets.[41] This is sometimes expressed in strikingly emotional language: "My heart recoils within me; my compassion grows warm and tender" (Hos. 11:8). In the New Testament through Jesus Christ God participates directly and personally in the very depth of human suffering and death, even to the point of experiencing God-forsakenness on the cross.[42] It is here one senses the unrestrained depth of compassion, dare we say the infinity of God's love, for humanity.

In light of this, the truth of impassibility—that God cannot be affected and changed by anything outside of God except by God's own will—must continue to be affirmed, for the cross of Jesus Christ is the strongest possible evidence of God's unchangeable love. But at the same time it must not prevent our saying that God can and did choose to enter into our history and share in our suffering. God is not impassive, but full compassion; God is pained by evil and suffering but rejoices at righteousness. God is affected by the world, not out of deficiency or weakness but because God chooses to be so affected out of love.[43]

If the cross can be affirmed as God's cross, how is it that this particular act is salvific? What has God accomplished in the atonement? It must first be said that the cross has its salvific meaning only because Jesus has been raised from the dead. The resurrection is at once God's reversal of the human verdict concerning Jesus and an affirmation that the way of Jesus as seen in his life and death is the way of God, a way that will be fully manifest in the eschatological Kingdom but is found now wherever God's will is done on earth as it is in heaven.

The cross then is inextricably linked to the rest of Jesus' life before and after, and therefore must be understood within the context of the biblical accounts. Theories of the atonement, whether *Christus victor,* Anselmic, or Abelardian, have a tendency to take on a life of their own apart from the story of Jesus. John R. W. Stott prefers to speak of "images" of the atonement, for while "theories are usually abstract and speculative concepts," biblical images of the atonement "are concrete pictures and belong to the data of revelation."[44] Likewise Colin Gunton directs us not to theories but to the "metaphors" of atonement with which the first Christians expressed the significance of the event of Jesus Christ for the world.[45] In line with the approach I take here, Gunton argues that "we are not able to speak of the action and being of God independently of the metaphors in which it is first expressed";[46] the language has been remolded under the impact of the event of the cross and has become revelatory of its meaning. Both Gunton and Stott first proceed to understand the metaphors or images of atonement within the context of the story of Jesus and the larger biblical narrative, and from there move to explore contemporary relevance.

Gunton focuses on three such metaphors, and while we cannot here do justice to his discussion, we can highlight their significance. What I especially want to note for each metaphor is the reversal of meaning which occurs when they are applied to Jesus and understood in terms of his story.

The first metaphor is "victory," drawn from the realm of military conflict. This is the moral victory over evil which occurred when Jesus went to the cross rather than adopt a way of life contrary to God. The death of Jesus is understood by the New Testament writers as the outcome of his life, the "logical consequence of the person he was and the choices he made."[47] The cross thus reverses the usual meaning of victory: "To be victorious does not mean butchering your opponent with weapons, but refusing to exercise power demonically in order to overcome evil with good."[48] In light of this, we have a new vision of the world, both in terms of recognizing its fallenness and in discerning the shape of God's liberation. We also see this victory as decisive but not yet final; God continues the work of overcoming evil until that victory is completed in the age to come.[49]

"Justice," the second metaphor, finds its natural home in the legal system. While victory places the emphasis on our bondage to sin and evil, justice focuses on our responsibility for sin: we have transgressed the law of God and are held accountable, and faced as well with the terrible consequences of our action.[50] Gunton highlights a number of theologically problematic misconstruals of this metaphor in Western

Christianity, including the portrayal of God as punitive rather than gracious and an emphasis on individual salvation to the exclusion of God's larger concerns for justice in the world. But rightly understood, this metaphor has the great strength of highlighting the offense of sin to God, not as a personal affront but rather as that which disrupts God's creation and causes suffering among God's creatures.[51] The concern is not with disobedience to an abstract or arbitrary law but with concrete sin in violation of the order of God's creation. What happens in the cross is that (in Barth's language) the Judge is judged in our place, reversing entirely our usual conception of justice. In this way God takes with utmost seriousness the terrible and unacceptable reality of sin while at the same time providing salvation for sinners.[52]

The third metaphor is "sacrifice," a term borrowed from the language of worship. Sin is here understood neither as bondage nor transgression but as uncleanness or the pollution of God's creation. Through the ritual of sacrifice, which in the Old Testament involved the slaughter of animals (or the giving of a suitable gift to God), the order and wholeness of the community within itself and in relation to God is reestablished.[53] While this is the direct background of the atonement metaphor, there are striking differences. Christ "entered once for all into the Holy Place, not with the blood of goats and calves, but with his own blood, thus obtaining eternal redemption" (Heb. 9:12). Here the sacrifice is once and for all, unnecessary to repeat; more importantly Jesus is not only the one who is sacrificed but the High Priest (Heb. 9:11), the one who makes the sacrifice. Thus unlike any other sacrifice, his death was not imposed but voluntary; and given who Jesus is, his voluntary sacrifice "is also and at the same time the gift of God."[54] The roles are reversed: before Israel had provided the sacrifice to God; now it is God who provides the sacrifice in an act of divine self-giving.[55]

We can see how in each of these instances the metaphor is refashioned by the story of Jesus to which it refers. But it should also be noted that none of these metaphors are adequate by themselves. A true understanding of the atonement is only possible when they are taken together and seen to mutually qualify and interpret one another.[56] Theories of the atonement tend to become fixed and exclusive; biblical metaphors interact with one another to create a far richer picture than would be possible even if all were considered separately.

Fundamental to all of these metaphors, and providing further enrichment for their meaning, are the concepts of "satisfaction" and "substitution." As Stott reminds us, satisfaction can be misconstrued such that it depicts God as accountable to some higher external standard, be it law, honor, or the moral order. In actuality these are not external but intrinsic to God's own character. What God must satisfy, then, is God's own self-consistency; God cannot save by contradicting either God's justice or mercy.[57] Given its terrible destructive effect on the creation, sin and evil must be condemned and judged; given God's love and redemptive purpose, humanity must be loved, forgiven, and transformed. Ultimately, both the judgement of sin and the salvation of sinners stem from God's love for the world.

The necessity that God remain faithful to the divine character underlies the idea of substitution, an aspect of atonement which has already been evident in each of the metaphors. This too can be severely misconstrued. We must not, says Stott, "speak of God punishing Jesus or of Jesus persuading God, for to do so is to set them over against each other as if they acted independently."[58] Substitution is an act of God, in which God through Jesus bears the consequences of our sin. As Gunton says,

> Jesus is our substitute because he does for us what we cannot do for ourselves. That includes undergoing the judgement of God, because were we to undergo it without him, it would mean our destruction.[59]

Substitution is thus a trinitarian activity, an act of divine love in which God undergoes judgement in our place in order to uphold the moral order of creation while at the same time restoring those who have violated that order.

Objections to substitutionary atonement often either depict God and Jesus in dualistic rather than trinitarian terms or fail to take seriously the problem of sin. God cannot forgive as if sin were of no consequence. It matters greatly that ethnic strife continues to fuel war and provoke genocide, that women and children are abused, that some people go hungry while others have more than they need, that the creation has been despoiled, that family relationships are riven by hurt and bitterness. It matters greatly that in our idolatry of material consumption and personal power and security we so often either manipulate or ignore rather than love and serve our neighbor for whom Christ died. Surely the term "wrath of God" is not too strong to describe the divine response. Surely the term "love of God" only begins to plumb the depth of what God does on the cross in order to reconcile, forgive, and provide new life.[60]

What is at stake here, as Gunton says so well, "is more than sins and feelings of guilt; it is the objective disruption of the life and fabric of the universe." We are "concerned with a breach of relationships so serious that only God can refashion them."[61] This is why a "subjective" and "exemplarist" theory of atonement, which envisions the example of Christ to be so striking as to engender a subjective change in the individual heart, may be pleasing to the autonomous individualism of the Enlightenment but remains insufficient and unconvincing apart from a substitutionary approach.[62]

This is not to say we are not to imitate Christ, nor that we are unaffected by the cross. It is to say that the problem of sin as an "objective disruption" and as a power within the human heart is much more serious than exemplary atonement allows. Beyond this, we must ask as well *why* the example of Jesus is so compelling as to affect us. Is it not precisely because he goes to the cross in our place out of love for us? Charles Wesley gives expression to the affective power of substitutionary atonement in these words:

> O Love divine! What hast thou done!
> Th' immortal God hath died for me!
> The Father's co-eternal Son
> Bore all my sins upon the tree.
> Th' immortal God for me hath died,
> My Lord, my Love is crucified.[63]

In the cross of Jesus Christ we see most clearly and definitively what it means to say "God is love;" and from it as well we begin to understand what it might mean for us to love as God has loved us.

CHAPTER 9

The Power of God

We have seen how God was redemptively active in biblical history, culminating in the event of Jesus Christ. I have argued that God's character or identity is revealed in these intentional actions, which are truthfully presented to us in scripture. Because Jesus Christ is the risen Lord and Savior who will come again in glory, there is no further revelation which can occur that will supersede the revelation of God in Christ. It is therefore definitive of God's character and purposes.

The focus of this chapter is on God's activity in the world today. *That* God is active today is generally conceded in Christian theology; *how* God is active and how that activity is to be recognized is more controversial. My first concern will be the latter question of how to recognize where God is at work today. I shall argue that the most important clue to God's present intention and action is the identity and purpose of God revealed in the biblical narrative, most especially in Jesus Christ.

This will not solve all the issues surrounding how God is at work, however. Two of these will be examined here. The first has to do with the nature of God's grace and human freedom, and will involve an analysis of the evangelical debate over "freewill theism." The second has to do with how much of the manifestation of the coming Kingdom can be expected in this life. For example, do we look for miraculous healings or social liberation in the present, or must these wait until Christ returns to fully establish his reign? We shall see that postmodernity permits a much more open attitude to what God is doing in the world than that characteristic of theologies based in Western modernity.

The Mission of God

The message of Jesus Christ, succinctly stated, was this: "The time is fulfilled, and the Kingdom of God has come near; repent, and believe the good news" (Mk. 1:15). It is the mission of God to establish the reign of God, such that God's will would be done on earth as it is in heaven. The Kingdom of God, the fulfillment of that mission and the complete establishment of that reign, was expected at the end of history. But in the life and ministry of Jesus, that future Kingdom had already come near. As he told messengers sent by the imprisoned John the Baptist, "the blind receive their sight, the lame walk, the lepers are cleansed, the deaf hear, the dead are raised, and the poor have good news brought to them. And blessed is anyone who takes no offense at me" (Mt. 11:5–6).

With the resurrection and ascension of Jesus, present expectation and future hope became inextricably linked. Jesus would come again in glory, establishing the final, universal reign of God over all creation. Yet at the same time, Jesus is already Lord over all things, having overcome even death itself. "God has made him both Lord and Messiah, this Jesus whom you crucified" (Acts 2:36). Although we await the final consummation, we are called in the present to hear the good news that in Jesus Christ the Kingdom has come near, and receive forgiveness and enter into the life of the Kingdom.

If the mission of God is to establish the Kingdom, we can see how God has begun to fulfill that goal, first through creating a distinctive people Israel and then by personally entering history through incarnation in Jesus Christ. In this one particular life and death God reveals to us the nature of the Kingdom under the conditions of the present age; moreover God effects redemption such that through faith in Christ we too can participate in the life and work of the Kingdom even now, before the final consummation.

The mission of God today continues through the presence and power of the Holy Spirit. Whereas in Christ God acted in history through incarnation in a single human being, with Pentecost God acts in history through indwelling a people. Incarnation entails an ontological identity: Jesus Christ was and is the second person of the Trinity, and thus reveals in his own intention and actions the very character and purposes of God. Indwelling is transformative, enabling persons and communities to grow in the knowledge and love of God and as a result to increasingly manifest in their intentions and actions the love and will of God.

This is the mission of God seen from the perspective of a Logos Christology, which emphasizes the divinity of Jesus. It must be joined, however, with a Spirit Christology which emphasizes Jesus as baptized by the Spirit.[1] Just as Jesus was empowered by the Spirit in his intentions and actions, so the church, the body of Christ, is similarly empowered by the indwelling Spirit, and continues the ministry of Jesus Christ throughout the world.

While the Spirit indwells the church, the Spirit is not confined to the church but is involved with all humanity and the entirety of creation.[2] There is both an upholding of creation and an ongoing creativity by God, but more than this is God's intention for love and righteousness to characterize creation as it does its Creator. This is why the Spirit reaches out to every human heart, creating a moral sensibility and enabling an obedient response even where the gospel itself is unknown.[3] God is at work throughout the earth, seeking to repair the fabric of human relationship which has been rent by sin. The church as the people of God are called and empowered to serve in this mission. As Murray Y. Dempster says, "the mission of the church is to witness to the truth that the kingdom of God which still belongs to the future has already broken into the present age in Jesus Christ and continues in the world through the power of the Holy Spirit."[4] Indeed, the Spirit constitutes the church as a missionary movement.

If Jesus Christ is the concrete embodiment of the life of the coming Kingdom in this present age, the Holy Spirit is the power of God enabling humanity to live now under the reign of God. Eschatology traditionally is about the "last things," but here it is also about living in the present in light of God's eschatological goal, as persons who already belong to the Kingdom of God. This is in contrast to a purely future eschatology which engenders despair and passivity in the face of present evil; it is also opposed to a purely realized eschatology which either fails to take seriously the pervasiveness of sin and evil or confines itself to an individual existential meaning.

More adequate to biblical revelation is an inaugurated eschatology which maintains a strong tension between the "already" and "not yet"[5] On one hand, Christ has not returned, and nothing in this present age can be confused with the Kingdom of God. Rather, the life of the age to come always stands over against the present, serving as the basis for a critical analysis which brings to light that which is in accord with God's character and purposes and that which is not. On the other hand, the Holy Spirit is already at work, an eschatological power in the midst of history. There is real hope even now, within the present age, as the Spirit brings to birth new life in a world marked by sin, suffering, and death.

What would it mean for the will of God to be done on earth as it is in heaven? The mission of God is holistic and all-encompassing—there is simply no aspect of creation of which Jesus is not Lord, or which is excluded from God's redemptive purpose. Thus the reign of God must be expressed throughout all aspects of creation, including the personal, social, creational, and cosmic dimensions.

It may be helpful for our gaining some sense of what the reign of God means to indicate those forces which are clearly opposed to God's rule. Certainly such a list would include sin, injustice, suffering, death, and Satan, which together constitute an interlocking and mutually reinforcing alternative to the Kingdom of God. Jesus' own ministry and death brought him in conflict with these forces, and his resurrection was God's triumph over them.

Sin involves those intentions and actions which are contrary to God's will. It consists of wrong or distorted relationships to God, others, and self; it implies misplaced loyalties (idolatry), ingratitude, confused values and priorities, the dehumanizing of others or their use for one's own end (injustice), too high an estimation of one's self (pride), or too low an estimation of one's worth or dignity (a denial of the *imago Dei*). Sin involves broken relationships: disobedience or rebellion against God, separation from one's neighbor. It produces guilt and shame.

Evangelical theology has always seen the heart of God's mission as redemption from sin. When at its most biblical, it understands the result of that redemptive act in Jesus Christ to be not only forgiveness and reconciliation, but a new life of love. Such a new life is essentially relational, involving love for God and one's neighbor. The broken relationships are restored and renewed in love, and to that extent the life of the Kingdom has begun to be realized in the midst of a fallen world. The worship, fellowship, and outreach of the church should be where this new life of the Kingdom is most clearly actualized through the power of the Spirit.[6]

More will be said concerning personal salvation in the next chapter, but it should be clear that salvation is not to be understood as excessively individualistic (although under the impact of Enlightenment concepts, evangelicalism has at times so misconstrued salvation, especially in America). Salvation is an essentially relational term, and necessarily involves the incorporation of persons into a new community.

This relational view is not only in accord with postmodern anthropology but is congruent with the communal understanding of personhood in both biblical culture and contemporary societies in the two-thirds world. The biblical view of persons-in-community is an alternative both to autonomous individualism and the kind of collectivism that denies individuality. Community is here understood as that which makes distinctive personhood possible; the fellowship and practices of Christian community is what enables persons to grow into mature disciples of Jesus Christ.

The concern for restoring broken relationships extends beyond the church to the institutions of human society. Because of its central importance to human life, evangelicals have rightly adopted a "pro-family" position with regard to public policy. However, not all that is promoted as pro-family reflects careful social analysis or freedom from ideological captivity. In an understandable reaction against the moral disintegration of the family in Western society, there is the danger of an idolatry of family, of making it an end in itself. As Rodney Clapp has perceptively argued, Kingdom of God and Christian community are the primary contexts within which biblical Christianity must understand the meaning and purpose of the family.[7]

Injustice is the social consequence of sin, and often becomes deeply embedded in the values, perceptions, and practices of cultures and institutions. The Kingdom of God challenges injustice on every level. It is clear in the Old Testament that God has a special concern for the poor and those most vulnerable, such as widows and orphans. Jesus continues and expands this concern. As Murray Dempster says,

> Jesus taught . . . that where God reigns, a new redemptive community is formed in which brothers and sisters enjoy an affirmative community; strangers are incorporated into the circle of neighborly love; peace is made with enemies; injustices are rectified; the poor experience solidarity with the human family and the creation; generous sharing results in the just satisfaction of human needs in which no one suffers deprivation; and all persons are entitled to respect, are to be treated with dignity, and are deserving of justice because they share the status of God's image-bearers.[8]

Such should characterize the Christian community both in its life together and ministry in the world.

Social injustice leads to suffering, but not all suffering is the result of injustice. All suffering, however, is of concern to God. In the Kingdom of God sickness and suffering will be nonexistent; Jesus manifested this reality through his healing ministry, a ministry continued in the early church through the power of the Spirit. Thus the people of God will continue to witness to God's intent through ministries of compassion to the sick, the hungry, the lonely, the grieving, and the victims of natural disasters.[9]

The suffering which is contrary to God's reign is involuntary suffering, the kind in which the one who suffers is a victim. This includes those who suffer due to natural disasters or societal injustice; the latter can be as blatant as racial violence or as subtle as the societal expectation that one "naturally" serves another because of gender or class. But there is another form of suffering and servanthood which is in accord with God's reign, when persons give of themselves out of love for others. When suffering for another is undergone freely in the name of Christ, it is a manifestation in the life of the Christian of the love that was in Christ.

Paul calls death the "last enemy to be destroyed" (I Cor. 15:26). It is a formidable enemy indeed, a foe whose reach extends to all life on the earth. In the Kingdom of God "death will be no more" (Rev. 21:4); Jesus himself raised the dead back to life as a manifestation of God's will toward life. But of ultimate significance is Jesus' own triumph over death, for with the resurrection he is not only raised but will die no more; so it shall be for all who have faith in Jesus Christ.

On the human level, death and sin are mutually reinforcing. When the fear of death becomes a conscious or (more often) unconscious concern, it distorts one's view of life. It can fuel a drive for individual security, which we try to satisfy through a multitude of transitory values, none of which truly gives us life. To live in this way is to be continually dissatisfied, always seeking more. In the process we are only able to see God and our neighbor as either obstacles to our desires or means to acquire what we want.

Jesus Christ frees us from the fear of death, for in his resurrection "death has been swallowed up in victory" (I Cor. 15:54). It is because Jesus is raised that we are set free to truly receive life not only in the future but in the present. For what is at stake here is not simply biological survival, but whether we can live a way of life that is in accord with God's reign as well as with who we were created to be. Jesus' own words make this clear,

> If any want to become my followers, let them deny them-
> selves and take up their cross and follow me. For those who
> want to save their life will lose it, and those who lose their life
> for my sake, and the sake of the gospel, will save it.
> (Mk. 8:34–35)

To be free from the fear of death is to be free to live life as it was meant to be, as disciples of Jesus Christ. It enables us to make God and our neighbor the center of our concern, just as we are the center of God's concern.

Death, however, not only threatens humanity, it hangs over the entire creation. Paul says that "the creation itself will be set free from its bondage to decay" (Rom. 8:21), and until Christ returns humanity has been given the responsibility for caring for the life of the creation. As Calvin B. DeWitt has noted, stewardship includes more than environmental concern, encompassing much that we have already discussed in this section. But there nonetheless is an urgent need for environmental stewardship as part of this larger calling.[10]

Resistance to death implies an entire range of missional activities, from protection of the unborn to fighting poverty, from combatting hunger to world peace. Evangelicals do not agree on specific public policy proposals with regard to these issues, nor on the exact shape of those ministries designed to deal with them on the personal and communal level. But because God is "pro-life," evangelicals cannot be consistent with their profession of faith unless they actively and creatively engage these problems.[11]

The victory of Jesus was not only over sin, injustice, suffering, and death but also over Satan and the spiritual power of evil. It is very difficult for a contemporary Western theology, even one that is evangelical, to take the demonic seriously as a spiritual reality. Yet with the postmodern globalization of theology, we will increasingly be challenged to expand our understanding of reality, especially where such indigenous theologies are most free of Western bias. Of course, more popular works on this subject abound in the West, some of which treat it cautiously and many which do not treat it with enough caution.

Certainly Jesus' ministry—unless one engages in a massive demythologization of gospel passages—encountered this reality both as temptation and in the form of demonic possession; Paul understands the demonic as spiritual powers at work in the created order. With Donald Bloesch I would agree that the "devil must be seen as a super-human intelligence with a strategy and agenda all his own,"[12] one which is diametrically opposed to the reign of God. In one sense Satan still can cause great harm and suffering by drawing persons away from God and their neighbor; in another sense Satan has already been defeated in the resurrection of Jesus Christ, a defeat which will become complete when Jesus returns in glory.

Marguerite Shuster and Paul Hiebert each provide a theological analysis which helps make sense of spiritual reality, and in the process offer clues to what the reign of God entails in light of the demonic. Shuster, who conceives of the demonic in terms of personal spiritual agency, describes humanity as continually interacting with the spiritual dimension. Rival spiritual powers, both divine and demonic, seek to order our wills through persuading us of very different construals of reality. Our intentions and actions are thus conformed to those perceptions and values that for us constitute reality, and we take on a different character depending on whether the source of those perceptions and values is Satan or the risen Christ. Indeed, our intentions and actions (what Shuster calls our will) become the avenues for either God or the devil to work through us to accomplish their intentions. One way we are open to demonic influence is our seeking power in the face of our own powerlessness and limitations. Paradoxically, the way to counter the power of Satan is not by a similar exercise of power but by the Word and Spirit operating through human weakness, and especially through such practices as fellowship, forgiveness, prayer, and praise that focus our attention on God and neighbor.[13]

Paul Hiebert, who is more reticent than Shuster concerning the ontological reality of the demonic, also sees the conflict between the two spiritual realms in terms of power. The question is not whether God has more power than the demonic, but whether the demonic can in some manner get God to use power in a demonic fashion.[14] This is what the temptations of Jesus were about, and thus Jesus' ministry and death were major defeats for the forces of evil. Seen from this perspective, Jesus' exorcisms were not as devastating to Satan as when he washed his disciples feet. And so it remains today: when the church under the power of the Spirit participates in ministries of proclamation, servanthood, compassion, and reconciliation, bringing the good news that the Kingdom of God has come near, Satan will "fall from heaven like a flash of lightening" (Lk. 10:18) but the angels in heaven will rejoice.[15]

We thus far have been focusing on the "already" of God's eschatological reign. There is now a need to be reminded of the "not yet." The world remains fallen, sin as the violation of God's will is found in us all, death has lost its sting but not its present reality, and Satan has not yet been consigned to the lake of fire. To recognize this is not at all to counsel despair or abandon hope, but it is the warn against presumption. Even as we are led and empowered by the Spirit to participate in God's mission, we must be careful not to simply identify our actions and accomplishments with God's reign. The Kingdom of God always stands over against our cultures and our churches, and when taken seriously this is a gracious means of helping us not only distinguish between them but to gain a sense of where the Spirit is directing us.

There is in particular the dangers of cultural accommodation, ideological captivity, and reductionism. Cultural accommodation occurs when we became too at home in our own particular culture, and begin to transform the gospel in light of cultural values instead of the reverse. Ideological captivity is when we try to make the gospel serve our agenda, be it capitalism or socialism, nationalism or internationalism, traditionalism or feminism, or the like. This does not mean that the gospel is necessarily hostile to these perspectives, only that it is the gospel which must be the determining and defining factor in every case. Finally, a reductionism occurs when one aspect of God's reign supplants the rest, as has so often happened in recent American history with evangelism and social concern. The eschatological reality of the coming Kingdom of God brings all of these distortions of the gospel under judgement, but thereby also brings with it the promise of new freedom to realize the reign of God in this present age.

The Grace of God and Human Freedom

If the foregoing sketch can be said to accurately (though not exhaustively) describe the mission of God, then how and in what ways is God carrying out that mission today? Part of the answer has already been given: God is at work through the church as it is empowered and led by the Spirit. We shall examine this aspect of God's work in chapter ten.

A logically prior consideration is how God's agency relates to human agency. We can begin to address this issue by noting the increasing dissatisfaction among many contemporary theologians with the traditional view of God designated "classical theism." Put in stark and overly simple terms, the God of classical theism is the detached, immutable, timeless, omnipotent, omniscient and impassible deity whose attributes are defined more by Greek philosophy than biblical revelation. We have already examined some of the theological difficulties posed by classical theism in chapter eight when we considered concepts of eternity and impassibility. Given the absolute control and perfect knowledge of such a God, history would seem to be merely the outworking of whatever God has predetermined and as a consequence human freedom would seem to consist of simply playing our preappointed roles.

The Christian tradition, as Donald Bloesch argues, "shows the unmistakable imprint of a biblical-cultural synthesis in which the ontological categories of Greco-Roman philosophy have been united with the personal-dramatic categories of biblical faith."[16] While it was entirely natural and appropriate for the intellectual defenders of Christianity to borrow from Greek philosophy to make their case, they nonetheless permitted those concepts of divinity to take root within Christian theology and seriously modify its doctrine of God.

We must not overstate the case. It was after all heterodox thinkers such as Arius who drank most deeply from the Hellenistic well, and perceptive theologians like Athanasius who discerned the danger this posed to biblical faith. The authority of the tradition for the contemporary church is in large part due to its faithful discernment of the gospel amid a host of competing claims. Yet in spite of their commitment to biblical revelation, classical theologians to a greater or lesser extent began to interpret that revelation through the lens of Neoplatonic and (later) Aristotelian philosophy.

The result was a kind of two-level approach to the doctrine of God. The "higher" level consisted of a God who is utterly simple and undivided, independent of the world, impassible, omnipotent, and so on. Biblical affirmations of almightiness, power, and faithfulness were defined in terms of Greek ideas of omnipotence and immutability. The "lower" level contained those other biblical ascriptions which seemingly were at odds with the perfection of God, such as having feelings or changing God's mind. These were described as anthropomorphisms, and thus not taken seriously as actually representing God's essential nature. It is this way of defining and dividing God's attributes in scripture that has made so many uneasy today.

In spite of its many strengths—some of which we'll note below—classical theism has had a number of serious consequences for biblical faith. To name just two in addition to those already noted, it makes prayers of petition and intercession something quite different than what they seem to be, which are requests for God to act in a way God might otherwise not do. The claim that such prayers have as their only real purpose the disposing of our hearts to receive what God gives and to serve where God directs seems a bit forced; if that's all we mean, why not simply pray that way?[17] Also, it makes little sense to speak of sin as a violation of God's will if in fact on some higher level everything that happens is God's will.

Of course, classical theologians were not unaware of these issues. In an illuminating study, William Placher has shown how Thomas Aquinas, Martin Luther, and John Calvin sought to uphold both the sovereign power of God and human agency. For them everything was determined by God, yet not only was human agency retained, they insisted that the results of a goodly amount of that agency could be appropriately termed sin. They held to these seemingly contradictory ideas not because they were unaware of the tension between them but because they were convinced both were the case. Insofar as they attempted an explanation, they referred to the mystery of God's transcendence. By this they meant that the nature and ways of God necessarily transcends human categories of thought;[18] what seems contradictory or paradoxical to us is due to our limitations and not to some defect in God's revelation.

As Placher tells the story, the "domestication" of God's transcendence begins with Protestant and Roman Catholic scholasticism, which attempted in various ways to clearly and rationally explain what had previously been assumed to be beyond human explanation.[19] In conjunction with this greater precision in understanding God, they also sought to rationally explain the operations of grace; among other things this led in Protestantism to the competing systems of the Calvinists and Arminians.[20]

It is Enlightenment modernity however, with its penchant for rational explanation and its jealously of human autonomy, that seriously began to misconstrue grace and transcendence. As they framed the issue, the question was one of relative power: the more God has, the less is retained by humanity; the more given humanity, the less can be exercised by God. Thus human freedom necessarily entailed keeping divine power safely in check. This the deists did by removing God entirely from creation; later liberals would achieve the same end by reconceiving God's involvement as a persuasive noncoercive influence.

Modernity in a similar way redefined transcendence. For theologians like Luther and Calvin, transcendence meant "otherness" and "mystery"—God is radically different from humanity and cannot be contained in human conceptuality. Transcendence and immanence were not opposites but complementary aspects of God's relationship with creation. But beginning with the deists spatial metaphors became dominant, and transcendence began to signify "distance" in clear contrast to immanence, which mean "nearness." Thus when process and feminist theologians attack classical theism for its distant God who wields absolute power at the expense of human freedom, they are really targeting not the God of classical Christianity but a modern distortion.[21]

Placher provides both the premodern and postmodern distance to identify and critique the misconstrual of classical Christianity by modernity. Moreover, he reminds us of the danger of limiting the ways of God to our capacity for understanding—mystery is indeed a necessary and appropriate category in any biblically serious theology. However, I do not believe he has fully delivered classical theism from all its difficulties. There is still the question of whether the insights of Greek philosophy assist or detract from a portrayal of God which is faithful to biblical revelation, insights which were heavily utilized by Augustine, Aquinas, and Calvin. For evangelical theology there is the further concern that the God of the classical-biblical synthesis is defended more in terms of Reformed scholasticism than of the Reformers themselves. That is, the classical theism that is so often portrayed as the biblical alternative to liberalism is the God whose transcendence has become subject to rational explanation.

Evangelicals seeking a more biblical portrayal cannot adopt what is often billed as the alternative to classical theism, the process model of God. Not that the process concept doesn't have certain commendable strengths—its dynamic, interacting God is an attractive contrast to the often static God of classical theism, especially in its scholastic form. But the process cure is in several ways worse than the disease. The God of process theology includes creation within the divine becoming such that God and creation are interdependent and mutually influence one another. Given this ontological identification of God and creation, which is a form of panentheism,[22] God cannot help but experience and constructively participate in the world. Trusting in such a God seems a bit superfluous, since God could hardly do otherwise under the circumstances.

Biblical theism posits a God who is ontologically distinct from the creation yet actively involved in it. To have faith in this God is a far more radical act of trust, based not on what this God must necessarily do but on what God has actually done in Israel and in Jesus Christ. The God revealed in Jesus Christ loves in freedom, creating and redeeming that which is ontologically different.

What is needed then is a model of God which preserves God's transcendent distinction from creation while upholding both divine and human agency within it. This Clark Pinnock has sought to provide in the form of "freewill theism" or the "open view" of God.[23] According to this model God is not a "solitary, domineering individual" but a social trinity of "diverse persons united in a communion of love and freedom." This relational view of God enables Pinnock to affirm that God "is self-sufficient in fullness" yet genuinely open to the world in love, interacting in a way that shares the richness of God's own divine fellowship.[24]

Creation is thus not necessary to complete a deficiency in God but is a freely chosen act of divine love. However "this act of creation does not entail that God controls and determines everything." Rather, God seeks creatures with whom God can enjoy a loving relationship and hence created human beings with a capacity to respond.[25] If this is the case, then the power of God must be exercised in a manner which supports rather than subverts God's purpose. Thus God shares power with humanity, giving them dominion over the earth, and running the risk of human sin in order to make possible human love and fellowship.[26] This is a self-limitation of God's power, but not a retreat into passivity. God remains actively engaged with humanity and the entire creation. Richard Rice, commenting on the biblical portrayal of divine activity, notes that

> at times God simply does things, acting on his own initiative and relying solely on his own power. Sometimes he accomplishes things through the cooperation of human agents, sometimes he overcomes creaturely opposition to accomplish things, sometimes he providentially uses opposition to accomplish something, and sometimes his intentions to do something are thwarted by human opposition.[27]

The issue this dynamic and varied description of God's activity raises is not whether God is omnipotent but in what ways is that power actually exercised. It also means that God is open to being affected by the world as well as affecting it.[28]

Critics of freewill theism often see this as a denial of God's omnipotence, since God is not said to control everything. Pinnock vigorously dissents, arguing that "it requires more power to rule over an undetermined world than it would a determined one." Indeed, he adds, "Only omnipotence has the requisite degree and quality of power to undertake such a project."[29]

This is a biblically persuasive yet nonetheless breathtaking revision of classical theism as we have come to know it. Though finding much here to applaud, Donald Bloesch worries that Pinnock and his allies have veered too close to process theology, in spite of their commendable intentions. He argues that freewill theism is characterized not by "God's aggressive action in the world but his receptively to the world";[30] moreover in their appropriate rejection of "the traditional concept of God as unrestrained power" they "too readily divorce the biblical concept of power from coercion."[31] I do not read them in this way. Freewill theists do at times overemphasize those aspects of God neglected by classical theism, but they seem to me to envision a God who at the same time both initiates action and responds to human action, at times even coercively.

More serious is Bloesch's critique of their understanding of freedom. He argues that freewill theists have an "anarchic or libertarian" view of freedom that would be more at home in the Enlightenment than in scripture. Biblical freedom is not the freedom to choose good or evil, but being freed from bondage to sin such that we can obey and serve God.[32] We are, he says, "saved by divine grace, not by human free will."[33]

Freewill theism does break with traditional Protestant teaching which understands original sin to mean total depravity, or the total corruption of the *imago Dei* in such a way that, apart from grace, humanity has no freedom to respond to God. But Pinnock is not captive to an Enlightenment view of human autonomy so much as he is convinced of the Eastern Orthodox position on sin and grace. "Eastern Orthodoxy has always rejected any doctrine of grace that denies freedom," says Pinnock with approval, "because freedom is essential to the image of God in us." Scripture, he argues, constantly assumes a human capacity to respond; salvation thus "requires the operation of both grace and the human will."[34]

To clarify Pinnock's position does not of course negate Bloesch's criticism. In terms of the general model of God, Bloesch's own proposal—a "dynamic biblical theism" which differs from classical theism "in envisaging God as a person who freely interacts with his creation rather than a first cause or principle of being."[35]—is remarkably similar to Pinnock's. What is needed to go with this interactive model is an understanding of grace which takes with utmost seriousness both human agency and the Protestant insistence on total corruption. As nominees for this task let me propose G. C. Berkouwer and John Wesley.

With Berkouwer we find a contemporary theologian who has recovered much of that original sense of God's transcendence which Placher has so carefully documented in Aquinas, Luther, and Calvin. According to J. C. DeMoor, Berkouwer was convinced there was "no competition, no rivalry, between the sovereign (re)creative activity of God's gracious Word and Spirit and the free, responsive activity of the human faith they evoke";[36] indeed there cannot be a contradiction between the sovereignty of grace and the free human response because no such contradiction can be found in scripture. In the process Berkouwer consistently rejected the false dilemmas which human rationality tried to impose on biblical revelation, such as a subject/object dualism. This DeMoor calls Berkouwer's "anti-polarity stance"; in it he evinces a suspicion of false dualities which anticipates to some extent that of Derrida.

According to DeMoor, Berkouwer believed it was "the infiltration of rationalism" into post-Reformation theology[37] which introduced an unbiblical tension between God and human agency. By reducing the sovereign grace of the living God to an eternal decree, Reformed scholasticism both depersonalized God and ruled out in advance "that Scripture could ever ascribe any decisive significance to the actions and reactions of man in the course of history."[38] Berkouwer instead envisions a God whose sovereign grace unfailingly accomplishes divine purposes precisely by granting humanity the freedom necessary to love and serve God. The power of God is not in compelling but in loving humanity.

What is at stake for Berkouwer can be illustrated by the story of the prodigal son. The Father loves the son and seeks his love in return. But because love cannot be compelled and still be love, neither can the Father compel the son to remain at home; the capacity to receive and give love necessarily includes the ability to reject love as well. Of course the Father had it in his power to prevent the son's departure, but to have done so would be contrary to the loving relationship which the Father desired. It is only in this sense God can be said to cause sin: out of love God does not compel humanity not to sin. What the Father does, in spite of the son's rejection of his love, is remain the Father, and it is his noncoercive love which enables and indeed causes his son's return.[39] Here is an understanding of omnipotence which has much in common with the interactive theism of Bloesch and Pinnock.

There are striking similarities between Berkouwer's description of grace and that of John Wesley. For Wesley God created us expressly for the purpose of loving God and others as we are loved by God; to love is at the heart of what is means to be created in God's image. God's great redemptive purpose is to fully restore in fallen humanity the capacity and disposition to love God and our neighbor. Grace for Wesley enables and invites persons into a relationship through which they grow in the knowledge and love of God.[40] By enable I do not mean merely assist, if that term implies a natural free will apart from grace. Wesley agrees with the Protestant Reformers that the *imago Dei* is totally corrupted—no part of our lives is untouched by sin, and therefore there is no natural inclination or capacity to respond to God. But because God does not want "any to' perish, but all to come to repentance" (2 Pet. 3:9) God's grace reaches out universally, to every human being, enabling and inviting all to return to relationship with God. This prevenient grace restores a measure of freedom, making possible a response that otherwise would be impossible. Thus Wesley rejects entirely the concept of individual autonomy advocated by the Enlightenment; freedom for Wesley is freedom from the sin which holds us captive and freedom to love in the same manner as God.

It should be evident that, with the exception of the initial effects of prevenient grace, Wesley rejects the typical Calvinist teaching that grace is irresistible. It cannot be if God is to accomplish the goal of enabling humanity to freely love in response to God's gracious love for them. However grace is for him more than unmerited favor—it is also transforming power, a work of the Holy Spirit, which begins with prevenient grace, extends to the new birth, and continues in sanctification, Christian perfection, and beyond. God is an active, powerful agent at work recreating and restoring the image of God in all who, enabled by grace, respond to God's initiative in faith.

Both Berkouwer and Wesley show God to be a loving personal agent whose gracious power is exercised not at the expense of human agency but in order to set persons free to love. God does not control all that happens, at least not in the usual sense, but God is actively and powerfully engaged in creation to bring about genuine redemption. The salvation that God seeks is not simply life beyond death; most centrally it is a relationship of love, a new life which lasts forever. It is to bring persons into this relationship that Jesus Christ died and was raised, and the Holy Spirit reaches out to all humanity in power and in love.

The Possibilities and Limits of Divine Power

While to speak of the "limits" of divine power may appear presumptuous to faithful adherents to historic Christianity, it is the very possibility of divine power which is a problem for modernity. The assumption of modern science—an assumption that was quickly extended to the social "sciences" as well—was that reality operated according to laws of nature which were discoverable by human reason. Through understanding these laws, a complete and satisfactory explanation could be found to account for the cause of all phenomena. We have already discussed in chapter eight the problem this posed for human freedom, leading many to adopt a Cartesian mind/body dualism as an alternative to a thoroughgoing materialism which denied human autonomy.

This modern view of reality posed problems as well for claims of divine activity in the world. The deists neatly solved the problem by describing God as the Creator of those laws of nature who subsequently did not intervene in their operations. Liberal theology from Schleiermacher on rejected this denial of divine involvement, and proposed instead an immanent God who worked in and through natural and historical processes. In both cases, the laws of nature were made secure against any miraculous intervention from the outside. Conservatives of course could not accept a denial of miraculous action by God; not only were miracles attested in scripture but certain central claims of the faith—exodus, incarnation, resurrection—depended on such divine activity. As a result, conservatives defended divine involvement as an intervention from the outside which at times violated the laws of nature. What all sides accepted without question was the scientific description of reality which understood causation in terms of a closed system of natural laws. But in a postmodern world it is this modern view of reality which is now being called into question, both as scientifically inadequate and as a peculiarly Western cultural bias.

With regard to the scientific critique, Nancey Murphy has described a postmodern shift from causal reductionism to a holistic approach that "recognizes that whole systems and their parts mutually condition one another."[41] The strategy of modern science was to explain more complex realities by reducing them to their component parts and then describing how those parts relate. Thus the cause of biological phenomena could ultimately be explained in terms of chemistry; chemistry in turn was explained through laws of physics. In spite of the great accomplishments made possible through this method of "bottom-up" causation it has become apparent that there are properties of higher-level, more complex entities which cannot be explained through studying the component elements. Rather, the whole is more than the sum of the parts and itself exerts causation "top-down." That is, some of the phenomena seen at "lower" levels of reality find their cause in participation within "higher" levels of organization; "chemical reactions do not work the same in a flask as they do within a living organism."[42]

What this means for a postmodern theology is that God need not be conceived as intervening from outside a closed system (conservative) or as immanent within that system (liberal). Murphy argues that just as we cannot satisfactorily explain phenomena without taking into account causal factors at higher levels of complexity, "so too divine acts may need to be recognized for a complete account of the direction of natural and human history." The theological challenge is to recognize "that God's intentional actions can bring about events above and beyond what could be accomplished" by merely sustaining the natural processes of the created order.[43] As we have seen, it is just this sort of proposal with which Marguerite Shuster attempted to account for both divine and demonic action; it is also congruent with the interactive approaches to divine action of Pinnock and Bloesch.

Murphy's analysis corresponds to an observation by William Abraham concerning historical causation:

> To ignore theological considerations as a working historian is one thing; to pronounce that they are always irrelevant is another. On the former view, the historian leaves open the possibility of a theistic explanation of events, while on the latter he must always remain ill at ease until he has found a naturalist explanation for every event of the past that is of interest to him.[44]

Put in Murphy's language, the historian can appropriately seek a "bottom-up" explanation; however, the historian has no grounds to rule out in advance "top-down" causality. To "proceed as if events can *only* be explained naturalistically," says Abraham, "is to embrace a disputed metaphysical doctrine."[45] As Murphy has shown, the metaphysical world is shifting, and reductionism either in science or history is problematic in a postmodern context.

Charles Kraft provides a complementary cultural analysis of the worldview of modern Western society. He argues that only God knows things as they are; we perceive reality through the filters of cultural assumptions and values, personal experience, and psychological makeup, all in turn touched by sin.[46] The mistake made by persons in the Western world is to confuse their perception of reality with reality itself.[47]

Because modern assumptions, rooted as they are in the Enlightenment, only permit natural causation, Westerners envision the "universe and all within it as machines" which operate according to natural laws, "without reference to God or other beings or powers that exist and operate outside the realm of what we consider 'natural' or 'normal'."[48]

Evangelicals in the West have become "practicing deists" who believe in God but do not expect God to really act in any significant way.[49]

There are two consequences of this worldview for theology and practice of Western Christians. First, the technological mindset through which science attempts to control and utilize nature is applied to ministry. Evangelism and missions, for example, become matters of knowledge and technique.[50] Even God is made "predictable and controllable." Of course, says Kraft, we ask God "to bless our plans," but "the plans and the control are basically *ours*, not his."[51] The second consequence was highlighted by Murphy's analysis as well: the occasional miracle is seen by definition as God's interference or interruption of normalcy. God is thus pictured in a semi-deistic fashion,

> well outside the human sphere, only occasionally stepping in to break a "natural" law here, to speed up a "natural" process there, to bring about an event that seemed "statistically very unlikely" here, or to create a "puzzling circumstance" there.[52]

The result of this "normality" is a lack of expectancy concerning divine action coupled with an unwarranted confidence in our own attempts to plan and control events.

Kraft contrasts this with the cultures of many non-Western people. Instead of picturing the universe as mechanistic, they are more apt to describe it in personal terms. Thus natural processes that Westerners seek to scientifically explain and control they interpret "as capricious— as being more like people rather than almost totally predictable like machines."[53] The consequence of this worldview can be fatalism, but it can also result in attempts to understand and appease the inhabitants of the spiritual realm which are seen as the cause of negative events.[54]

From this it should be clear that Kraft does not endorse any particular cultural worldview; rather each has its own particular strengths and weaknesses. While non-Western cultures with a supernaturalist bias tend to focus only on ultimate causes, modern Western societies limit explanations to immediate causes.[55] Or, in Nancey Murphy's terms, many non-Western cultures interpret causality "top-down" while Western modernity understands causality solely as "bottom-up." Kraft argues that the Kingdom perspective of Jesus Christ can enter and transform every cultural context, maintaining the distinctiveness of each human culture while modifying it in terms of God's ultimate purpose and values.[56] Jesus presents us with a "new normalcy," which means that a range of phenomena from "miracles" to loving the unlovable are normal occurrences for those who belong to the Kingdom of God.[57]

If with Murphy and Kraft we throw open the postmodern door to divine activity, including that kind usually termed "miraculous," we are faced with two questions. The first is, if the limits on divine action by modernity are mistaken, then why isn't God acting in each and every instance for which there is a valid need? In other words, are there other limits constraining divine activity than the improper ones proposed by modernity? Second, if God is acting in distinctive ways, how do we identity such activity as that of God?

We can address the first question in terms of the already/not yet distinction discussed earlier in this chapter. In this present age God justifies and sanctifies persons even (to adopt a Wesleyan view) perfecting them in love. However, as Wesley insisted, "involuntary transgressions" remain; we never reach a point in this life where we fully obey the perfect will of God. Likewise God heals the sick, sometimes through natural processes, sometimes through medicine or surgery, and sometimes miraculously. However, as long as we remain in this age we face the reality of sickness and finally death (though it does not have the last word); even Lazarus whom Jesus raised from death still returned to the grave. God also liberates people from oppression, enabling entire societies to become more just and compassionate. However, no society on earth perfectly reflects the justice and love of the Kingdom of God. Only in the Kingdom itself will sin, sickness, death, and injustice be no more. In this age we can expect genuine anticipations of that Kingdom, at times powerfully, but not its fullness until Jesus returns in glory.

This provides a general framework for understanding the true limitations of God's power. They are self-limitations which naturally result from divine faithfulness: God will not act in the present in such a way that undercuts God's ultimate purpose. The present age is the arena of God's redemptive activity in the lives of persons, calling them into relationship with God and one another. The end of history will not come until this mission of God is complete.

There, is however, the more specific question of why and how God is at work in particular circumstances, especially those involving human suffering. This has always been a difficult theological issue, and we cannot pretend to solve it here.[58] We can nonetheless lift up certain factors which must be considered in addressing this question.

I have elsewhere explored one important aspect of the issue of divine activity through a comparison of charismatic theologies of healing. There I framed the discussion around a tension between God's faithfulness and God's freedom. By "faithfulness" I meant that God is always true to both God's character and promises, while "freedom" referred to God's ability to choose how and whether to act.[59] Those terms are similar to the language of character and agency introduced in the previous chapter. What I argued in my article and wish to emphasize here is that it is a theological mistake to resolve this tension in favor of either of the two poles.

We can see this danger in the healing theologies of Kenneth Hagin Sr. and Agnes Sanford, which for all their differences have in common the resolution of the tension in favor of faithfulness.[60] Because they understand divine healing to be an absolute promise of God on the condition of faith, they depict it in terms of spiritual laws which operate automatically: the requisite faith thus necessarily secures the promised healing. Sanford argues that "God works immutably and inexorably by law. . . . He has never from the beginning until now healed anyone by the interposition of an arbitrary or capricious force."[61] But in her attempt to avoid an arbitrary God she ends up conceiving God as operating with the regularity of a law of physics, even describing God analogous to natural processes like electricity and gravity. The indebtedness of these approaches to modernity is evident in the claim to have discovered spiritual laws within scripture which operate on something like a cause and effect basis just as do the natural laws of science. The answer to why one is not healed in these theologies is clear: it is lack of faith, the fault not of God but human beings. In the process the idea of God as a personal agent is diminished as well.

The opposite danger would be to conceive of God as free to the point of being arbitrary, disconnected from either God's character or promises. Understandably there are no charismatic healing theologies which take this approach. However, some like Kathryn Kuhlman and Charles Farah do lean much more in the direction of emphasizing God's freedom.[62] For them, divine healing is a sovereign act of God, in Farah's words, "a mystery . . . we will never fully understand. We box God in . . . and God refuses to dance to our tune."[63] Arguing that what healing practitioners like Hagin call faith is really presumption, Farah calls for faith in God whether or not we receive the healing we seek. While convinced healing is God's general will, he says we often do not know God's will in particular circumstances. In these, Farah is content to "rest easy in the sovereignty of a God whose 'ways are not my ways; whose thoughts are not my thoughts.'"[64]

The question Farah leaves open is what Kraft calls normalcy—how normal is divine healing among the people of God? What can we expect God to do? Some practitioners of healing ministry like Francis MacNutt, John Wimber, and Ken Blue want to assert this normalcy more strongly without compromising God's freedom, and therefore offer a more integrated approach.[65] Because God is a loving God, they understand healing to be the ordinary will of God; however they recognize as well that God does not always heal as we would like. While faith is acknowledged as an important factor in prayer for healing, the failure to receive healing is not automatically attributed to a lack of faith. None of these have developed a fully satisfactory theology of healing, and all would join Farah in honoring an element of mystery and sovereignty in God's activity. Their integrative approach does have the advantage of affirming God's faithfulness and freedom and depicting the divine/human relationship as between active and involved personal agents. This comports well with the interactive theism proposed earlier in this chapter.

What is missing from these theologies is a sense of the priorities within God's mission. Here is where John Wesley offers a helpful corrective. Wesley believed God healed both through medicine and miraculously, but unlike many in the holiness movement a century later, he did not view healing as a twin promise of God alongside salvation. Healing was important, because it was important to a loving God who will ultimately put an end to sickness and death. But it was not as important as salvation itself, understood as the restoration of the image of God within the person such that they manifest in their lives the love which characterizes the triune God. Consequently to elevate healing to the level of salvation is as great an error as to ignore it. Prayer for healing should be a natural and normal feature of the Christian community, but is always in service to the greater goal of growing in love.[66]

This gives us as well the criteria for recognizing any act, miraculous or otherwise, as a potential act of God. Is such an act in character with God's intentions and actions as revealed in Christ? Does this action further God's purposes, such that God's will is done on earth as in heaven? To answer questions like this calls for discernment by a community that has been shaped by scripture and worship and devoted to prayer. Such a context encourages openness to the guidance of the Holy Spirit.[67]

In the case of signs and wonders, such discernment can avoid the error of calling God the author of an event simply because it is miraculous, as well as seeking such phenomena as ends in themselves. As charismatic theologian Thomas Smail reminds us,

> the significant thing about the dramatic signs is not their miraculous quality as such, but that they are signs of the activity of the risen Jesus, and they open our eyes to see with fresh clarity that the basis of the whole Christian life in all its personal and corporate dimensions is his renewing work.[68]

Signs and wonders point us to Christ and the Kingdom of God.

The power of God has a christological shape, but a christological shape ultimately means the cross. God does heal the sick, but it is not God's purpose to remove every problem or cure every misfortune. What God is most centrally about is transforming our lives through the Holy Spirit and empowering us to take up our cross as disciples of Jesus Christ. What we then learn through the power of the Spirit is what Paul wrote to the church in Rome:

> Who shall separate us from the love of Christ? Will hardship, or distress, or persecution, or famine, or nakedness, or peril, or sword? . . . No, in all these things we are more than conquerors through him who loved us. For I am convinced that neither death, nor life, nor angels, nor rulers, nor things present, nor things to come, nor powers, nor height, nor depth, nor anything else in all creation, will be able to separate us from the love of God in Christ Jesus our Lord. (Rom. 8:35, 37–39)

CHAPTER 10

The People of God

If the gospel of Jesus Christ is true, there should be evidence of it today. The claim that the crucified Jesus is Lord and offers new life through the Spirit is scarcely credible if no new life is to be found. This evidence—indeed the only evidence that will make a difference in a postmodern world—is communities of people who in their life together and relationships to others manifest the life that was in Christ. This chapter is about those communities and that new life.

I have organized it around the themes of pardon, holiness, and power. This is traditional language from the Wesleyan, Holiness, and Pentecostal movements, although in my usage of these terms I expand their meaning. In particular, I am as concerned to speak of communities which experience and embody these three realities as I am persons.

"Pardon" in this discussion refers to forgiveness both received and given; "holiness" to Christian affections and related virtues, most especially love; and "power" to empowerment for ministry, within the fellowship and without. While there is no attempt to argue for a chronological sequencing of these as discrete events of grace in each person's life, there is nonetheless a logical relationship.[1] Put briefly, it is pardon which makes holiness possible, and holiness that gives content and direction to empowerment. I will emphasize all three as both life-changing events and ongoing realities, mutually interacting with one another to enable Christian growth.

The Christian life is related to God and is rooted in community. It is related to God in that it is both a response to what God has done in Jesus Christ and a growing actualization of the life of God within persons and communities. It is rooted in community because it is there—through scripture, sacraments, hymns, and prayer—that the reality of God is experienced, persons enter into a relationship with God, and grow in that relationship over time. By dwelling in the biblical narrative the Christian life receives its particular shape and the Christian believer is enabled to see the world as it truly is.

Pardon: Learning the Truth About Ourselves

Forgiveness of sins is a radically creative act of God. As L. Gregory Jones has said it is a mistake "to think of Christian forgiveness primarily as absolution from guilt; the purpose of forgiveness is the restoration of communion, the reconciliation of brokenness."[2] Through forgiveness we are renewed because we are brought into new relationships with God and one another. It is, in Colin Gunton's words, "an ontic change, because to enter a new set of relationships—and particularly this one—is to be a new creation."[3]

This understanding of forgiveness in terms of entering new relationships is difficult for modernity to grasp. Autonomous individuals might give or receive forgiveness, but they remain fundamentally who they are prior to the act of forgiveness. Forgiveness in Christian terms is intrinsically relational and therefore life-changing; postmodernity, which views personhood as in many ways the product of relationship and context, can perhaps understand the impact of forgiveness better.

I say perhaps because there are problems with the concept of forgiveness which may well persist in the postmodern period. Two tendencies which reflect these problems are analyzed by Jones. The first underestimates the problem of sin and trivializes the meaning of forgiveness. According to this account, our problem is not so much the sin we do as the hurt we receive, often unintentionally, from others. At home in the therapeutic culture that dominates so much of Western life, it portrays forgiveness not as a way of reconciliation but as a means of inner healing, a way to keep our individual and private selves from wallowing in bitterness. Issues of God's judgement and our own culpability are ignored.[4]

The second tendency depicts a world not populated by basically decent people struggling with inner hurt, but as a place of force and violence. In such a world only force, not forgiveness, is strong enough to counter the evil we face. Lacking that force, despair or suicide become the only other alternatives.[5] The effect of forgiveness in such a world is to trivialize the evil and encourage its continuance.

What neither of these recognize is that forgiveness rooted in the death and resurrection of Jesus is "not a distorted and distorting weakness" but an "alternative form of power."[6] As such it is both a denial and an affirmation. What it denies is that sin and evil ultimately reign. We have already seen how Jesus, by going to the cross, denied the power of evil to determine his life—he refused to use demonic means to defeat the demonic.

What it affirms is the reign of God, even in the present age. Forgiveness is a fundamentally creative act, opening new possibilities and enabling broken relationships to be healed. It is the alternative to the terrible logic of retribution which in our day has fueled violence and hatred from North Ireland to Bosnia, from Palestine to Rwanda, from Somalia to the cities of North America. It is the alternative to broken relationships in families and neighborhoods and in the workplace. The good news, says Colin Gunton, "is that the cycle of offence and retribution is broken . . . by something different: by the creative re-establishment of human relations on a new basis."[7] Forgiveness permits those new relationships. It is the central form which love must take in a fallen world.

What was startling about the new approach to forgiveness inaugurated by Jesus is that it is offered without preconditions. What disturbed many about Jesus' pronouncement of forgiveness was not only that in so doing he presumed divine authority, but he forgave without prior repentance. Judaism certainly believed that God forgives sin, and does so graciously, but normally this would follow repentance and, if possible, restitution. The concern is whether forgiveness which does not first insist on repentance takes sin seriously—a concern which becomes even more urgent when forgiveness is transposed into therapeutic terms while the world seems captive to hatred and violence.[8]

In the discussion of the atonement in chapter eight we addressed one side of the question of taking sin seriously. There we saw that the forgiveness which God offers is costly ultimately because it costs the life of the Son of God—indeed, death becomes an experience of the triune God. The logic of substitution is that the offense of sin to God and its damage to the creation is affirmed in the strongest possible manner while forgiveness and new life are offered to sinful humanity who God nonetheless loves. Thus, *God* takes sin very seriously indeed.

The other side of the question is whether *we* take sin seriously, both in our own lives and in our world. The sad and at times terrible fact is that Christians all too often have not, and as a result been all too at home in the destructive ways which characterize human society. We have even contributed to its destructiveness in the name of Christ. The reasons for this are manifold, but theologically one important factor has been a tendency to abstract the atonement and forgiveness of sins from the biblical narrative of the life, death, and resurrection of Jesus Christ which gives them meaning. When atonement becomes a transaction divorced from the context in which it occurred it becomes difficult to understand its purpose. The forgiveness which is given through Christ is not an end in itself, but a means to an end: it enables holiness of heart and life, the restoration of communion with God and neighbor, participation in the life of love which characterizes the triune life of God. Jesus, as we saw in the previous chapter, came announcing the inbreaking of the Kingdom of God; his life, death and resurrection embodied and inaugurated the reign of God on earth. The forgiveness he pronounces and which his cross makes available is in service to delivering persons from a life ruled by sin and initiating them into a new life, under the reign of God.

The failure to see this leads to antinomianism, which portrays grace and law as mutually exclusive. For the antinomian, to receive forgiveness is not to enter into a new way of life, but to feel forgiven while remaining unchanged. One is delivered from hell, not from sin, but one's sinful way of life is no longer of any consequence, for Christ bore the punishment for our sins. Thus an abstract transaction leads to a "forgiveness" which becomes an end in itself, trivializing sin.[9]

Legalism, the opposite misunderstanding, also fails to take sin seriously, for it has too benign a view of sin's effects on the human heart. What legalists fail to realize is that we not only disobey God's law but that we *are* sinners, and inescapably participate in social and institutional systems which encourage, reinforce, and require persons to live their lives oriented toward sin and away from God. This way of life becomes internalized and "natural," even though from the standpoint of the Kingdom of God it is based on a vision of the world that is distorted and on values that are illusory. It disrupts our relationships, encourages idolatry, and involves us in patterns of manipulation or domination of others. This is why repentance as a precondition of grace is unrealistic—it simply does not take seriously the corrupting hold of sin on our lives, as well as the subtle ways that grasp is manifested. In the end, legalism not only underestimates sin but devalues the atonement as well.[10]

Thus what is needed is nothing less than an act of God which breaks the power of sin in our lives and enables us to live a new life. This occurs foundationally in Jesus Christ, whose particular life, death, and resurrection has universal import. But it is the present work of the Holy Spirit, who is universally present to all persons, to enable those who respond to that forgiveness to work out its implications in their own particular lives and relationships.

There are at least three elements in this work of the Spirit. First, the Spirit enables us to see our lives and relationships truly, from the standpoint of the Kingdom of God. Our vision, distorted as it is by cultural perceptions at variance to God's reign, is gradually given proper clarity and focus. What we come to see is the truth about our lives. Wherein we have elevated ourselves above others, the judgement of God graciously brings us down. Whether our self-elevation (tradition-ally called pride) is achieved through a favorable comparison to another person or membership in a group of people defined by class, race, ethnicity, or gender, it greivously distorts our relationships with others. The temptations to elevate ourselves are manifold: our culture encour-ages it, the praise and esteem of others may lull us into it, and our insecurities may cry out for it as a remedy. Yet this self-elevation is always an illusion, for it denies the truth that all persons are created in God's image and all are loved by God, even unto death on a cross. The Holy Spirit enables us to see through this self-deception.

Wherein we have some to see ourselves as less than we are, the judgement of God graciously lifts us up. This too is sin, and is encour-aged by particular circumstances and cultural conditioning. Such self-abnegation also distorts our relationships with others, but the Holy Spirit exposes it as the untruth it is in the light of the Kingdom of God. Repentance in this case is to claim our worth and dignity before God, and to live faithfully in that knowledge. Self-abnegation and self-eleva-tion can together form a pattern, in which the experience of the former in one set of relationships leads to the practice of the latter in another, as a kind of cure for a diminished self. But the only lasting cure is the experience the liberating forgiveness of God in Christ Jesus, which enables genuine relationships of love.

Second, the Spirit then enables us to repent and, wherever possible, to engage in acts of reconciliation. When forgiveness has truly been received, repentance is the natural and necessary result.[11] It is natural because forgiveness implies that we have need to be forgiven, and, having received grace, we are enabled by the Spirit to then honestly face our sin. It is necessary because lack of repentance implies a failure to accept forgiveness, or that forgiveness has taken a distorted, antinomian form. True forgiveness changes one's life—it moves one from one way of life to another, and reconstitutes relationships in ways that call for repentance. It is, says Gunton, "about the free acknowledgement of

offenses alongside a refusal to allow them to define future relationships."[12]

Third, the Spirit incorporates us into a new community which has
forgiveness and repentance at its heart. Through practices of the community such as baptism, eucharist, searching the scripture, proclamation, and prayer—what Wesley calls means of grace—the Spirit enables
us to participate ever anew in the narrative of what God has done in
Jesus Christ. Through indwelling this narrative we are continually
reminded of the larger context of the forgiveness which we have received.[13] We see it not as an isolated act but as God's way of enabling us
to enter into and live the life of the Kingdom.

In the fellowship we ourselves practice forgiveness and repentance;
in Jones' terms we "embody forgiveness." Insofar as our communities
are characterized by these practices, they manifest in the present the life
of the coming Kingdom. They also become schools of forgiveness,
wherein we learn in concrete terms how to live with others in reconciliation and love by both giving and receiving forgiveness.

The early Methodists understood this. They practiced forgiveness
and repentance in class meetings, where together they sought to learn
what it means to be faithful disciples of Jesus Christ. In their band
meetings, they freely confessed sins to one another in a context of grace
and forgiveness. Thus for the early Methodists, forgiveness and reconciliation was practiced as part of the ongoing life of the community.[14]
Likewise the early Pentecostals sought to embody forgiveness. Steve
Land shows that "restitution and reconciliation" was the expected result
of pardon and repentance. Thus "confession and repentance of sin was
not only a belief in the righteousness of God in Christ but also a
declaration to walk in the light, to walk righteously in the world."[15] In
other words, pardon led to holiness as its purpose and goal.

As Jones says so well, "We need God and others both to discover
who and whose we are and also because it is only through our life
together that we can fulfill our destiny for communion in God's Kingdom."[16] The final truth about ourselves is not that we are sinners before
God. It is that we are persons created and loved by God, and meant for
loving fellowship with God and one another. Through forgiveness we
enter into that fellowship; by giving and receiving forgiveness we learn
the costly yet joyful reality of reconciliation and love.

Holiness: Growing in Truth and Love

It should be clear from the foregoing discussion that the forgiveness spoken of here is not just any forgiveness—it is the forgiveness given by God in and through Jesus Christ. It has its own particular pattern and shape which Christians, as glad recipients of that forgiveness, then seek to embody in their own lives. There is no way to understand Christian forgiveness apart from the particular narrative of what God has done in Jesus Christ.

Insofar as forgiveness has been of interest to modernity at all, it has been described in allegedly neutral terms, by philosophical analyses which either attempt to describe it as a universal human phenomenon without relation to God at all or relate it to a general philosophical theism. As L. Gregory Jones has shown, these approaches necessarily misconstrue Christian forgiveness by abstracting it from the narrative of the triune God which gives it definition.[17] From a postmodern perspective, of course, it can be seen that this objective analysis is in fact rooted in certain Western philosophical traditions and actually depends on a rendering of reality different than that of the Christian narrative.

This narratively-shaped particularity applies not only to forgiveness but to the Christian life as a whole. God's forgiveness as an initial experience is the entry point into that new life and makes it possible, for its effect is to restore the loving relationship with God which sin has disrupted. It thus begins a new life, marked by new relationships with God and others. As John Wesley insisted, to love God and one's neighbor is essentially what salvation *is*, a gracious and wonderful gift of God in which we begin to be once again the people we were created to be. Is it any wonder that evangelicals utilize the scriptural language of "new birth" or being "born again" to name this entrance into new life? Traditional terms also include regeneration, sanctification, and holiness of heart and life, but at its heart to love in this way is to participate in the very life of the triune God. Charles Wesley could aptly term those perfected in love as "transcripts of the Trinity."[18]

In this section I will offer a way of describing the Christian life which shows how such a life is framed and shaped by the Holy Spirit through the biblical narrative. This will involve explicating the relationship between the distinctive Christian affections which largely constitute that life and the means of grace which are the specific practices through which our relationship with God and the neighbor is experienced and lived. In the process I will address several potential misunderstandings of affections and means of grace, some of which have been encouraged by modernity.

"True religion," argued Jonathan Edwards, "chiefly consists in holy affections."[19] In making this claim, Edwards is doing more than his stated task of defending the Great Awakening from both its critics and its own excesses; he is at the same time challenging a pervasive bias of Enlightenment modernity. We can perhaps appreciate better his accomplishment if we first see what he was against.

In chapter eight we examined the dualism of mind and body which was everywhere assumed by post-Cartesian philosophy. Somewhat paralleling this was a presumed conflict between reason and passion for the control of the will. The dominant tendency was to elevate reason and argue that, for the will to be rightly ordered, the mind or reason must exert control over the passions of the body. This was the position of the critics of the awakening: they were rationalists who viewed with alarm the heightened emotions which the revival evoked.

The counter tendency would be to elevate emotion. The excesses of the awakening were largely due to enthusiasts who put great stock in intense emotional experience or unusual bodily manifestations. A more acceptable approach for Enlightenment religious thinkers was the later romanticism which protested against an unfeeling and somewhat abstract rationalism.

Edwards was not satisfied with the presumed conflict between passion and reason which underlay these various positions. He was seeking a more holistic anthropology, one that saw emotion not as an inconvenience but as integral to our humanity. At the same time his understanding of affections was neither as episodic or unusual as that of the enthusiasts, nor as general or common as that of the romantics. Affections were always particular, and Christian affections were distinctively Christian.

It is this holistic anthropology coupled with an emphasis on the distinctiveness of the Christian affections which made Edwards' position attractive to John Wesley in the eighteenth century[20] and recommends it to many who are schooled in the post-critical strand of postmodernity in our day. Don E. Saliers proposes a contemporary retrieval of the language of the affections, at once informed by contemporary thinking and faithful to Edwards' own usage.[21] In a parallel move Robert C. Roberts speaks of "emotion-dispositions," by which he means something very much like what Edwards and Saliers mean by affections.[22] My own discussion is rooted in the tradition of Edwards and Wesley and indebted to the insights of Saliers and Roberts.

The affections are the most central of the "fruits of the Spirit" or "virtues" that together constitute the Christian life. The term "fruits of the Spirit" is a reminder that the affections are the work of the Holy Spirit. The term "virtue" implies that these are traits of character acquired through engaging in practices or disciplines which the Spirit utilizes as means of grace. What I am proposing here is thus related to the contemporary revival of "virtue ethics" or the "ethics of character"; however, by using the term "affections" I want to emphasize more the experiential aspects of the Christian life, especially in response to what God has done in Jesus Christ.

Affections are at one and the same time dispositions, way of perceiving, and necessarily relational. As dispositions they are traits of character which incline us to think, act, and feel in certain ways. They can be distinguished from the more episodic feelings which they sometimes produce: affections are rooted in the heart, while feelings come and go. Thus we might *feel* hopeful or thankful on a particular occasion; we can *be* hopeful or thankful people throughout all circumstances in life. As Saliers says (here drawing on Edwards), it is "when religious emotions become deep and abiding motives" that we can "speak of them as holy affections which are the distinguishing marks of true religious faith."[23] For Edwards, mature Christian affections are habitual; Wesley agreed and termed such habitual affections "holy tempers."[24]

The Christian life consists of a pattern of these affections. For Saliers it includes "gratitude to God for creation and redemption, awe and holy fear of the divine majesty, repentant sorrow over our sins, joy in God's steadfast love and mercy, and love of God and neighbor."[25] Roberts enumerates such emotions "as hope, peace, joy, compassion, and gratitude."[26] Each has a role to play in making our lives discernably Christian, but some have a more central role—they are governing affections which form the core of the Christian character. For both Edwards and Wesley, the unquestionably central affections are love of God and neighbor. This is so for Wesley because salvation is essentially God restoring the *imago Dei* in humanity, and as God is love, so are we to manifest love in all our relationships.

Another way to refer to that which orients and directs the affections is to speak of having a "passion." The term "passion" is complicated by its various usages. As a synonym for emotion, it has been used in Enlightenment thought to emphasize the unpredictability and irrationality of the emotions—they "happen" to us or we "suffer" them, and to that extent we lose rational control. In patristic theology, the "passions" were not generic terms for emotions, but rather referred to those kinds of emotions which took us away from life rooted in God.[27] Here, passion means something like an overriding concern, all-consuming pursuit. For example, we speak of persons having a passion for gardening, meaning much of their lives are given over to this interest. Roberts describes the Christian life as centered on a "passion for the Kingdom of God," which consists of "an overriding enthusiasm for the life of perfect fellowship with God and neighbor in the promised Kingdom."[28] Likewise, Steven Land sees Pentecostal affections as oriented around a "passion for the Kingdom."[29] It is both the character of God as love and the reign of God which provide the orchestration and impetus that patterns the affections.

If affections are dispositions, it is easy to see how they are also ways of seeing, or, in Roberts' terms, "construals." For Roberts emotion-dispositions are "concerns," such as a concern or passion for the Kingdom; they in turn dispose us to a variety of emotions which are fundamentally construals "of one's circumstances . . . in a way relevant to some such concern."[30] Saliers describes affections as enabling us to evaluate our world through disposing us to think, feel, and act in certain ways. For example, how we construe oppression in Haiti, starvation in Somalia, or increased homelessness in our own city depends very much on the affections which constitute our character. Christian affections lead us to see the world in terms of the Christian story and to interpret it in that light.

Finally, affections are necessarily relational, that is, they take objects. We do not simply love, but we love God and our neighbor; we do not just hope in general, but place our hope in the promises of God. This means that affections are not the sort of virtues that can be possessed apart from a relationship with God. This is why Wesley could insist at one and the same time that salvation is by grace and yet we are really changed: our very real transformation of heart and life occurs within a graciously initiated and sustained relationship with God through the power of the Holy Spirit.

It is the object of the affection that ultimately determines the content of that affection, that is, the disposition to think, feel, and act in certain ways. Thus hope in laying up treasures on earth and hope in the Kingdom of God are not simply two different objects of the same hope, they are fundamentally two different kinds of hope, and imply two very different ways of life. The same could be said for love of God and love of money. The object of the affection qualifies and shapes the affection itself.

This feature of an affection provides the conceptual link with much of the discussion in the previous chapters. For if Christian affections are Christian because they take God and the things of God as objects, the definitive and true account of the objects of those affections is found in the biblical narrative. Thus it is scripture itself, containing as it does narratives, metaphors, and the like, that is the primary means through which the Holy Spirit transforms our lives and relationships, conforming them to the truth of God.[31]

I will say more about this below, when I talk of means of grace. But first, we must make further distinctions between various types of fruits of the Spirit. The affections are chief among the virtues but do not constitute them all. Roberts identifies three types of fruits of the Spirit— emotions, styles, and strengths—each of which contributes to a Christian character and life.

By "styles" Roberts means such "attitudes and patterns of behavioral response" as "gentleness, nurturing the poor and the abandoned, forgiveness, mercy, long-suffering, and kindness to enemies."[32] Rather than being concerns like the emotions, the styles are described as ways in which we imitate God. L. Gregory Jones speaks of forgiveness along the same lines: through practicing forgiveness under the guidance of those who excel at it in the Christian community, we learn how to forgive others in a variety of circumstances. Drawing on Alasdair MacIntyre, he likens learning to forgive to learning a craft:

> On the one hand, we are learning what it is about ourselves that needs to be transformed if we are to become holy people; on the other hand, we are learning how to diagnose and discern the craft of forgiveness in the situations and contexts that we and others face in the world around us.[33]

There is, then, a change in us as well as a learned skill in the discernment of circumstances.

I would want to frame the difference between affections and styles somewhat differently than Roberts. He says for both emotions and styles that to acquire them as virtues one must act in conformity with them. Thus, the way to be a hopeful person is to act hopeful; the behavior shapes the character. I think this is true for styles and in a secondary way for affections. What is primary about the affection, however, is that they are graced responses to God's gracious acts: we have gratitude because of what God has done, we hope because of what God has promised. So I would agree that with a style like forgiveness, we learn to forgive others in the manner which God forgives, but with an affection like love, "we love because he first loved us." (I Jn. 4:19) Further, the imitation of Christ (styles) is only possible because we have experienced and responded to that which God has done in Christ (affections).[34]

It is the affections and styles which make the Christian life distinctive, because both in different ways are dependent on the distinctive redemptive act of God in Christ for their shape and direction. This is not the case for Roberts' third category, the "strengths." Including such traits of character as "steadfastness, self-control, patience, perseverance, and courage,"[35] the strengths are necessary to enable any character, Christian or otherwise, to remain strong and persist over time. Like the styles, these become part of our character precisely as we practice them in community.

What makes affections—and thereby, the Christian life—distinctive is the objects which they take. As Saliers explains,

> The more deeply an emotion is "lived into," the more it involves understanding the specific objects toward which the emotion is directed, and the specific occasion which prompts the emotion. Again, the function of literature and poetry, and much of Scripture as well, is to arouse, sustain, and articulate deep emotions, not by "causing" certain subjective feelings, but by offering evaluative images and descriptions of reality.[36]

As Christians "live into" the affections by way of biblical narrative and imagery, they grow in the knowledge and love of God. They learn, in Roberts' language, to construe the world in terms of the Christian story.[37] Thus, contrary to the expectations of Western modernity, belief and emotion are not either unconnected or in conflict as much as they are integrally related in the lives of people.

This "living into" the affections occurs as Christians engage in a range of practices or "spiritual disciplines," or in Wesleyan terms "means of grace." There has been a recovery of spiritual disciplines throughout the church; in evangelicalism this has been fueled by the significant and influential writings of Richard J. Foster as well as important books by Dallas Willard, James Earl Massey, and M. Robert Mulholland.[38] Wesley's Methodists had a three-fold rule or discipline which encompassed a number of practices. They were to do no harm, do good to the bodies and souls of persons ("acts of mercy") and regularly participate in both public worship and daily devotions ("acts of piety"). These latter practices consisted of such means of grace as searching the scriptures, prayer, fasting, the Lord's Supper, and engaging in Christian conversation.[39]

Evangelicals from non-sacramental traditions have had a strong suspicion of "ritual," and some Protestants have had an aversion to "discipline." The concern was to avoid a dead, empty formalism in worship and works-righteousness in the Christian life.[40] But the problem, as Wesley so clearly saw, was not with liturgy (written or otherwise) or discipline, but whether such practices drew one into a relationship with God. He was convinced that the Holy Spirit used these means of grace to transform human lives, and enabled our participation in them; growth in our relationship with God and our neighbor occurred insofar as we then actively used the means of grace with open and receptive hearts. Or, as we noted in chapter four, we experience the presence of God in and through means of grace as we come to them in faith, understood as a "spiritual sense." Richard Foster makes the same point when he describes the disciplines "as a means of receiving" the grace of God—they "allow us to place ourselves before God so that He can transform us."[41]

In chapter four we said the identity and presence of God is encountered and experienced as one participates in the communal, liturgical, and devotional life of the church. We are now in a position to see how these "acts of piety" enable Christian affections to be formed and shaped as we grow in our relationship with God. Through scripture and other means of grace we come to a deeper knowledge of God's identity, that is, those intentions and actions which reveal the character of God. At one and the same time we are drawn ever more into a relationship with the God depicted in scripture; we not only know about God, we actually know God as a living reality in our lives. The affections are evoked, sustained, and deepened as we indewll the scriptures, receive the eucharist, and offer prayer and praise to God.

The affections as responses to God are not imitations of God—we do not normally think of God having gratitude or hope. But the affections are the seedbed of the styles through which we seek to learn the way of life which Jesus embodied. The one exception to this is one of the most important: love of neighbor is both an affection and style, both a response to God's love and a cultivation of Jesus' way of life. It is the "acts of mercy" which provide the occasion for learning how to forgive, have compassion, and even be righteously angry in a manner appropriate to Christ and the reign of God. Such styles are attained first and foremost in community, where we learn to love and forgive one another. Then, with the ongoing support and guidance in discernment that comes with participation in such a community, we seek as well to embody Christ's way of life in the more difficult arena of the world at large.

This call for our active participation in a full range of spiritual disciplines runs counter to a common misunderstanding of "spiritual" as being opposed to "bodily." Modernity, with its dualism of mind and body, has only exaggerated this tendency. The way to Christian growth is not simply to reach the intellect but the whole person. As Dallas Willard argues, embodied existence necessitates practices which focus on the body and its habitual emotions and behaviors.[42] Such a correspondence of Spirit and body was fundamental to Pentecostal worship, as Steven Land has shown, as well as to the practices of African-American spirituality and Holiness revivalism from which it was derived.[43]

The goal of participation in the means of grace is to enable God to graciously restore us to the image of God in which we were created. This is not simply the goal of individuals, but the community itself is called to and promised transformation such that it reflects in its life the life of God. Such a life, as we have seen, is distinctive: it is characterized by the same love which the triune God is, and which was revealed in the life, death, and resurrection of Jesus Christ. To live and grow in such a life is fundamentally what constitutes salvation through Jesus Christ in the power of the Spirit.

It is at this point that the sort of religious pluralism which envisions all the world religions as resting on a common religious experience is seriously flawed. Such a pluralism attempts to construe diverse religious beliefs and practices as secondary expressions of a universal experience; in this way some liberals have sought to apply to other religions the same sort of approach which has proved so problematic in Christianity. As we have seen, it is precisely the beliefs about God and the resulting practices which make certain kinds of experience possible. Put simply, the different beliefs and practices of the various world religions necessarily lead to quite different religious experiences. Rather than pursue a decidedly modern strategy of identifying a universal experience (and in the process potentially impose yet another western metanarrative on the rest of the world), a postmodern approach will take religious difference with much greater seriousness.

This is not to say that they Holy Spirit is only at work among Christians—I would insist the Spirit is at work in all persons in the form of prevenient grace. Nor it is to say that God's will is only done, when it is done at all, by Christians—if the Spirit is at work everywhere, it would be surprising indeed if there was not evidence of it in the form of the love and forgiveness which was revealed in Jesus Christ. Nor does this mean that only Christians have salvation, if by "salvation" one means life with God after death—evangelicals are conflicted on this point[44]; my own preference, again based on prevenient grace, is that God reaches out to all persons and they are accountable for their grace-enabled response.[45]

What this does mean is that Christian salvation in its primary sense of new life in Christ is a necessarily different salvation than that envisioned by other religions, and is different because its depiction of God and God's purposes are different.[46] For the Christian life, what it means to love and hope and forgive is bound up in Jesus Christ and his cross. Because this Jesus is risen, the expectation is that the love revealed in Christ will ultimately transform the world.

Power: Living the Truth in Love

Holiness in terms of the affections and other virtues not only characterizes the Christian life of persons but more fundamentally the life of the Christian community itself. It is the body of believers, when faithful in their worship, fellowship, and mission, who together enact intentions consistent with those revealed in Jesus Christ. The key qualification is faithfulness, for we recognize that no Christian community is completely faithful to all that God intends. Nonetheless, wherever a Christian community struggles to discern and follow the leading of the Holy Spirit, there will be found the will of God being done on earth as it is in heaven.

As we have seen, the fruits of the Spirit are necessary to give the community its character, motivation, and vision. This does not by itself equip the community for ministry, however. Empowerment for ministry is accomplished by the Holy Spirit, who apportions diverse gifts of the Spirit to the various members of the community. There are some twenty gifts mentioned in four key New Testament passages (Rom. 12:6–8, I Cor. 12:1–11, I Cor. 12: 28–30, and Eph. 4:11–16); in addition other gifts have been identified in scripture and tradition.[47]

Fundamentally, both "fruits" and "gifts" are *charisms* or gifts of grace. However, the distinction between them is important. The fruits of the

Spirit have to do with our character, with who we are; the gifts of the Spirit equip us for ministry, and relate to what we do. Fruits of the Spirit are meant to characterize every Christian life as well as the relationships which constitute the community—all are meant to love, hope, and have faith. Gifts are apportioned differently among the members of the community—"All these are activated by one and the same Spirit, who allots to each one individually just as the Spirit chooses" (I Cor. 12:11). Each gift is a "manifestation of the Spirit," provided for "the common good" (I Cor. 12:7). This means that it is only as all the gifts are being utilized that the church becomes "the body of Christ," continuing the work of Christ in the world in the power of the Spirit.

Kenneth Kinghorn makes a distinction between the gifts of the Spirit and the ministries of the community. A single gift, such as the gift of teaching, could be exercised through a variety of ministries, such as preaching, writing, or counseling.[48] At the same time, any single ministry could utilize a range of gifts, and therefore involve Christians coming together to serve in a particular way.

While the Christian community is itself distinctive because of the character it bears, and thus is necessarily in tension with the surrounding culture, it at the same time includes diversity within itself. It is not only diverse gifts and ministries I have in mind here, but the persons who are given those gifts. What Juan Sepúlveda says regarding Pentecostal communities in Latin America should apply to those of Christians everywhere. First,

> Persons marked by abandonment, solitude and impotence found in the Pentecostal group a community which accepted them without conditions and integrated them as one of their own, and already this act alone changed their lives. . . . Immediately one feels important, that one's life has value, that God does, in fact, love each and every one, because the community has already shown it to them.[49]

That is, the community is open and receptive to all persons, without regard to socio-cultural distinctions. This counter-cultural openness to diversity has marked genuine Christian revival, from the New Testament church in Antioch to communities today. Such receptivity to persons is a sign of a prior and foundational receptivity to Christ and the Spirit.

Second,

> The new person, who is incorporated into the Pentecostal community through conversion, receives, and is acknowledged by the church to

have received, a gift which will enable him or her to begin to participate in carrying out the evangelizing mission of the church.[50]

The reception of a gift imparts a new status to the Christian, their status in the Kingdom of God. This is a status the culture can neither give nor take away, a point recognized by the poor and marginalized through the centuries, most notably by African-American slaves. Their identity and worth as human beings comes not from cultural definition but divine love; the evidence for this is that every Christian of whatever background had an essential role in the community's participation in the mission of God.

Christian ministry is essentially a cooperative endeavor, requiring the use of everyone's gifts if the work of Christ is to be done.[51] The gifts, then, are for the building up of the community and its reaching out in service to others. This is a point which is apt to be forgotten in the modern, individualistic West. There it is a more "natural" assumption that spiritual gifts are personal possessions rather than for the community and world, and empowerment becomes not a means to ministry but an end in itself. Clark Pinnock rightly warns that "God did not pour the spirit out for us to exult in it as a private benefit. The purpose was (and is) to empower witnesses to God's kingdom (Acts 1:8)."[52]

The early Pentecostals were more perceptive in this regard than many, Pentecostal or otherwise, are today. To seek personal empowerment for ends other than those of God's Kingdom necessarily contradicts the purpose of spiritual gifts. This is why they consistently rooted the exercise of gifts in the prior reality of holiness. As Steven Land concludes, "Purity precedes power in the logic of early Pentecostal faith development because one must be a witness in character and deeds."[53] The affections and styles which constitute Christian character provide both shape and vision to the gifts and ministries.

That the goal of empowerment is the reign of God and consequently the transformation of persons and cultures means not only that the community receives spiritual gifts but that it must be led by the Spirit. As Pinnock says, the "Spirit is the power behind mission, and the church is the instrument of it, not the initiator,"[54] a concept that is contrary to modernity's penchant for instrumental reason. It is not that reason is set aside, but is utilized in conjunction with prayer and other means of grace to help discern what the Spirit is saying to the church. Because the mission is God's, it must "be initiated and empowered by the Spirit"; it "cannot be carried out by human wisdom and strength alone."[55]

This admonition by Pinnock has special relevance when we remember the issue of true and false contextualization from chapter seven. Cultural norms combine with sinful proclivities to deaden a congregation's faithfulness. As Pinnock observes,

> No one is naturally disposed to join Jesus in the business of confronting the powers of evil or in the costly action of embodying the new order. . . . It is almost impossible unless the church keeps the vision alive and before us.[56]

The Spirit through the means of grace provides the community with a vision of the Kingdom and consequently the resources to critically evaluate the patterns and norms of one's culture and life.

That those patterns and norms need critical evaluation is shown by recalling the concerns of the postmodern ultra-critics. In a world of "difference," they argued, cultural identity is often maintained over against those who are different, the "other." The strategies for dealing with the "other" are numerous—in a penetrating analysis, Miroslav Volf identifies elimination, assimilation, domination, and abandonment as the common means of maintaining social or ethnic or cultural purity in the face of external diversity.[57] But in the end, Christians must name each of these strategies as sin.

The reason is the life that Jesus led. As the incarnate Son of God, anointed by the Holy Spirit, he transgressed cultural barriers and subverted cultural hierarchies between gender, class, and race; by transgressing them he showed them not to be divinely ordered but the constructs of a fallen world. But it is the barriers and hierarchies that are the constructs, not the differences; the call of the gospel is for diversity without separation.

What is at stake for Christians in this is the central affection and style of love for neighbor. Given the postmodern concern for cultural diversity and the persistence of conflict between various national, racial, ethnic, or cultural groups, it deserves our attention.

Put simply, without the guidance of the Spirit through the biblical narrative, and without a receptive, prayerful community seeking to discern the leading of the Spirit, Christians will inevitably fall captive to cultural definitions of the other. We know this is the case because it has happened so often. Speaking of this Christian complicity, Volf notes the disturbing fact that

> our coziness with the surrounding culture has made us so blind to many of its evils that, instead of calling them into question, we offer

our own version of them—in God's name and with a good conscience.[58]

Instead of mounting a cultural critique in light of the Kingdom of God we perpetrate the evil in the name of Christ.

We spoke of "difference" in terms of gender in chapter seven, so here let us briefly examine race and class. Indian evangelical Vinay Samuel said at the Lausanne II Conference on World Evangelism that "the most serious thing is the image around the world that evangelicals are soft on racial justice." While many signs and wonders can be duplicated within the other religions of India, "they cannot duplicate the miracle of black and white together, of racial injustice being swept away by the power of the gospel."[59] The great shame in America is, of course, the Christian complicity with slavery and the normalization of racism in the churches. As Mark Noll has shown, this alone disqualifies America from being a "Christian" nation in the manner some have claimed.[60] This is not solely an evangelical failure, nor should the protests of early nineteenth century Holiness revivalists and other Christians against slavery go unacknowledged. But the fact remains that the bulk of the church was complacent, and denominations tended to become institutionalized along racial lines.

There have been recent signs of change in various segments of evangelicalism. The National Association of Evangelicals and the National Association of Black Evangelicals have joined together to produce congregational resources to counter racism. The Southern Baptist Convention has recently passed a resolution expressing its regret for past racism. More breathtakingly, the Pentecostal Fellowship of North America, which had consisted of only predominantly white denominations, expressed regret for its racism, disbanded, and participated in the formation of a new organization led by a bishop in the predominantly black Church of God in Christ.[61] Finally, the Promise Keepers movement of Christian men has made elimination of racism one of its central goals.[62] These are hopeful developments, the beginning of what will be a long journey of justice and reconciliation.

Of course, the problem of race is larger than relations between white and black. In America, there is the equally historic racism experienced by Native Americans, as well as that experienced by the growing and highly diverse communities of Hispanics and Asian-Americans.[63] Large segments of evangelicalism can be found among each of these peoples, and they have their own distinctive contributions to make to evangelical Christianity.

More concrete acts of repentance and reconciliation are occurring on the local level, along with long term commitment to change. Some evangelicals are moving into the inner cities, learning what it means to be a good neighbor to the residents and participating in multi-racial congregations.[64] Others in suburban congregations are supporting these efforts not simply from afar but through personal involvement. This will bear fruit if those in the city—many of whom are themselves evangelical Christians—are not only embraced but respected for the character of their lives, the gifts they have been given, and the vision they possess of the Kingdom of God. That is, the goal is to become one people of God while accepting, celebrating, and learning from our diversity.

Such has been the case where genuine friendship has developed between persons of different races. Recent books by Spencer Perkins and Chris Rice, and Glen Kehrein and Raleigh Washington, have traced the painful and wonderful journey of black and white friendship among evangelicals.[65] What is so evident in these accounts is, given our American culture, how difficult the task of interracial friendship can be, even among strongly committed Christians. Yet at the same time these are books of hope, in which the Holy Spirit is in the end more powerful than even racism and prejudice.

As America and indeed most of the world becomes increasingly diverse, the problem of racism will continue to haunt Christians. There is no other direction which is faithful to Christ than to struggle to overcome the barriers and attitudes which separate us, and to genuinely honor our differences. As Spencer Perkins says, "A world confused about race needs to see a gospel with guts enough to break the idols of race, not only through our words but also through our deeds."[66]

At least in America, the problem of class is even more insidious than race, if only because it is more subtle. Evangelicals have had a long history of involvement with the poor. Of course, such involvement in itself does not ensure that the poor are really received as persons of dignity and worth—the poor can be patronized or romanticized instead. Yet I think it is fair to say that evangelicals continue to be faithful in this regard, as the already mentioned inner city ministries bear witness.

Yet the question of class is larger than involvement with the poor—it cuts across all social and economic lines. It is unfortunately the case that all too often evangelicals and other Christians tend to view persons of other classes through lenses supplied by their own. This is exacerbated by the fact that congregations tend to consist of either poor, blue collar, or upper middle class members, each assuming the cultural stereotypes of the other. How well do we actually know one another? How often do we misconstrue persons of other classes because we do not understand the practices which constitute their way of life?[67] Our segregation along class and ethnic lines limits our ability to see others as they truly are, and thus constricts the effect of compassion.

Perhaps an even greater challenge than race and class in a world of postmodern diversity is to love one's neighbor when that neighbor is one's enemy. Jesus' command is as direct as it is difficult:

> You have heard that it was said, "You shall love your neighbor and hate your enemy." but I say to you, love your enemies and pray for those who persecute you, so that you may be children of your Father in heaven. . . . Be perfect, therefore, as your heavenly Father is perfect (Mt. 5:43–45, 48).

To frame this as an admonition to love as God loves might seem presumptuous, for what does God know about the suffering and death inflicted by human beings on one another? It would be, except that God has directly experienced betrayal, suffering, death, and even godforsakenness in Jesus Christ. Love of enemies marked the life and even the death of Jesus, and it was again and again replicated in the lives of persecuted Christians, beginning at least with Stephen (Acts 7:60).

None of this discounts the difficulty of loving one's enemies. How indeed can one love the neighbor who continually spreads untruth or the co-worker who persists in undercutting you behind your back for fear you will get the promotion he or she so dearly covets? And if this is difficult, as it most surely is, how does one love those who do emotional and bodily harm to ourselves or to those we love—the murderer or rapist, for example? How does one love the concentration camp guard or the soldier who commits unspeakable acts of terror and violence against one's people in the name of "ethnic cleansing?" Out of such suffering and persecution comes a cry for God's justice—surely the injustice of this world is not now to be set aside as if it was of no consequence.

We have already seen one terrible consequence of sin and injustice: the death of the Son of God on the cross. But we must also remember the purpose of Jesus' death and resurrection is to restore a bruised and broken creation. The command to love our enemies and the cry for justice are both deeply rooted in God's ultimate purpose to establish peace, love, and justice throughout the earth.

Both Gregory Jones and Miroslav Volf have dealt with the issue of love for enemies with great sensitivity. They eschew easy answers. It is the strength of their accounts that they take seriously both the necessity of loving one's enemies and the requirement that justice be done. It may be that the best approach is not to abstract a moral principle but to tell stories of Christians who have struggled to love their enemies in a range of circumstances. They do not all have to agree on what such a practice would mean for their struggle to be faithful and to have meaning and integrity.

The danger of loving one's enemies is that it seems to trivialize suffering and undermine justice. But Jones and Volf also point to the danger of failing to love one's enemies. As Volf says, the victims of conflict "often find themselves sucked into a long history of wrongdoing in which yesterday's victims are today's perpetrators and today's perpetrators tomorrow's victims."[68] Jones identifies a further problem: "the habit of hatred and the desire for vengeance not only perpetuate the cycle of violence; they also constrict and thereby distort the vision of the hater."[69] The failure to love our enemy can turn us into enemies as well, putting at risk our living the new life we have received.

We have been looking at love for our enemies in instances of great suffering. But this phenomenon of hatred and becoming an enemy occurs in much less extreme circumstances. Most recently in America, we have seen a pattern of hating and vilifying one's opponents in the political arena. Unfortunately some evangelicals have all too eagerly participated in this sort of activity, and they are often the ones who provide the definition of "evangelical" in the minds of the public.

This has led Richard Mouw, among others, to call for Christian civility in the public life, arguing that the holding of deep convictions concerning matters of great importance does not require incivility toward those who disagree.[70] We have seen with regard to Christian affections that the intensity of feeling expressed is not a sign of the depth of the affection; rather it is the faithful integrity of a life lived over time. Whether our politics tends to the right or left and whatever our partisan allegiances it is imperative that our public words and deeds not contradict the Christ we profess. The way we stand for deep convictions says as much about the truth of the gospel as do those convictions themselves.

All this is to suggest the pervasiveness of culture in determining how we see our neighbor, and how difficult it is in the best as well as the worst of circumstances to (as Volf says) genuinely embrace the other.

We need a narrative that enables us to make sense of our world, giving us critical distance over against our own culture. We need a community of persons who are shaped by the story and who help one another to live it out. Above all, we need a Holy Spirit who will bring us into a transforming relationship with God and empower us to truly live the new life in Christ.

Thus while the ultra-critics have raised the postmodern concern for "difference" and the "other," it is the post-critics' description of narratively-shaped communities—aided considerably by a vigorous doctrine of the Holy Spirit—which provides resources for a way to address that concern which is faithful to the gospel. For in a postmodern world, the persuasiveness of the truth claims of Christianity will depend on communities of persons whose characters reflect and who struggle to enact the love which was revealed in Christ. As Lesslie Newbigin has said, "the only hermeneutic of the gospel" is "a congregation of men and women who believe it and live by it." Such a community "has at its heart, the remembering and rehearsing," through word and sacrament, of the "words and deeds" of Jesus. "Insofar as it is true to its calling" the participants in the community "find that the gospel gives them the framework of understanding, the 'lenses' through which they are able to understand and cope with the world."[71]

These communities will not be free of ambiguity nor immune from conflict, as if Jesus had already returned in glory. But they will manifest in their own life together and in their relations to those around them the truth that the Jesus who was crucified is risen from the dead. It is in seeing here, in the varied contexts and situations of life, what it means to say Jesus is Savior and Lord that postmodern people may be persuaded that he is their Savior and Lord as well.

SELECT BIBLIOGRAPHY
OF EVANGELICAL THEOLOGIANS

This bibliography is an introduction to significant theologians, perspectives, and works in evangelical theology. For the most part it is limited to theologians proper, excluding biblical scholars, historians, ethicists, and philosophers. The primary sources include books but not articles; preference was given to more recent or comprehensive works. They are listed chronologically by date of publication. Secondary sources on a theologian are placed under that theologian's name after the primary sources. I have also listed the ecclesial or contextual tradition to which the theologians belong, but it is important to recognize that not all are influenced by it to the same degree.

Among the secondary sources, I have referenced several collections of essays on theologians by simply using the last name of the editors. The complete information on these sources is:

Elwell, Walter, A., ed., *Handbook of Evangelical Theologians* (Baker, 1993)

Ford, David F., ed., *The Modern Theologians*, Second Edition (Blackwell, 1996)

George, Timothy, and David S. Dockery, eds., *Baptist Theologians* (Broadman, 1990)

Marty, Martin E., and Dean G. Peerman, eds., *A Handbook of Christian Theologians*, Enlarged Edition (Abingdon, 1984)

Musser, Donald W., and Joseph L. Price, eds., *A New Handbook of Christian Theologians* (Abingdon, 1996)

◆ ◆ ◆

ABRAHAM, WILLIAM J. (Wesleyan)

The Divine Inspiration of Scripture (Oxford, 1981)

Divine Revelation and the Limits of Historical Criticism (Oxford, 1982)

The Coming Great Revival: Recovering the Full Evangelical Tradition (Harper & Row, 1984)

The Logic of Evangelism (Eerdmans, 1989)

Waking From Doctrinal Amnesia (Abingdon, 1995)

ANDERSON, RAY S. (Reformed)

Historical Transcendence and The Reality of God (Eerdmans, 1975)

BENTLEY, WILLIAM H. (African-American)

The Relevance of a Black Evangelical Theology for American Theology (BECN, 1981)

The Christology of Black Theology (National Black Christian Students Conference, 1986)

BERKHOF, HENDRIKUS (Reformed)

Christian Faith (Eerdmans, 1979)

BERKOUWER, G. C. (Reformed):

Modern Uncertainty and Christian Faith   (Eerdmans, 1953)

Studies in Dogmatics (Eerdmans):

    1. *Faith and Sanctification* (1952)

    2. *The Providence of God* (1952)

    3. *Faith and Justification* (1954)

    4. *The Person of Christ* (1954)

    5. *General Revelation* (1955)

    6. *Faith and Perseverance* (1958)

    7. *Divine Election* (1960)

    8. *Man: The Image of God* (1962)

    9. *The Work of Christ* (1968)

    10. *The Sacraments* (1969)

    11. *Sin* (1971)

    12. *The Return of Christ* (1972)

    13. *Holy Scripture* (1975)

    14. *The Church* (1976)

A Half Century of Theology (Eerdmans, 1977)

Anderson, Ray S., "Evangelical Theology" in Ford

DeMoor, J. C., *Towards a Biblically Theo-Logical Method* (J. H. Kok, 1980)

Smedes, Lewis B., "G. C. Berkouwer" in *Creative Minds in Contemporary Theology*, ed. Philip Edgcumbe Hughes (Eerdmans, 1969), pp. 63–98

Watts, Gary L., "G. C. Berkouwer" in Elwell

BLOESCH, DONALD G. (Reformed)

Essentials of Evangelical Theology, 2 Vols. (Harper & Row, 1978)

The Future of Evangelical Christianity (Doubleday, 1983)

Freedom for Obedience (Harper & Row, 1987)

Christian Foundations, 7 vols (projected, InterVarsity Press):
   A Theology of Word and Spirit (1992)
   Holy Scripture (1994)
   God the Almighty (1995)
   Jesus Christ (1997)
McKim, Donald K., "Donald G. Bloesch" in Elwell
Olson, Roger E., "Donald G. Bloesch" in Musser/Price

CALLEN, BARRY L. (Wesleyan Holiness)
God as Loving Grace (Evangel, 1996)

CARNELL, EDWARD JOHN (Baptist)
Christian Commitment (Macmillan, 1957)
The Case for Orthodox Christianity (Westminster, 1959)
The Kingdom of Love and the Pride of Life (Eerdmans, 1960)
The Case for Biblical Christianity (Eerdmans, 1969)
Lewis, Gordon R., "Edward John Carnell" in Elwell
Rosas, L. Joseph III, "Edward John Carnell" in George/Dockery
Sims, John A., *Edward John Carnell: Defender of the Faith* (Univ. Press of
   Amer. 1979)
Wozniak, Kenneth W., *Ethics in the Thought of Edward John Carnell* (Univ.
   Press of Amer. 1983)

CHRISTENSEN, LARRY, ed. (Lutheran Charismatic)
Welcome, Holy Spirit (Augsburg, 1987)

COSTAS, ORLANDO E. (Latin American)
Christ Outside the Gate (Orbis, 1982)
Liberating News (Eerdmans, 1989)
Pope-Levison, Priscilla, *Evangelization from a Liberation Perspective* (Peter
   Lang, 1991), Chapter 11

DEARTEAGA, WILLIAM (Independent Charismatic)
Quenching the Spirit (Creation House, 1992)

DELCOLLE, RALPH (Roman Catholic Charismatic)
Christ and the Spirit (Oxford, 1994)

DUNNING, H. RAY (Wesleyan Holiness)
Grace, Faith, and Holiness (Beacon Hill, 1988)

DYRNESS, WILLIAM A. (Reformed)
Learning About Theology from the Third World (Zondervan, 1990)

ERICKSON, MILLARD J. (Baptist)
Christian Theology (Baker, 1983–1985)

The Word Became Flesh (Baker, 1991)
The Evangelical Mind and Heart (Baker, 1993)
Evangelical Interpretation (Baker, 1993)
Where is Theology Going? (Baker, 1994)
God in Three Persons (Baker, 1995)
Dockery, David S., "Millard J. Erickson" in George/Dockery
Hustad, L. Arnold, "Millard J. Erickson" in Elwell

FACKRE, GABRIEL (Ecumenical)
The Christian Story, Vol. 1 (Eerdmans, 1978, revised 1984, 1996)
The Christian Story, Vol. 2 (Eerdmans, 1987)
Ecumenical Faith in Evangelical Perspective (1993)

FINGER, THOMAS (Anabaptist)
Christian Theology: An Eschatological Approach, 2 vols. (Herald, 1985–1989)
Self, Earth, and Society (InterVarsity, 1997)

FRAME, JOHN H. (Reformed)
The Doctrine of the Knowledge of God (Baker, 1987)

GARRETT, JAMES LEO, JR. (Baptist)
Systematic Theology (Eerdmans, 1990–1995)

GELPI, DONALD L. (Roman Catholic Charismatic)
Pentecostalism: A Theological Viewpoint (Deus, 1971)
Pentecostal Piety (Paulist, 1972)
Charism and Sacrament: A Theology of Christian Conversion (Paulist, 1976)

GRENZ, STANLEY J. (Baptist)
Revisioning Evangelical Theology (InterVarsity, 1993)
The Millennial Maze (InterVarsity, 1992)
Theology for the Community of God (Broadman, 1994)
Women in the Church (with Denise Muir Kjesbo) (InterVarsity, 1995)

GRIDER, J. KENNETH (Wesleyan Holiness)
A Wesleyan-Holiness Theology (Beacon Hill, 1994)

GROOTHUIS, REBECCA MERRILL (Reformed, Christians for Biblical Equality)
Women Caught in the Conflict (Baker, 1994)
Good News for Women (Baker 1997)

GUNTON, COLIN E. (Anglican)
Yesterday and Today (Eerdmans, 1983)
Enlightenment and Alienation (Eerdmans, 1985)
The Actuality of Atonement (Eerdmans, 1989)

The Promise of Trinitarian Theology (T & T Clark, 1991)
Christ and Creation (Eerdmans, 1992)
The One, the Three, and the Many (Cambridge, 1993)
A Brief Theology of Revelation (T & T Clark, 1995)

HENRY, CARL F. H. (Baptist)
God, Revelation, and Authority, 6 vols. (Word, 1976–83)
Evangelicals in Search of Identity (Word, 1976)
Confessions of a Theologian (Word, 1986)
Christian Countermoves in a Decadent Culture (Multanomah, 1986)
Twilight of a Great Civilization (Crossway, 1988)
Toward a Recovery of Christian Belief (Crossway, 1990)
The Identity of Jesus of Nazareth (Broadman, 1992)
gods of this age or . . . God of the Ages? (Broadman, 1994)
Anderson, Ray S., "Evangelical Theology" in Ford
Erickson, Millard J., "Carl F. H. Henry" in Musser/Price
Fackre, Gabriel, "Carl F. H. Henry" in Marty/Peerman
Grenz, Stanley J. and Roger E. Olson, *20th Century Theology* (InterVarsity, 1992), Chapter 10
Mohler, Richard Albert, Jr., "Carl F. H. Henry" in George/Dockery
Patterson, Bob E., *Carl F. H. Henry* (Word, 1983)
Purdy, Richard A., "Carl F. H. Henry" in Elwell

HOCKEN, PETER (Roman Catholic Charismatic)
One Lord, One Spirit, One Body (The Word Among Us, 1987)
The Glory and the Shame (Eagle, 1994)

HORTEN, STANLEY M., ed. (Pentecostal)
Systematic Theology: A Pentecostal Perspective (Logion, 1994)

HUMMEL, CHARLES E. (Charismatic)
Fire in the Fireplace: Contemporary Charismatic Renewal (InterVarsity, 1993)

JEWETT, PAUL K. (Reformed)
Neo-Evangelical Theology (Eerdmans):
  1. *God, Creation, and Revelation* (1991)
  2. *Who We Are, Our Dignity as Human* (1996)

JOHNSTON, ROBERT K. (Baptist)
Evangelicals at an Impasse (John Knox, 1979)

JONES, L. GREGORY (Wesleyan)
Transformed Judgement: Toward a Trinitarian Account of the Moral Life (Notre Dame, 1989)

Reading in Communion [with Stephen Fowl] (Eerdmans, 1991)

Embodying Forgiveness (Eerdmans, 1995)

KASSIAN, MARY (Council for Biblical Manhood and Womanhood)

The Feminist Gospel (Crossway, 1992)

KRAFT, CHARLES (Third Wave Charismatic)

Christianity With Power (Servant, 1989)

KRAUS, C. NORMAN (Anabaptist)

Jesus Christ Our Lord: Christology from a Disciple's Perspective (Herald, 1987)

LAND, STEVEN J. (Pentecostal)

Pentecostal Spirituality (Sheffield, 1993)

LEWIS, C. S. (Anglican)

Mere Christianity (Macmillan, 1943–1952)

Miracles (Macmillan, 1947)

Christian Reflections (Eerdmans, 1967)

God in the Dock (Eerdmans, 1990)

Christensen, Michael J., *C. S. Lewis on Scripture* (Abingdon, 1979)

Holmer, Paul L., *C. S. Lewis: The Shape of His Faith and Thought* (Harper & Row, 1976)

Payne, Leanne, *Real Presence: The Holy Spirit in the Works of C. S. Lewis* (Cornerstone, 1979)

LEWIS, GORDON R. AND BRUCE A DEMAREST (Baptist)

Integrative Theology, 3 vols. (Zondervan, 1987–1994)

LINTS, RICHARD (Reformed)

The Fabric of Theology (Eerdmans, 1993)

MCGRATH, ALISTER. (Anglican)

The Making of Modern German Christology (Blackwell, 1986)

The Genesis of Doctrine: A Study in the Foundations of Doctrinal Criticism (Blackwell, 1990)

Spirituality in an Age of Change (Zondervan, 1994)

Evangelicalism and the Future of Christianity (InterVarsity, 1995)

A Passion for Truth (InterVarsity, 1996)

Bauman, Michael, "Alister E. McGrath" in Elwell

MIDDLETON, RICHARD AND BRIAN J. WALSH (Reformed)

The Transforming Vision: Shaping a Christian Worldview (InterVarsity, 1984)

Truth is Stranger Than It Used to Be (InterVarsity, 1995)

MONTGOMERY, JOHN WARWICK (Lutheran)
History and Christianity (Bethany House, 1964)
The Suicide of Christian Theology (Bethany, 1970)
Faith Founded on Fact (Trinity Press, 1978)

MOODY, DALE (Baptist)
The Word of Truth (Eerdmans, 1981)
Stiver, Danny R., "Dale Moody" in George/Dockery

MUHLEN, HERIBERT (Roman Catholic Charismatic)
A Charismatic Theology: Initiation in the Spirit (Paulist, 1979)

MURPHY, NANCEY (Anabaptist)
*Beyond Liberalism & Fundamentalism: How Modern and Postmodern Philoso-
phy Set the Theological Agenda* (Trinity, 1996)

NASH, RONALD (Reformed)
The Word of God and the Mind of Man (Zondervan, 1982)
The Concept of God (Zondervan, 1983)
Christian Faith and Historical Understanding (Zondervan, 1984)
Faith and Reason (Zondervan, 1988)
Worldviews in Conflict (Zondervan, 1992)
Is Jesus the Only Savior? (Zondervan, 1995)

NEWBIGIN, LESSLIE (Reformed)
The Gospel in a Pluralist Society (Eerdmans, 1989)
Truth to Tell (Eerdmans, 1991)
Proper Confidence (Eerdmans, 1995)
Truth and Authority in Modernity (Trinity, 1996)

O'CONNER, EDWARD D. (Roman Catholic Charismatic)
The Pentecostal Movement in the Catholic Church (Ave Maria, 1971)

ODEN, THOMAS C. (Wesleyan)
After Modernity . . . What? (Zondervan, 1990)
Systematic Theology 3 vols. (Harper and Row):
    1. *The Living God* (1987)
    2. *The Word of Life* (1989)
    3. *Life in the Spirit* (1992)
The Transforming Power of Grace (Abingdon, 1993)
Clendenin, Daniel B., "Thomas Oden" in Elwell
Pugh, Jeffrey C., "Thomas C. Oden" in Musser/Price

PACKER, JAMES I. (Anglican Reformed)
"Fundamentalism" and the Word of God (Eerdmans, 1958)

Evangelism and the Sovereignty of God (InterVarsity, 1961)

Knowing God (InterVarsity, 1973)

Knowing Man (Cornerstone, 1979)

A Quest for Godliness: The Puritan Vision of the Christian Life (Crossway, 1990)

Rediscovering Holiness (Servant, 1992)

God has Spoken: Revelation and the Bible (Baker, 1994)

Truth & Power: The Place of Scripture in the   Christian Life (Shaw, 1996)

Catherwood, Christopher, *Five Evangelical Leaders* (Harold Shaw, 1986)

Lewis, Donald and Alister McGrath, eds., *Doing Theology for the People of God* (InterVarsity, 1996)

Nicole, Roger, "J. I. Packer" in Elwell

PADGETT, ALAN G. (Wesleyan)

God, Eternity and the Nature of Time (St. Martin's, 1992)

PADILLA, C. RENÉ (Latin American)

Mission Between the Times (Eerdmans, 1985)

Conflict and Context: Hermeneutics in the Americas [ed., with Mark Lou Branson] (Eerdmans, 1986)

PANNELL, WILLIAM (African-American Baptist)

My Friend, the Enemy (Word, 1968)

Evangelism From the Bottom up (Zondervan, 1992)

The Coming Race Wars (Zondervan, 1993)

PETERSEN, DOUGLAS (Pentecostal)

Not by Might Nor By Power: A Pentecostal Theology of Social Concern for Latin America (Regnum, 1996)

PINNOCK, CLARK H. (Baptist)

Biblical Revelation (Moody, 1971)

Grace Unlimited [ed.] (Bethany, 1975)

Reason Enough: A Case for the Christian Faith (InterVarsity, 1980)

The Scripture Principle (Harper & Row, 1981)

Three Keys to Spiritual Renewal (Bethany, 1985)

The Grace of God, the Will of Man [ed.] (Zondervan, 1989)

Theological Crossfire [with Delwin Brown] (Zondervan, 1990)

Tracking the Maze (Harper & Row, 1990)

A Wideness in God's Mercy (Zondervan, 1992)

The Openness of God [ed.] (InterVarsity, 1994)

Flame of Love: A Theology of the Holy Spirit (InterVarsity, 1996)

Johnston, Robert K., "Clark H. Pinnock" in Elwell

Rakestraw, Robert V., "Clark H. Pinnock" in George/Dockery

Roennfeldt, Ray C. S., *Clark H. Pinnock on Biblical Authority* (Andrews University, 1990)

RAMACHANDRA, VINOTH (Sri Lankan)

The Recovery of Mission: Beyond the Pluralist Paradigm (Paternoster, 1996; Eerdmans, 1997)

Gods That Fail (Paternoster, 1997)

RAMM, BERNARD (Baptist)

The Pattern of Religious Authority (Eerdmans, 1957)

The Witness of the Spirit (Eerdmans, 1959)

Special Revelation and the Word of God (Eerdmans, 1961)

After Fundamentalism (Harper & Row, 1983)

Offense to Reason (Harper & Row, 1985)

An Evangelical Christology (Thomas Nelson, 1985)

Day, Alan, "Bernard Ramm" in George/Dockery

Grenz, Stanley J. and Roger E. Olson, *20th Century Theology* (InterVarsity, 1992), Chapter 10

Vanhoozer, Kevin J., "Bernard Ramm" in Elwell

RO, BONG RIN, AND RUTH E. SHENAUR, eds.

The Bible and Theology in Asian Contexts: An Evangelical Perspective on Asian Theology (Asia Theological Association, 1984)

SALLY, COLUMBUS, AND ROBERT BEHM (African-American Baptist)

Your God Is Too White (InterVarsity, 1970); Reprinted as: *What Color is Your God?* (Citadel, 1988)

SAMUEL, VINAY, AND CHRIS SUGDEN

Sharing Christ in the Two Thirds World (Eerdmans, 1983)

SCHAEFFER, FRANCIS (Reformed)

Escape From Reason (InterVarsity, 1968)

The God Who is There (InterVarsity, 1968)

True Spirituality (Tyndale, 1971)

He is There and He is Not Silent (Tyndale, 1972)

No Final Conflict (InterVarsity, 1975)

How Should We Then Live? (Revell, 1976)

Catherwood, Christopher, *Five Evangelical Leaders* (Harold Shaw, 1985)

Duriez, Colin, "Francis Schaeffer" in Elwell

Morris, Thomas V., *Francis Schaeffer's Apologetics: A Critique* (Moody, 1976)

Ruegsegger, Ronald W., ed., *Reflections on Francis Schaeffer* (Zondervan, 1986)

SKINNER, TOM (African-American Baptist)
How Black is the Gospel? (Lippincott, 1970)
Words of Revolution (Zondervan, 1970)

SMAIL, THOMAS A. (Reformed Charismatic)
Reflected Glory: The Spirit in Christ and Christian (Eerdmans, 1975)
The Forgotten Father (Eerdmans, 1980)
The Love of Power or the Power of Love [with Andrew Walker and Nigel Wright] (Bethany, 1994)

SNYDER, HOWARD (Wesleyan)
The Problem of Wineskins (InterVarsity, 1975)
The Community of the King (InterVarsity, 1977)
The Radical Wesley (InterVarsity, 1980)
Liberating the Church (InterVarsity, 1983)
A Kingdom Manifesto (InterVarsity, 1985)
Models of the Kingdom (Abingdon, 1991)
Earth Currents (Abingdon, 1995)

SPYKMAN, GORDON (Reformed)
Reformational Theology (Eerdmans, 1992)

STORKEY, ELAINE (Anglican, Christians for Biblical Equality)
What's Right With Feminism (Eerdmans, 1986)

STOTT, JOHN R. W. (Anglican)
Basic Christianity (Eerdmans, 1958; rev. InterVarsity, 1971)
Christ the Controversialist (Tyndale, 1970)
Christian Mission in the Modern World (InterVarsity, 1977)
The Cross of Christ (InterVarsity, 1986)
Evangelical Essentials [with David Edwards] (InterVarsity, 1988)
The Contemporary Christian (InterVarsity, 1992)
Catherwood, Christopher, *Five Evangelical Leaders* (Harold Shaw, 1985)
Eden, Martyn, and David F. Wells, ed., *The Gospel in the Modern World: A Tribute to John Stott* (InterVarsity, 1991)
Williams, Peter, "John R. W. Stott" in Elwell

SULLIVAN, FRANCIS A. (Roman Catholic Charismatic)
Charisms and Charismatic Renewal (Servant, 1982)

SUURMOND, JEAN-JACQUES (Reformed)
Word and Spirit at Play: Towards a Charismatic Theology (Eerdmans, 1995)

THIELICKE, HELMUT (Lutheran)
Between Heaven and Earth (Harper & Row, 1965)
The Trouble With the Church (Harper & Row, 1965)
I Believe: The Christian's Creed (Fortress, 1968)
How Modern Should Theology Be? (Fortress, 1969)
Death and Life (Fortress, 1970)
The Hidden Question of God (Eerdmans, 1977)
The Evangelical Faith, 3 vols. (Eerdmans, 1974–1982)
Modern Faith and Thought (Eerdmans, 1990)
Anderson, Ray S., "Evangelical Theology" in Ford
Bromiley, Geoffery, "Helmut Thielicke" in Marty/Peerman
Fry, C. George, "Helmut Thielicke" in Elwell

TORRANCE, THOMAS F. (Reformed)
Theology in Reconstruction (Eerdmans, 1965)
Space, Time and Incarnation (Oxford, 1969)
Theological Science (Oxford, 1969)
God and Rationality (Oxford, 1971)
Theology and Reconciliation (Eerdmans, 1976)
Space, Time and Resurrection (Eerdmans, 1976)
The Ground and Grammar of Theology (Univ. of Virginia, 1980)
The Mediation of Christ (Eerdmans, 1983)
Reality and Evangelical Theology (Westminster, 1982)
The Trinitarian Faith (T & T Clark, 1988)
The Christian Doctrine of God, One Being Three Persons (T & T Clark, 1996)
Colyer, Elmer M., "Thomas F. Torrance" in Musser/Price
Hardy, Daniel W., "Thomas F. Torrance" in Ford

TREMBATH, KERN ROBERT
Evangelical Theories of Inspiration (Oxford, 1987)
Divine Revelation (Oxford, 1991)

VAN TIL, CORNELIUS (Reformed)
The Defense of the Faith (P & R, 1985)
Common Grace and the Gospel (P & R, 1964)
A Christian Theory of Knowledge (P & R, 1969)
An Introduction to Systematic Theology (P & R, 1974)
Frame, John M.,*Cornelius Van Til: An Analysis of His Thought* (P & R, 1995)
Frame, John M., "Cornelius Van Til" in Elwell.
Roberts, Wesley A., "Cornelius Van Til" in David F. Wells, ed., *Reformed Theology in America* (Eerdmans, 1985

VILLAFAÑE, ELDIN (Hispanic Pentecostal)
The Liberating Spirit: Toward an Hispanic American Pentecostal Social Ethic (Eerdmans, 1993)

VOLF, MIROSLAV (Croatian Pentecostal)
Work in the Spirit: Toward a Pneumatological Theology of Work (Oxford, 1991)
Exclusion and Embrace: A Theological Exploration of Identity, Otherness, and Reconciliation (Abingdon, 1996)
Trinity and Community: An Ecumenical Ecclesiology (Eerdmans, 1997)

WAINWRIGHT, GEOFFREY (Wesleyan)
Doxology: A Systematic Theology (Oxford, 1980)

WELLS, DAVID F. (Reformed)
The Person of Christ (Crossway, 1984)
Turning to God (Baker, 1989)
No Place for Truth (Eerdmans, 1993)
God in the Wasteland (Eerdmans, 1994)

WILLIAMS, J. RODMAN (Presbyterian Charismatic)
The Era of the Spirit (Logos, 1971)
The Pentecostal Reality (Logos, 1972)
The Gift of the Holy Spirit Today (Logos, 1980)
Renewal Theology, 3 vols. (Zondervan, 1988–1992)

WOOD, LAURENCE W. (Wesleyan Holiness)
Pentecostal Grace (Zondervan, 1980)

NOTES

Introduction

1. For a survey of theories of truth accompanied by theological reflection, see Nancey Murphy, "Christianity and Theories of Truth," *Dialog* 34:2 (Spring, 1995), pp. 99–104. A fine survey of how five evangelical theologians understand truth is James Emery White, *What is Truth?* (Nashville: Broadman & Holman, 1994).

Chapter 1: The Evangelical Family

1. William J. Abraham, *The Coming Great Revival: Recovering the Full Evangelical Tradition* (San Francisco: Harper & Row, 1984), p. 10.

2. Ibid., p. 10.

3. Ibid., p. 9.

4. Donald W. Dayton, "Some Doubts About the Usefulness of the Category 'Evangelical,'" in Donald W. Dayton and Robert K. Johnston, eds., *The Variety of American Evangelicalism* (Downers Grove: InterVarsity, 1991), p. 251.

5. Abraham, *The Coming Great Revival*, p. 48.

6. Richard Lints, *The Fabric of Theology: A Prolegomenon to Evangelical Theology* (Grand Rapids: Eerdmans, 1993), pp. 54–55.

7. Abraham, *The Coming Great Revival*, p. 9.

8. Robert K. Johnston, "American Evangelicalism: An Extended Family," in Dayton and Johnston, *The Variety of American Evangelicalism*, pp.255–56. But see Dayton's critique on p. 250.

9. Alister McGrath, *Evangelicalism and the Future of Christianity* (Downers Grove: InterVarsity, 1995), pp. 55–56.

10. Stanley J. Grenz, *Revisioning Evangelical Theology: A Fresh Agenda for the 21st Century* (Downers Grove: InterVarsity, 1993), pp. 30–31.

11. Ibid., p. 45.

12. Ibid., pp. 31–32.

13. Ibid., pp. 32–33.

14. Ibid., p. 33.

15. Ibid., p. 34.

16. I first encountered this typology in Donald W. Dayton, "Karl Barth and Evangelicalism: The Varieties of a Sibling Rivalry," *TSF Bulletin*, May-June 1985, pp. 18–23. See also his "Whither Evangelicalism?" in Theodore Runyon, ed., *Sanctification and Liberation* (Nashville: Abingdon, 1981), pp. 142–63; and "The Use of Scripture in the

Wesleyan Tradition" in Robert K. Johnston, ed., *The Use of the Bible in Theology: Evangelical Options* (Atlanta: John Knox Press, 1985), pp. 121–36.

17. Richard Quebedeaux, *The Young Evangelicals* (San Francisco: Harper & Row, 1974), p. 14. In *The Worldly Evangelicals* (San Francisco: Harper & Row, 1978), Quebedeaux divides evangelicalism into a right, center, and young evangelical left.

18. Gabriel Fackre, "Evangelical, Evangelicalism," in Alan Richardson and John Bowden, eds., *The Westminster Dictionary of Christian Theology* (Philadelphia: Westminster, 1983), p. 191.

19. Donald G. Bloesch, "Evangelicalism," in Donald W. Musser and Joseph L. Price, eds., *A New Handbook of Christian Theology* (Nashville: Abingdon, 1992), pp. 170–71. See also his *The Future of Evangelical Christianity: A Call for Unity Amid Diversity* (Garden City: Doubleday, 1983), Chapter III.

20. I consider neo-orthodox theologians like Barth, "catholic and evangelical" theologians like Braaten and Jensen, and "post-liberals" like George Lindbeck and Hans Frei to be the theological next-door neighbors of evangelicalism. The reason they are not normally included in the evangelical family is they have not been active participants within it. Rather, their dialogue partners have tended to be the liberal theologians with whom they disagree. While they certainly belong to the broader stream of historic Christian orthodoxy, their influence on evangelicalism has been largely through their writings. A recent dialogue between evangelicals and postliberals explores the continuities and divergences between them; see Timothy R. Phillips and Dennis L. Okholm, eds., *The Nature of Confession: Evangelicals & Postliberals in Conversation* (Downers Grove: InterVarsity, 1996).

21. Two works written by evangelicals on Reformation theology are Alister E. McGrath, *Reformation Thought: An Introduction*, rev. ed. (Oxford: Blackwell, 1993) and Timothy George, *Theology of the Reformers* (Nashville: Broadman, 1988).

22. Roman Catholic charismatics, who might well be seen as part of the evangelical family, would certainly dissent from Protestant distinctives. But there are Protestants, the "catholic evangelicals" in Donald Bloesch's typology, who seek to maintain evangelical essentials "within the context of catholic faith." (Bloesch, *The Future of Evangelical Christianity*, p. 49). Some seek to incorporate the Reformation emphases within the larger tradition; among these are evangelicals who actually have become Eastern Orthodox (Peter Gillquist) or Roman Catholic (Thomas Howard). See Thomas Howard, *Evangelical is Not Enough* (San Francisco: Ignatius, 1984). Others have gravitated to the Anglican tradition—an account of which can be found in Robert E. Webber, *Evangelicals on the Canterbury Trail* (Waco: Word, 1985). Still others stand clearly in the Reformation or in the tradition of the religious awakenings, but seek to constructively draw upon the wider tradition of patristic and medieval theology and spirituality to renew the contemporary church. Besides Bloesch and Webber notable figures in this strand of catholic evangelicalism include Richard Lovelace, Thomas F. Torrance, and Thomas C. Oden. See also Robert E. Webber, *Common Roots: A Call to Evangelical Maturity* (Grand Rapids: Zondervan, 1978) and Robert Webber and Donald Bloesch, eds., *The Orthodox Evangelicals* (Nashville: Thomas Nelson, 1978). This tendency has been analyzed and found wanting by John Seel in *The Evangelical Forfeit* (Grand Rapids: Baker, 1993), pp. 95–102, 111–114. Alister McGrath, while respecting the spiritual resources of these catholic traditions, urges

evangelicals to draw more deeply on the spirituality of the Reformation, puritanism, and pietism (*Evangelicalism and the Future of Christianity*, pp. 119–137).

23. See Mark A. Noll's discussion of the relation of Turretin to the Princeton theologians in his introduction to Mark A. Noll, ed., *The Princeton Theology 1812–1921* (Grand Rapids: Baker, 1983), pp. 29–30.

24. On Pietism see Howard W. Snyder, *Signs of the Spirit* (Grand Rapids: Zondervan, 1989); Dale Brown, *Understanding Pietism* (Grand Rapids: Eerdmans., 1978); and Ted A. Campbell, *The Religion of the Heart* (Columbia: The University of South Carolina Press, 1991), pp. 70–98; and McGrath, *Evangelicalism and the Future of Christianity*, p. 25.

25. On Puritanism see J. I. Packer, *A Quest for Godliness: The Puritan Vision of the Christian Life* (Wheaton: Crossway, 1990); and McGrath, *Evangelicalism and the Future of Christianity*, pp. 24–25.

26. On the Wesleyan awakening, see Richard P. Heitzenrater, *Wesley and the People Called Methodists* (Nashville: Abingdon, 1993); on the English revival more generally see Campbell, *The Religion of the Heart*, pp. 99–129; on the Great Awakening in America see Edwin Scott Gausted, *The Great Awakening in New England* (New York: Harper & Brothers, 1957); on the linkage of the awakenings in Great Britain and America see Michael J. Crawford, *Seasons of Grace* (New York: Oxford University Press, 1991).

27. August Hermann Francke established a vast social ministry which influenced John Wesley, among many others. Wesley's contemporary, William Wilberforce, was another social activist who led the fight against slavery. For Wesley's own social concern, see Theodore W. Jennings, *Good News to the Poor: John Wesley's Evangelical Economics* (Nashville: Abingdon, 1990) and Manfred Marquardt, *John Wesley's Social Ethics: Praxis and Principles* (Nashville: Abingdon, 1992).

28. New critical editions of the works of Wesley and Edwards are now being published by Abingdon and Yale University Press respectively. The best accounts of Wesley's theology is Randy L. Maddox, *Responsible Grace: John Wesley's Practical Theology* (Nashville: Kingswood, 1994), and Kenneth J. Collins, *The Scripture Way of Salvation* (Nashville: Abingdon, 1997). On Edwards see Conrad Cherry, *The Theology of Jonathan Edwards: A Reappraisal* (Bloomington: Indiana University Press, 1966); Robert W. Jenson, *America's Theologian: A Recommendation of Jonathan Edwards* (New York: Oxford University Press, 1988); and Nathan O. Hatch and Harry S. Stout, eds., *Jonathan Edwards and the American Experience* (New York: Oxford University Press, 1988.

29. On Wesley's use of Edwards, see Gregory S. Clapper, *John Wesley on the Affections* (Metuchen: Scarecrow, 1989) and Richard B. Steele, *"Gracious Affections" and "True Virtue" According to Jonathan Edwards and John Wesley* (Metuchen: Scarecrow, 1994).

30. The term "Arminian" designates a movement in seventeenth century Dutch Reformed theology named after Jacobus Arminius, who opposed the strict Calvinistic position on predestination, irresistible grace, and human freedom. Condemned by the Synod of Dort (1618), Arminianism became popular in England, where it designated a wide range of views from natural human free will to Wesley's more orthodox position of universal prevenient grace.

31. For a history of the Holiness movement, see Melvin E. Dieter, *The Holiness Revival of the Nineteenth Century* (Metuchen: Scarecrow, 1980). For the theology of that

movement, see Donald W. Dayton, *The Theological Roots of Pentecostalism* (Grand Rapids: Zondervan, 1987).

32. The classic study is Timothy L. Smith, *Revivalism and Social Reform in Mid-Nineteenth Century America* (Nashville: Abingdon, 1957). An important recent work is Donald W. Dayton, *Discovering an Evangelical Heritage* (San Francisco: Harper & row, 1976).

33. See Albert J. Raboteau, *Slave Religion: The "Invisible Institution" in the Antibellum South* (Oxford: Oxford University Press, 1978); James O. Stallings, *Telling the Story: Evangelism in Black Churches* (Valley Forge: Judson, 1988); and two essays in David F. Wells and John D. Woodbridge, eds., *The Evangelicals* (Nashville: Abingdon, 1975): William Pannell, "The Religious Heritage of Blacks," pp. 96–107 and William H. Bentley, "Bible Believers in the Black Community," pp. 108–121.

34. See Noll, ed., *Princeton Theology*, including the editor's introduction, pp. 11–48. See also the essays by Mark A. Noll, David F. Wells, and W. Andrew Hoffecker in David F. Wells, ed., *Reformed Theology in America* (Grand Rapids: Eerdmans, 1985).

35. See the discussion in Noll, ed., *Princeton Theology*, pp. 30–33; and in George M. Marsden, *Fundamentalism and American Culture* (New York: Oxford University Press, 1980), pp. 14–16, 110–16.

36. From Hodge's *Systematic Theology*, as cited in Noll, ed., *Princeton Theology*, p. 130.

37. See W. Andrew Hoffecker, *Piety and the Princeton Theologians* (Grand Rapids: Baker, 1981); and Noll, ed., *Princeton Theology*, pp. 33–34.

38. See James D. Bratt, *Dutch Calvinism in Modern America* (Grand Rapids: Eerdmans, 1984), pp. 14–33. For a comparison with the Princeton theology, see Marsden, *Fundamentalism and American Culture*, p. 115. In addition to the Dutch tradition, another significant alternative to Old Princeton was Reformed evangelicalism in Scotland, which included such theologians as James Orr and James Denney. See Alan P. F. Sell, *Defending & Declaring the Faith: Some Scottish Examples 1860–1920* (Carlisle, U.K.: Paternoster, 1987).

39. David O. Moberg, *The Great Reversal: Evangelism and Social Concern*, rev. ed. (Philadelphia: Lippincott, 1977). See also Marsden, *Fundamentalism and American Culture*, pp. 85–93.

40. These are cited by Dayton in "Pentecostal/Charismatic Renewal and Social Change: A Western Perspective," *Transformation* 5:4 (October/December, 1988), pp. 8–9.

41. From Charles Finney, *Reflections on Revival*, ed. Donald W. Dayton (Minneapolis: Bethany Fellowship, 1979). Dayton has shown how later evangelicals have edited Finney's works to remove references to social change, then printing the abridged version as if it were the original. See *Discovering an Evangelical Heritage*, pp. 19–24.

42. Quoted in W. H. Daniels, *Moody: His Word, Work, and Workers* (New York: Hitchcock and Walden, 1877).

43. For a comparative study of various millennial positions see Stanley J. Grenz, *The Millennial Maze* (Downers Grove: InterVarsity, 1992); Robert G. Clouse, ed., *The Meaning of the Millennium: Four Views* (Downers Grove: InterVarsity, 1977); and Millard J. Erickson, *Contemporary Options in Eschatology* (Grand Rapids: Baker, 1977).

44. On dispensationalism see Timothy P. Weber, *Living in the Shadow of the Second Coming: American Premillennialism 1875–1982* (Chicago: The University of Chicago Press, 1987); and Marsden, *Fundamentalism and American Culture*, pp. 43–71.

45. On Scofield, see Marsden, *Fundamentalism and American Culture*, pp. 59–60.

46. The best overall study is Marsden, *Fundamentalism and American Culture*; on *The Fundamentals* see pp. 118–23. See also George M. Marsden, *Understanding Fundamentalism and Evangelicalism* (Grand Rapids: Eerdmans, 1991), pp. 9–61; and Quebedeaux, *The Young Evangelicals*, pp. 8–9.

47. Marsden, *Fundamentalism and American Culture*, p. 117 and Quebedeaux, *The Young Evangelicals*, p. 9.

48. Marsden, *Fundamentalism and American Culture*, especially pp. 141–98; and Quebedeaux, *The Young Evangelicals*, pp. 5–10.

49. Ernest R. Sandeen, *The Roots of Fundamentalism: British and American Millenarianism, 1800–1930* (Grand Rapids: Baker, 1970).

50. Marsden, *Fundamentalism and American Culture*, pp. 72–101.

51. For descriptions of fundamentalism, see Marsden, *Fundamentalism and American Culture*, pp. 199–228; Marsden, *Understanding Fundamentalism and Evangelicalism*, pp. 1–4; and Quebedeaux, *The Young Evangelicals*, pp. 19–28.

52. On the history of Pentecostalism, see Vinson Synan, *The Holiness-Pentecostal Tradition* (Grand Rapids: Eerdmans, 1977) and Vinson Synan, ed., *Aspects of Pentecostal-Charismatic Origins* (Plainfield: Logos, 1975).

53. The most thorough and perceptive analysis of the development of Pentecostal theology is D. William Faupel, *The Everlasting Gospel: The Significance of Eschatology in the Development of Pentecostal Thought* (Sheffield: Sheffield Academic Press, 1996).The best account of Pentecostal theology and spirituality in terms of its contemporary significance is Steven J. Land, *Pentecostal Spirituality: A Passion for the Kingdom* (Sheffield: Sheffield Academic Press, 1993).

54. For a critique of cessationism see Jon Ruthven, *On the Cessation of the Charismata: The Protestant Polemic on Miracles* (Sheffield: Sheffield Academic Press, 1994). Proponents of four views—cessionist, open but cautious, third wave, and pentecostal/charismatic—debate one another in Wayne A. Grudem, ed., *Are Miraculous Gifts for Today?* (Grand Rapids: Zondervan, 1996).

55. On the Charismatic Movement see Charles E. Hummel, *Fire in the Fireplace: Charismatic Renewal in the Nineties* (Downers Grove: InterVarsity, 1993); Michael P. Hamilton, ed., *The Charismatic Movement* (Grand Rapids: Eerdmans, 1975); Richard Quebedeaux, *The New Charismatics II*; and Vinson Synan, *In the Latter Days: The Outpouring of the Holy Spirit in the Twentieth Century*, rev. ed. (Ann Arbor: Servant Publications, 1991). Some of the best works in Charismatic theology include Larry Christensen, ed., *Welcome Holy Spirit: A Study of Charismatic Renewal in the Church* (Minneapolis: Augsburg, 1987) [Lutheran]; Thomas a Smail, *Reflected Glory: The Spirit in Christ and Christians* (Grand Rapids: Eerdmans, 1975) [Anglican/Reformed]; Edwin O'Conner, *The Pentecostal Movement in the Catholic Church* (Notre Dame: Ave Maria Press, 1971) [Roman Catholic]; and Francis A. Sullivan, *Charisms and Charismatic Renewal* (Ann Arbor: Servant Publications, 1982) [Roman Catholic].

56. A helpful survey of Charismatic views of Spirit-baptism is H. I. Lederle, *Interpretations of "Spirit Baptism" in the Charismatic Renewal Movement: Treasures Old and New* (Peabody: Hendrickson, 1988).

57. The best overall defense of independent Charismatic theology is William DeArteaga, *Quenching the Spirit: Examining Centuries of Opposition to the Moving of the Holy Spirit* (Lake Mary: Creation House, 1992).

58. See C. Peter Wagner, *The Third Wave of the Holy Spirit* (Ann Arbor: Servant Publications, 1988) and Charles H. Kraft, *Christianity With Power* (Ann Arbor: Servant Publications, 1989). See also the essays in Gary S. Greig and Kevin N. Springer, eds., *The Kingdom and the Power* (Ventura: Regal, 1993).
59. Bernard L. Ramm, *The Christian View of Science and Scripture* (Grand Rapids: Eerdmans, 1954). One of the most recent of Henry's many books on culture is *Gods of this Age or ... God of the Ages?* (Nashville: Broadman & Holman, 1994).
60. Carl F. H. Henry, *The Uneasy Conscience of Modern Fundamentalism* (Grand Rapids: Eerdmans, 1947).
61. A helpful survey is Robert Booth Fowler, *A New Engagement: Evangelical Political Thought, 1966–1976*. See also Craig M. Gay, *With Liberty and Justice for Whom?: The Recent Evangelical Debate Over Capitalism* (Grand Rapids: Eerdmans, 1991). Collections of essays representing a variety of evangelical positions can be found in Augustus Cerillo, Jr. and Murray W. Dempster, eds., *Salt and Light: Evangelical Political Thought in Modern America* (Grand Rapids: Baker, 1989); and Richard John Neuhaus and Michael Cromartie, eds., *Piety & Politics: Evangelicals and Fundamentalists Confront the World* (Washington: Ethics and Public Policy Center, 1987).
62. See Ronald J. Sider, *Rich Christians in an Age of Hunger* (Downers Grove: InterVarsity, 1977) and *Completely Pro-Life* (Downers Grove: InterVarsity, 1987). See also his recent *One-Sided Christianity?* (Grand Rapids: Zondervan, 1993).
63. See Jim Wallis, *Agenda for Biblical People* (New York: Harper & Row, 1976), and his more recent *The Soul of Politics: Beyond the "Religious Right" and "Secular Left"* (San Diego: Harcourt, Brace, 1995) and *Who Speaks for God?* (New York: Doubleday, 1996).
64. Edward John Carnell, *The Case for Orthodox Theology* (Philadelphia: Westminster, 1959).
65. Bernard Ramm, *Special Revelation and the Word of God* (Grand Rapids: Eerdmans, 1961) and *After Fundamentalism: The Future of Evangelical Theology* (San Francisco: Harper & Row, 1983).
66. Harold Lindsell, *The Battle for the Bible* (Grand Rapids: Zondervan, 1976).
67. More will be said on this issue in chapter five. Two helpful surveys of evangelical positions are Gabriel Fackre, *The Christian Story*, (Grand Rapids: Eerdmans, 1987), 2:60–73; and Robert K. Johnston, *Evangelicals at an Impasse* (Atlanta: John Knox, 1979).
68. George Marsden has noted that it is these post-fundamentalist evangelicals who "have been the strongest party in this coalition" and "have attempted to speak of set standards for evangelicals generally." Such attempts to unify a "diverse movement by fiat" are seen by Marsden as "artificial." George Marsden, "Introduction: The Evangelical Denomination," in Marsden, ed., *Evangelicalism in Modern America* (Grand Rapids: Eerdmans, 1984), p. xvi.
69. Donald W. Dayton, "'The Search for Historical Evangelicalism': George Marsden's History of Fuller Seminary as a Case Study," *Christian Scholars Review* XXIII:1 (September, 1993), p. 18. This entire issue is a symposium around "What is Evangelicalism?" See also Kenneth J. Collins, "Children of Neglect: American Methodist Evangelicals," *Christian Scholars Review* XX:1 (September, 1990), pp. 7–16.
70. John H. Gerstner, "The Theological Boundaries of Evangelical Faith," in Wells and Woodbridge, eds., *The Evangelicals*, p. 27.
71. This seems to be Mark A. Noll's concern in *The Scandal of the Evangelical Mind* (Grand Rapids: Eerdmans, 1994), where he finds the Holiness movement, Pente-

costalism, and dispensationalism to have all contributed to the decline of evangelical thought in America. His specific examples seem to focus on dispensationalism alone, however. Noll's thesis has been strongly criticized by several historians and theologians, including the present author. See my review in the *Wesleyan Theological Journal* 31:1 (Spring, 1996), pp. 224–28.

72. Dayton, *Discovering an Evangelical Heritage*, p. 131.

73. Ibid., p. 132.

74. Gordon Rupp, *Principalities and Powers* (Nashville: Abingdon, 1952), pp. 90–112.

75. Johnston, "Family," in Dayton and Johnston, eds., *The Variety of American Evangelicalism*, p. 264.

76. Ibid., p. 266.

77. Ibid.

Chapter 2: Theology in the Midst of Modernity

1. Among the introductory surveys of the history of philosophy which are written from the perspective of theology are Colin Brown, *Christianity & Western Thought*, Vol.1 (Downers Grove: InterVarsity, 1990); Diogenes Allen, *Philosophy for Understanding Theology* (Atlanta: John Knox, 1985); and J. Deotis Roberts, *A Philosophical Introduction to Theology* (Philadelphia: Trinity Press International, 1991). They, in turn, reference more technical analyses.

2. Thomas C. Oden, *After Modernity . . . What?: Agenda for Theology* (Grand Rapids: Zondervan, 1990), p. 45.

3. As do J. Richard Middleton and Brian J. Walsh in *Truth is Stranger Than It Used to Be: Biblical Faith in a Postmodern Age* (Downers Grove: InterVarsity, 1995), p. 14. Oden dates it from the French Revolution in 1789. See *After Modernity . . . What?*, p. 44.

4. Lesslie Newbigin, *Proper Confidence: Faith, Doubt & Certainty in Christian Discipleship* (Grand Rapids: Eerdmans, 1995), p. 21.

5. Allen, *Philosophy.* p. 181.

6. Compare the extensive and appreciative discussion of Reid by Colin Brown (*Christianity*, pp. 259–68) with the brief dismissal by Diogenes Allen (*Philosophy for Understanding Theology*, pp. 192–93). There has been a renaissance of sorts in the study of Reid, especially by evangelical philosophers Alvin Plantinga and Nicholas Wolterstorff, who seek to critically appropriate his insights. See the essays by Wolterstorff and Paul Helm in Hendrik Hart, Johan van der Hoeven, and Nicholas Wolterstorff, eds., *Rationality in the Calvinian Tradition* (Washington: University Press of America, 1983), pp. 43–89. A helpful discussion of the issues involved is found in Kelly James Clark, *Return to Reason* (Grand Rapids: Eerdmans, 1990), which shows how Reid is being used by these philosophers to undergird a presuppositionalist apologetic. This rethinking of Reid is in contrast to the evidentialist use of Reid in the nineteenth Century.

7. Lesslie Newbigin, *The Gospel in a Pluralist Society* (Grand Rapids: Eerdmans, 1989), p. 15.

8. For a selection of primary sources around the debate over deism in Great Britain, see E. Graham Waring, ed., *Deism and Natural Religion: A Source Book* (New York: Frederick Ungar Publishing Co., 1967).

9. Kenneth Cauthen, *The Impact of American Religious Liberalism* (New York: Harper & Row, 1962), p. 5.

10. "Bishop Spong: 'I'm a Seeker of the Truth,'" *The Atlanta Journal/The Atlanta Constitution*, December 12, 1992, p. E6.

11. Cauthen, *The Impact of American Religious Liberalism*, p. 9.

12. Ibid., pp. 10–11.

13. Ibid., p. 21.

14. Ibid., pp. 11–12.

15. David L. Edwards and John Stott, *Evangelical Essentials: A Liberal-Evangelical Dialogue* (Downers Grove: InterVarsity, 1988), p. 30.

16. Ibid., p. 31.

17. Ibid., p. 39.

18. Ibid., pp. 39–40.

19. Ibid., p. 39.

20. Ibid., pp. 104–5.

21. Ibid., p. 104.

22. Clark H. Pinnock and Delwin Brown, *Theological Crossfire: An Evangelical/Liberal Dialogue* (Grand Rapids: Zondervan, 1990), p. 22.

23. Ibid., p. 23.

24. Ibid., p. 39.

25. Ibid., p. 40.

26. Ibid., p. 52.

27. Ibid., p. 45.

28. For a description of various evidential approaches, see Kenneth S. Kantzer, "Unity and Diversity in Evangelical Faith," in Wells and Woodbridge, ed., *The Evangelicals*, p. 42.

29. Josh McDowell, *Evidence That Demands a Verdict* (San Bernadino, Calf.: Campus Crusade for Christ, 1972).

30. John Warwick Montogmery, *History and Christianity* (Minneapolis: Bethany House Publishers, 1964), pp. 16–21. For another evidentialist position, see R. C. Sproul, John Gerstner, and Arthur Lindsley: *Classical Apologetics: A Rational Defense of the Christian Faith and Critique of Presuppositional Apologetics* (Grand Rapids: Zondervan, 1984).

31. Ibid., p. 26.

32. Ibid., pp. 26–35.

33. Ibid., p. 49.

34. Ibid., pp. 50–58.

35. Ibid., p. 61.

36. Ibid., pp. 63–78.

37. Ibid., pp. 79–80.

38. Ibid., pp. 43–44.

39. Ibid., p. 75.

40. Ibid.

41. For a similar critique by a very different theologian, see Wolfhart Pannenberg, *Basic Questions in Theology* (Philadelphia: Fortress, 1907), pp. 1:43–46.

42. Carl F. H. Henry, *Toward a Recovery of Christian Belief* (Wheaton: Crossway, 1990), p. 44.

43. For a summary of the views of Van Til and Clark, see Kantzer, in Wells/Wood-bridge, p. 48–51. An appreciative yet critical analysis of Van Til can be found in John M. Frame, *Cornelius Van Til: An Analysis of His Thought* (Phillipsburg: P & R Publishing, 1995).

44. Henry, *Toward a Recovery of Christian Belief*, pp. 105–106. For another defense of presuppositionalism, see Ronald H. Nash, *The Word of God and the Mind of Man* (Grand Rapids: Zondervan, 1982).

45. Ibid., p. 105; see also pp. 51, 60.

46. Ibid., pp. 40, 60.

47. Ibid., p. 64.

48. Ibid., p. 68.

49. Ibid., p. 80.

50. Ibid., p. 81; see also p. 53.

51. Ibid., pp. 55, 59.

52. Ibid., p. 110

53. Ibid., p. 95.

54. Bloesch, *The Future of Evangelical Christianity*, pp. 89–90.

55. Ibid., p. 90.

56. Donald G. Bloesch, *A Theology of Word and Spirit: Authority & Method in Theology* (Downers Grove: InterVarsity, 1992), p. 202.

57. Ibid., p. 21.

58. Ibid., p. 22; see also p.61.

59. Ibid.; see also p. 19.

60. Bloesch, *The Future of Evangelical Christianity*, p. 123.

61. Bloesch, *A Theology of Word and Spirit*, p. 12.

62. Ibid., p. 18.

63. Ibid., p. 23; see also p. 44.

64. Ibid., p. 47.

65. Ibid., p. 19; see also p. 11.

66. Ibid., pp. 19–20.

67. Ibid., p. 59.

Chapter 3: Theology at the End of Modernity

1. Stanley J. Grenz, "Star Trek and the Next Generation: Postmodernism and the Future of Evangelical Theology," in David S. Dockery, ed., *The Challenge of Postmodernism: An Evangelical Engagement* (Wheaten: Victor, 1995), pp. 94–95.

2. Middleton and Walsh, *Truth is Stranger Than It Used to Be*, p. 41.

3. Roger E. Olson, "Whales and Elephants Both God's Creatures But Can They Meet?: Evangelicals and Liberals in Dialogue," *Pro Ecclesia* IV: 2 (Spring, 1995), p. 174.

4. Lints, *The Fabric of Theology*, p. 200; see also pp. 218–22.

5. Ibid., pp. 199–200, see also pp. 201–203.

6. Grenz, "Star Trek," in Dockery, *The Challenge of Postmodernism*, p. 94.

7. Ibid., p. 94.

8. Walter Lowe, *Theology and Difference: The Wound of Reason* (Bloomington: Indiana University Press, 1993), p. 23.

9. Ibid., p.24.

10. Ibid., pp. 25–26. Lowe argues that Kant, in contrast, maintains a dialectic between nature and history.

11. The doctrine of God of nineteenth century liberal theology, derived as it was from human experience, was especially vulnerable to Feuerbach's critique. In the twentieth century, the theologies of Karl Barth and Paul Tillich can be understood in part as attempts to avoid the idolatry described by Feuerbach, albeit in very different ways.

12. For an analysis of Freud, Marx, and Nietzsche and their significance for Christian theology see Merold Westphal, *Suspicion & Faith: The Religious Uses of Modern Atheism* (Grand Rapids: Eerdmans, 1993).

13. Middleton and Walsh, *Truth is Stranger Than It Used to Be*, p. 29. Their discussion of deconstruction is especially helpful in laying out the issues clearly and appreciatively.

14. Ibid., p. 34.

15. Ibid., p. 35.

16. As cited in ibid., p. 70.

17. As do evangelicals such as Stanley J. Grenz, who discusses all three in *A Primer on Postmodernism* (Grand Rapids: Eerdmans, 1996) and Roger Lundin, *The Culture of Interpretation: Christian Faith and the Postmodern World* (Grand Rapids: Eerdmans, 1993), who discusses Derrida and Rorty, pp. 185–99. The postliberal William C. Placher interprets Foucault and Rorty as relativists in *Unapologetic Theology: A Christian Voice in a Pluralist Conversation* (Louisville: Westminster/John Knox, 1989), pp. 92–102. Thomas C. Oden, in *After Modernity . . . What?*, considers the ultra-critics to be hypermodern rather than genuinely postmodern. For a range of evangelical definitions and assessments, see Timothy R. Phillips and Dennis L. Okholm, eds., *Christian Apologetics in the Postmodern World* (Downers Grove, Il.: InterVarsity, 1995) and David S. Dockery, ed., *The Challenge of Postmodernism*.

18. Lowe, *Theology and Difference*, p. 13. What follows is indebted to Lowe's discussion of Derrida on pp. 13–16.

19. Ibid., p. xi.

20. Ibid. p. 70.

21. A point made by John Patrick Diggins, *The Promise of Pragmatism* (Chicago: The University of Chicago Press, 1994), p. 457.

22. See for example Leander E. Keck's call for a "hermeneutic of affirmation" in *The Church Confident* (Nashville: Abingdon, 1993), pp. 63–67. Keck argues that the hermeneutic of suspicion, rightly used, "interrogates evidence in order to find the truth;" however it all too frequently has become a "hermeneutic of alienation" which "interrogates it in order to document an alleged truth already in hand." (p. 59). This is a post-critical sensibility concerning the role of suspicion and affirmation.

23. Paul Ricoeur, *Freud and Philosophy: An Essay on Interpretation* (New Haven: Yale University Press, 1970), p. 27.

24. Ibid., p. 28. Ricoeur himself is not clearly a postmodern thinker, although he has influenced many who are.

25. The "early" Wittgenstein of the *Tractatus Logico-Philosophicus* (1921) understands language in terms of the Kantian distinction between fact and value. Analyzed according to the rules of logic, statements were seen as having to do with one or the other but not both. The "later" Wittgenstein of the *Philosophical Investigations* (1953)

no longer grounds his view of language in logical distinctions abstracted from life, but in the varied and particular practices of life itself. As a result, he came to see language as having a multitude of forms and usages. For a perceptive interpretation of the later Wittgenstein, see Fergus Kerr, *Theology After Wittgenstein* (New York: Blackwell, 1986). For an example of his use in a post-critical philosophy of religion see Jerry H. Gill, *On Knowing God* (Philadelphia: Westminster, 1981).

26. A point made by Kerr, *Theology After Wittgenstein*, p. 137.

27. Alasdair MacIntyre, *After Virtue* (Notre Dame: University of Notre Dame Press, 1981), p. 38.

28. Ibid., pp. 50–51.

29. Ibid., p. 207.

30. Ibid., p. 203–4.

31. Ibid., p. 201.

32. Ibid., p. 204.

33. Ibid., p. 245.

34. Alasdair MacIntyre, *Whose Justice? Which Rationality?* (Notre Dame: University of Notre Dame Press, 1988), p. 351.

35. Ibid., p. 356.

36. Ibid., p. 357.

37. Ibid., p. 350.

38. Ibid., p. 362. MacIntyre's "epistemological crisis" seems to result in something like the "paradigm shift" which Thomas Kuhn argues for in *The Structure of Scientific Revolutions* (Chicago: The University of Chicago Press, 1970).

39. Ibid., p. 365.

40. Drusilla Scott, *Everyman Revived: The Common Sense of Michael Polanyi* (Grand Rapids: Eerdmans, 1995), pp. 48–51. The original edition was published in 1985. See also how Jerry Gill uses Polanyi in *On Knowing God* (Philadelphia: Westminster, 1981).

41. Ibid., p. 52.

42. Ibid., p. 73.

43. Ibid., p. 47.

44. Michael Polanyi, *Knowing and Being* (Chicago: University of Chicago Press, 1960), p. 133. Quoted in Scott, *Everyman Revived*, p. 59.

45. Scott, *Everyman Revived*, p. 68.

46. Ibid., p. 77. This is similar to Kuhn's "paradigm shift."

47. Ibid., p. 70.

48. Ibid., p. 74.

49. Seminal postliberal texts include Hans Frei, *The Eclipse of Biblical Narrative* (New Haven: Yale University Press, 1974) and *The Identity of Jesus Christ* (Philadelphia: Fortress, 1975), Paul Holmer, *The Grammar of Faith* (New York: Harper & Row, 1978), and George Lindbeck, *The Nature of Doctrine: Religion and Theology in a Postliberal Age* (Philadelphia: Westminster, 1984). Besides Hauerwas other notable postliberal theologians include George Hunsinger, William Placher, David Kelsey, Garret Green, Ronald Thiemann, and George Stroup.

50. On this see Olson, "Whales and Elephants." Among the theologians discussed by Olson are William Abraham, Stanley Grenz, and Clark Pinnock. See also Nancey Murphy, *Beyond Liberalism & Fundamentalism: How Modern and Postmodern Philosophy*

Set the Theological Agenda (Valley Forge: Trinity Press International, 1996) for a perceptive analysis of both modernity and postmodernity. She considers the post-critical strand (which she terms "Anglo-American") to be more authentically post-modern than the ultra-critical (or "Continental") strand. Among the post-critical figures she draws upon are Wittgenstein, MacIntyre, epistemologist W. V. O. Quine, and linguistic philosopher J. L. Austin.

Chapter 4: The Resurrection of the Crucified Jesus

1. Jürgen Moltmann, *Theology of Hope* (New York: Harper & Row, 1967), p. 165.
2. Lesslie Newbigin, *Truth to Tell: The Gospel as Public Truth* (Grand Rapids: Eerdmans, 1991), p. 11. See also Newbigin, *Pluralist Society*, p. 11.
3. Thomas F. Torrance, *Space, Time & Resurrection* (Grand Rapids: Eerdmans, 1976), p. 17.
4. Ibid.
5. Peter Carnley, *The Structure of Resurrection Belief* (Oxford: Oxford University Press, 1987), p. 148.
6. For perceptive discussions of these difficulties see Carnley, ibid., pp. 148–82 and Stephen T. Davis, *Risen Indeed: Making Sense of the Resurrection* (Grand Rapids: Eerdmans, 1993), pp. 22–42.
7. Newbigin, *Truth to Tell*, p. 35.
8. Ibid., p. 28. See also Newbigin, *The Gospel in a Pluralist Society*, pp. 8–12.
9. Torrance, *Space, Time & Resurrection*, p. 31.
10. Ibid.
11. Newbigin, *The Gospel in a Pluralist Society*, p. 47.
12. The central theme of Newbigin, *Proper Confidence: Faith, Doubt, and Certainty in Christian Discipleship* (Grand Rapids: Eerdmans, 1995).
13. Carnley, *The Structure of Resurrection Belief*, p. 184. Carnley discusses this approach in detail on pp. 183–222.
14. Ibid., p. 259.
15. Ibid., p. 263.
16. John Wesley, "On Dissipation," in Albert C. Outler, ed., *Sermons III* (Nashville: Abingdon, 1986), pp. 118–19. Vol. 3 of *The Works of John Wesley*.
17. Ibid., p. 120.
18. John Wesley, "Walking by Sight and Walking by Faith," in Albert C. Outler, ed., *Sermons IV* (Nashville: Abingdon, 1987), p. 58. Vol. 4 of *The Works of John Wesley*.
19. Wesley, "On Dissipation," p. 120.
20. Ibid., p. 122.
21. John Wesley, "An Earnest Appeal to Men of Reason and Religion," in Gerald R. Cragg, ed., *The Appeals to Men of Reason and Religion* (Oxford: Oxford University Press, 1975), p. 46. Vol. 11 of *The Works of John Wesley*.

For discussions of Wesley's understanding of faith as a spiritual sense, see Randy L. Maddox, *Responsible Grace*, pp. 27–28; Theodore H. Runyon, "The Importance of Experience for Faith," in Randy L. Maddox, ed., *Aldersgate Reconsidered* (Nashville: Abingdon, 1990); and Rex D. Matthews, "'With the Eyes of Faith': Spiritual Experience and the Knowledge of God in the Theology of John Wesley," in Theodore H. Runyon, ed., *Wesleyan Theology Today* (Nashville: Abingdon, 1985).
22. Wesley, "Earnest Appeal," pp. 47–48.

23. Conrad Cherry, *The Theology of Jonathan Edwards*, p. 29. For a full discussion of Edwards' position see Chapter 11.

24. Thomas F. Torrance, *God and Rationality* (Oxford: Oxford University Press, 1971), p. 166.

25. Bloesch, *A Theology of Word and Spirit*, p. 14. See also pp. 49–53.

26. Torrance, *God and Rationality*, p. 166.

27. Bloesch, *A Theology of Word and Spirit*, p. 15.

28. Ibid., p. 50.

29. Helmut Thielicke, *The Evangelical Faith* (Grand Rapids: Eerdmans, 1974), 1:152.

30. Ibid., p. 153. Thielicke understands our identity to be in Christ rather than in ourselves, an alien righteousness. I agree instead with Wesley, who speaks of our being transformed in ourselves, though always dependent on and never apart from Christ.

31. Bloesch, *A Theology of Word and Spirit*, p. 15. J. C. DeMoor argues that the opposition to a false subject/object polarity is at the heart of G. C. Berkouwer's theological method as well. See his *Towards a Biblically Theo-logical Method* (Kampen: J. H. Kok, 1980).

32. Carnley, *The Structure of Resurrection Belief*, pp. 297–326.

33. For a more complete discussion see Henry H. Knight III, *The Presence of God in the Christian Life: John Wesley and the Means of Grace* (Metuchen: Scarecrow, 1992).

34. John Wesley, "Minutes of Some Late Conversations" in *The Works of the Rev. John Wesley, M.A.*, Thomas Jackson, ed. (Grand Rapids: Baker, 1978), Vol. 8, p. 276.

Chapter 5: The Inadequacies of Propositionalism

1. His major work, a mature statement of the heart of his theology, is his six volume *God, Revelation and Authority* (Waco: Word, 1976–83). A much shorter exposition of a position similar to Henry's is found in Ronald H. Nash, *The Word of God and the Mind of Man* (Grand Rapids: Zondervan, 1982).

2. Henry, *God, Revelation and Authority*, 2:20–21.

3. Ibid., p. 44.

4. Ibid., 3:248.

5. Ibid., p. 203.

6. Ibid., p. 456.

7. Ibid., p. 457.

8. Ibid.

9. James I. Packer, *"Fundamentalism" and the Word of God* (Grand Rapids: Eerdmans, 1958), p. 93.

10. Ibid., p. 94.

11. Henry, *God, Revelation and Authority*, Vol. 4, p. 129. The influence of thought does not, however, mean "divine causation of each and every word choice" (p. 141). Packer defines inspiration as "a supernatural, providential influence of God's Holy Spirit upon the human authors which caused them to write what He wished to be written. ..." (*"Fundamentalism" and the Word of God*, p. 77). Packer seems more concerned than Henry to understand verbal inspiration as implying something like word choice; "If the words were not wholly God's, then their teaching would not be wholly God's." (p. 90).

12. Henry, *God, Revelation and Authority*, Vol. 4, p. 142.

13. Packer, *"Fundamentalism" and the Word of God*, p. 82.

14. Notice that Henry argues deductively: biblical authority implies verbal inspiration which in turn implies inerrancy. This is a consequence of his presuppositionalist method. Evidentialists argue inductively: they provide evidence for inerrancy, which then implies inspiration, and that in turn gives the Bible authority. This approach is typical of Hodge and Warfield as well as contemporary evidentialists like John W. Montgomery, John Gerstner and Harold Lindsell. One of the finest expositions of propositional revelation, which integrates both of these methods, is *Biblical Revelation: The Foundation of Christian Theology* (Chicago: Moody, 1971), which is the culminating work of the "early" Clark H. Pinnock. In all cases, their arguments are correlated with an interpretation of the Bible's own claims concerning its authority, inspiration, and inerrancy.

15. Henry, *God, Revelation and Authority*, Vol. 4, p. 201.

16. Ibid., p. 202.

17. Packer, *"Fundamentalism" and the Word of God*, p. 104.

18. See David N. Livingston, *Darwin's Forgotten Defenders* (Grand Rapids: Eerdmans, 1987), pp. 120–21. Note how Warfield used Darwinian insights to counter racist arguments for the multiple origin of humanity by defending a common origin. For a careful discussion of how Hodge and Warfield understood inerrancy, see Moises Silva, "Old Princeton, Westminster, and Inerrancy" in Harvie M. Conn, ed., *Inerrancy and Hermeneutic* (Grand Rapids: Baker, 1988), pp. 67–80.

19. Henry, *God, Revelation and Authority*, Vol. 4, p. 205.

20. Harold Lindsell, *The Battle for the Bible*. Francis Schaeffer was another early enlistee in this battle. See his *No Final Conflict: The Bible Without Error in All That It Affirms* (Downers Grove, IL.: InterVarsity, 1975).

On the other side of the evangelical spectrum were Dewey M. Beegle, *Scripture, Tradition, and Infallibility* (Grand Rapids: Eerdmans, 1973) and Stephen T. Davis, *The Debate About the Bible* (Philadelphia: Westminster, 1977). Most evangelical scholars found themselves variously located between these two positions.

21. This led to a massive publication of papers defending inerrancy. Among these are Norman L. Geisler, ed., *Inerrancy* (Grand Rapids: Zondervan, 1980); Norman L. Geisler, ed., *Biblical Errancy: Its Philosophical Roots* (Grand Rapids: Zondervan, 1981); Gordon Lewis and Bruce Demarest, ed., *Challenges to Inerrancy* (Chicago: The Moody Press, 1984); John Hannah, ed., *Inerrancy and the Church* (Chicago: Moody, 1984); and Earl Radamacher and Robert Preus, ed., *Hermeneutics, Inerrancy, and the Bible* (Grand Rapids: Zondervan, 1984). These were all sponsored by the ICBI. Additional collections of essays on this topic are D. A. Carson and John Woodbridge, eds., *Scripture and Truth* (Grand Rapids: Zondervan, 1983) and Harvie M. Conn, ed., *Inerrancy and Hermeneutic* (Grand Rapids: Baker, 1988).

An important dialogue on inerrancy was held in 1987, sponsored by the six Southern Baptist seminaries. It is published as *The Proceedings of the Conference on Biblical Inerrancy 1987* (Nashville: Broadman, 1987).

22. William J. Abraham, *An Introduction to the Philosophy of Religion* (Englewood Cliffs: Prentice-Hall, Inc., 1985), pp. 104–113.

23. Henry, *God, Revelation and Authority*, 3:222. Note entire argument on pp. 216–29.

24. Ibid., p. 239. Note his entire argument on pp. 230–47.

25. McGrath, *A Passion for Truth: The Intellectual Coherence of Evangelicalism* (Downers Grove, Il.: InterVarsity, 1996), p. 170.
26. Torrance, *Reality and Evangelical Theology* (Philadelphia: Westminster, 1982), p. 17; see also p. 70.
27. Ibid., p. 16. Compare this concern for a living relationship with God through scripture with this analogy by J. I. Packer: "Imagine your boss handing to you, one of his employees, a policy memorandum written by some of his personal staff and assuring you as he does so that it exactly expresses his mind. ... By studying the memo [the employee] comes to know the boss's mind with a precision not otherwise attainable. So it is with members of the Christian church as they study their Bibles." Here the focus is on information cognitively received. See his essay on "The Adequacy of Human Language," in Geisler, ed., *Inerrancy*, p. 221.
28. William J. Abraham, *Divine Revelation and the Limits of Historical Criticism* (Oxford: Oxford University Press, 1982), p. 15.
29. Donald G. Bloesch, *Holy Scripture* (Downers Grove: InterVarsity, 1994), p. 49. See also Colin E. Gunton's defense of propositions within revelation in *A Brief Theology of Revelation* (Edinburgh: T. & T. Clark, 1995), pp. 7–13.
30. Henry, *God, Revelation and Authority*, Vol. 3, p. 453; see also Vol. 4, p. 120. While the suspicion of metaphor goes back to Aristotle, the zenith of that suspicion was reached in the Enlightenment, wherein thinkers like Thomas Hobbes could term it an abuse of language, inherently deceitful. See the discussion of metaphor in Colin E. Gunton, *The Actuality of Atonement: A Study of Metaphor, Rationality and the Christian Tradition* (Grand Rapids: Eerdmans, 1989), pp. 29–30. If one accepts the Enlightenment premise, then an apologetic concern will necessarily lead in the direction of Henry's insistence on propositionalism.
31. Ibid., p. 364. See his entire argument on pp. 362–66 and in Vol. 4 on pp. 117–21.
32. Bloesch, *Holy Scripture*, p. 286 .
33. Abraham, *Divine Revelation and the Limits of Historical Criticism*, p. 11.
34. Clark H. Pinnock, *The Scripture Principle* (San Francisco: Harper & Row, 1984), p. 19.
35. William J. Abraham, *The Divine Inspiration of Holy Scripture* (Oxford: Oxford University Press, 1981), p. 67.
36. Pinnock, *The Scripture Principle*, p. 63. Abraham likewise argues that "divine speaking" is only one type of inspiration, but has been equated with the whole. See Abraham, *Inspiration*, pp. 58–62. John Goldingay proposes four "models" for understanding the diversity within scripture: witnessing tradition (narrative), authoritative canon (scriptural commands), inspired word (prophecy) and experienced revelation (psalms, apocalypses, epistles, and wisdom literature). He suggests we first carefully define each model in terms of the type of literature to which it most naturally refers prior to our stretching the model to apply to the entirety of scripture. See his *Models for Scripture* (Grand Rapids: Eerdmans, 1994) and *Models for Interpretation of Scripture* (Grand Rapids: Eerdmans, 1995).
37. Bloesch, *Holy Scripture*, p. 118.
38. Abraham, *The Divine Inspiration of Scripture*, pp. 63–67. Kern R. Trembath, building on Abraham's proposal, argues that the Bible is not the product of inspiration but the means. To view the Bible as the product of inspiration inevitably tends to invest it with characteristics which only belong to God. Inspiration for Trembath is

the enhancement of our understanding of God which comes at God's initiative by means of the unique instrument of scripture. See his *Evangelical Theories of Biblical Inspiration: A Review and Proposal* (New York: Oxford University Press, 1987). While sympathetic with the dynamic he proposes I am reluctant to abandon inspiration as a property of the scriptural text. My own proposal in the next chapter is an attempt to maintain the traditional evangelical view without confusing scripture with God.

39. Pinnock, *The Scripture Principle*, p. 103.

40. Ibid., pp. 103–104. Colin Gunton describes inspiration as the "affirmation that God the Spirit enabled members of a community in a particular time to articulate what it was about that particular configuration of events that is uniquely significant for the salvation of the world." See Gunton, *A Brief Theology of Revelation*, p. 76.

41. Bloesch, *Holy Scripture*, p. 88.

42. One early collection of essays which sought to keep evangelicalism open to a wider range of views on inerrancy and infallibility was Jack Rogers, ed., *Biblical Authority* (Waco.: Word, 1977). Included are essays by Rogers, Pinnock, Beverly Mickelsen, Bernard Ramm, and David Hubbard. There has been a marked antipathy of Wesleyan-Holiness evangelicals to an insistence on strict inerrancy. Both H. Orton Wiley and A. M. Hills, perhaps the leading Holiness theologians of this century, held to a dynamic theory of inspiration and to the idea that the scriptures were without error in their teaching on doctrine and practice. Hills in fact believed there were inconsequential errors in the autographs. More recently, H. R. Dunning and J. Kenneth Grider endorse dynamic inspiration and believe the focus on inerrancy as an issue is either misplaced (Dunning) or of no great importance (Grider); scripture is authoritative and reliable in terms of its purpose, which is soteriological. See H. Ray Dunning, *Grace, Faith, and Holiness* (Kansas City: Beacon Hill Press, 1988), pp. 55–76; and J. Kenneth Grider, *A Wesleyan-Holiness Theology* (Kansas City: Beacon Hill Press, 1994), pp. 63–85. Steven J. Land sees doctrines of infallibility and inerrancy as a reduction of "a much fuller doctrine of the Word of God" involving its dynamic interaction with the Holy Spirit(cf. *Pentecostal Spirituality*, p. 74). Scott A. Ellington argues similarly that the framework of the inerrancy debate is more a product of Enlightenment academia than the church and is at odds with the Pentecostal emphasis on a living experience with God through scripture ("Pentecostalism and the Authority of Scripture," *Journal of Pentecostal Theology* 9, 1996, pp. 16–38).

43. See Robert K. Johnston, *Evangelicals at an Impasse*, pp. 15–47 and Gabriel Fackre, *The Christian Story*, Vol. 2, pp. 62–73. Both typologies make a fundamental distinction between inerrancy and infallibility. They may be summarized and integrated as follows, with representative figures in each category in brackets:

INERRANCY: Scripture contains no error
  DETAILED INERRANCY (Johnston): No errors in the autographs
    TRANSMISSIVE INERRANCY (Fackre): Divine preservation insures received text is without error [Harold Lindsell]
    TRAJECTORY INERRANCY (Fackre): Divine guidance insures received text is substantially without error [Carl F. H. Henry, James I. Packer]
  I RENIC INERRANCY (Johnston)/INTENTIONAL INERRANCY (Fackre): No error in terms of authorial intention; recognition that error means different things for different literacy forms [Clark H. Pinnock]

INFALLIBILITY: Scripture is trustworthy; it does not deceive

CO MPLETE INFALLIBILITY (Johnston): Message of the whole of scripture is infallible

UNITIVE INFALLIBILITY (Fackre): Scripture has an overall coherent message [G. C. Berkouwer]

ESSENTIALIST INFALLIBILITY (Fackre): The more comprehensive statements in scripture (the essential affirmations) interpret the less comprehensive [Donald G. Bloesch]

PARTIAL INFALLIBILITY(Johnston)/CHRISTOCENTRIC INFALLIBILITY (Fackre): Christ is the standard for judging what is or is not authoritative in scripture [Dewey Beegle, Paul K. Jewett]

44. Pinnock, *The Scripture Principle*, p. 78.

45. Ibid., p. xx. Bernard Ramm much earlier than Pinnock expressed concern that the term "propositional revelation" was imprecise because "it fails to do justice to the literary, historical and poetic elements of special revelation." See his *Special Revelation and the Word of God*, pp. 154–155.

46. Bloesch, *Holy Scripture*, p. 37.

47. Ibid., p. 128. See his entire discussion of inerrancy on pp. 105–117.

48. Gunton, *A Brief Theology of Revelation*, p. 66.

49. Pinnock, *The Scripture Principle*, p. 49. See Pinnock's elaboration of this point in "The Work of the Holy Spirit in Hermeneutics," *Journal of Pentecostal Theology* 2 (April, 1993), pp. 3–23.

50. Grenz, *Revisioning Evangelical Theology*, p. 114.

51. Land, *A Passion for the Kingdom*, p. 100.

Chapter 6: The Promise of Narrative

1. Frei, *The Eclipse of Biblical Narrative*.

2. Stephen Crites, "The Narrative Quality of Experience," in Stanley Hauerwas and L. Gregory Jones, eds., *Why Narrative? Readings in Narrative Theology* (Grand Rapids: Eerdmans, 1989), pp. 65–88.

3. Hans W. Frei, *Theology and Narrative: Selected Essays*, George Hunsinger and William C. Placher, eds (Oxford: Oxford University Press, 1993), p. 208.

4. Gary Comstock describes these two tendencies as "purist" and "impurist;" the "purist" category includes the postliberals. See his "Two Types of Narrative Theology," *Journal of the American Academy of Religion* 55:4 (Winter, 1987), pp. 687–720.

5. Gerard Loughlin, *Telling God's Story* (Cambridge: Cambridge University Press, 1996), p. 44.

6. Ibid., pp. 50–51. See his comparison of "story" and "narratives" on pp. 52–63.

7. Gabriel Fackre, *The Christian Story*, Revised Edition (Grand Rapids: Eerdmans, 1984), 1:8.

8. Ibid., p. 9.

9. Ibid., p. 5.

10. Eric Auerbach, *Mimesis* (Princeton: Princeton University Press, 1968), p. 15.

11. Frei, *The Eclipse of Biblical Narrative*, p. xiv.

12. Ibid., p. 14.

13. Ibid., p. 30.
14. Auerbach, *Mimesis*, p. 73.
15. Frei, *The Eclipse of Biblical Narrative*, p. 142.
16. Loughlin, *Telling God's Story*, p. 70.
17. Frei, *The Identity of Jesus Christ* speaks of this narrative portrayal in terms of "intention-action" and "self-manifestation" description. Frei argues that, in contrast to Cartesian mind/body dualism, narrative describes the self holistically: intentions are enacted and selves are embodied agents. See especially pp. 91–137.
18. See Lindbeck, *The Nature of Doctrine*, especially pp. 32–41.
19. George W. Stroup, *The Promise of Narrative Theology* (Atlanta: John Knox Press, 1981), especially pp. 132–69.
20. Ibid., p. 171.
21. McGrath, *A Passion for Truth*, p. 107.
22. Lindbeck, *The Nature of Doctrine*, p. 114.
23. Mark I. Wallace, *The Second Naiveté: Barth, Ricoeur, and the New Yale Theology* (Macon, Ga.: Mercer University Press, 1990), p. 89.
24. Carl F. H. Henry, "Narrative Theology: An Evangelical Appraisal," *Trinity Journal* 8:1 (Spring, 1987), p. 4.
25. Bloesch, *A Theology of Word and Spirit*, p. 133; see also pp. 17, 30, 188.
26. McGrath, *A Passion for Truth*, p. 153.
27. Ibid., p. 154. See McGrath's full critique on pp. 148–161. See also the discussion by McGrath, Lindbeck, Fackre, and others in Phillips and Okholm, eds., *The Nature of Confession*.
28. Lindbeck, *The Nature of Doctrine*, p. 63.
29. Ibid., pp. 68–69.
30. Ibid., p. 64.
31. Ibid.
32. Ibid.
33. Wallace, *The Second Naiveté*, p. 106.
34. Ibid.
35. Bruce D. Marshall, "Aquinas as Postliberal Theologian," *The Thomist* 53 (1989), p. 365. This is a most careful analysis of Lindbeck which distinguishes between his different uses of the word "truth." See especially pp. 357–70. Steven J. Land makes a similar point when he says "For Pentecostals, to know God is to be in a right relation, to walk in the light and in the Spirit. ... For example, to say 'God is with us' without being with God is to lie or merely to speculate." See his *Pentecostal Spirituality*, p. 37.
36. Lindbeck, *The Nature of Doctrine*, p. 66. Jeffrey Hensley concurs that Lindbeck is often misread as an antirealist, and suggests the reason for this is Lindbeck's epistemological antifoundationalism. See his "Are Postliberals Necessarily Antirealists? Reexamining the Metaphysics of Lindbeck's Postliberal Theology," in Phillips and Okholm, eds., *The Nature of Confession*. See also, in the same volume, David K. Clark, 'Relativism, Fideism & the Promise of Postliberalism."
37. Hans Frei, "Response to 'Narrative Theology: An Evangelical Appraisal'," *Trinity Journal* 8:1 (Spring, 1987), p. 24.
38. Ibid., pp. 23–24.

39. Ibid., p. 24. See also George Hunsinger's analysis in "What Can Evangelicals & Postliberals Learn from Each Other? The Carl Henry–Hans Frei Exchange Reconsidered" in Phillips and Okholm, eds., *The Nature of Confession.*

40. This seems to be Wallace's point in *The Second Naiveté*, p. 106.

41. Fackre, *The Chrisitan Story*, 1:5. In the second volume of *The Christian Story* Fackre affirms propositional truth while criticizing propositionalism. "When a text comes alive under the power of the Spirit and does a transforming work, it is *through* not around the objective truth claims made by that text. ... Biblical assertions, whatever their genre, do make truth claims of an objective sort, affirmations about the nature of reality to which the proper answer is 'yes' or 'no.'" "They correspond or conform to something or someone in time or beyond it" (p. 249).

42. Bloesch, *Holy Scripture*, p. 270.

43. Ibid., p. 274. Joseph Byrd likewise argues that "while most Pentecostals understand the Bible as historically literal, their preaching generally demonstrates that they believe the biblical narratives have a symbolic nature as well as a historical nature." He proposes a Pentecostal adaptation of the post-critical hermeneutics of Paul Ricoeur. See his article "Paul Ricoeur's Hermeneutical Theory and Pentecostal Proclamation" in *Pneuma* 15:2 (Fall, 1993), p. 210.

44. Clark H. Pinnock, *Tracking the Maze* (San Francisco: Harper & Row, 1990), p. 154. Bloesch likewise speaks of "myth that becomes fact in content without ceasing to be myth in form." See *Holy Scripture*, 276.

45. Ibid., p. 164.

46. C. S. Lewis, *God in the Dock* (Grand Rapids: Eerdmans, 1970), p. 67.

47. Pinnock, *Tracking the Maze*, p. 160.

48. Bloesch, *Holy Scripture*, p. 269.

49. Pinnock, *Tracking the Maze*, p. 161. This is not to say that Elisha's axehead or Lot's wife become any less important to the understanding of the truth of a passage should they turn out not to be historical fact. As Timothy B. Cargal has said (here about Pilate washing his hands) "it is the issue of its function within the story that is more significant than its historical reliability." See his article "Beyond the Fundamentalist-Modernist Controversy: Pentecostals and Hermeneutics in a Postmodern Age" in *Pneuma* 15:2 (Fall, 1993), p. 185. One does not have to abandon strict inerrancy to utilize literary insights. Tremper Longman III holds to the detailed historicity of scripture while nonetheless recognizing and respecting its predominantly narrative and poetic quality. He argues that a literary approach to biblical interpretation is compatible with a strong affirmation of the inerrancy and infallibility of scripture. See his "Story Tellers and Poets in the Bible: Can Literary Artifice Be True?" in Harvie M. Conn, ed., *Inerrancy and Hermeneutic* (Grand Rapids: Baker, 1988), pp. 137–49.

50. Bloesch, *Holy Scripture*, p. 269; see also p. 274.

51. Pinnock, *Tracking the Maze*, p. 160.

52. Bloesch, *Holy Scripture*, p. 269.

53. Torrance, *Reality and Evangelical Theology*, p. 37; see also Bloesch, *Scripture*, p. 267.

54. Bloesch, *Holy Scripture*, p. 266.

55. Torrance, *Reality and Evangelical Theology*, p. 66.

56. Ibid., p. 64.

57. Ibid., p. 60. Torrance is here reflecting the influence of Karl Barth. It is fair to say that Barth has been seriously misunderstood by rational propositionalist evangelicals, who insist that by failing to adhere to the kind of rational orthodoxy they represent Barth has either fallen into Kantian subjectivism or is inescapably contradictory. What they miss is Barth's very biblical resistance to the epistemological dualism of Enlightenment modernity. It is this feature that makes Barth so attractive to Torrance, Bloesch, and Bernard Ramm, all of whom critically appropriate his insights.

For surveys of evangelical responses to Barth see Philip R. Thone, *Evangelicals and Karl Barth* (Allison, Pa.: Pickwick, 1995) and Gregory Bolich, *Karl Barth and Evangelicalism* (Downers Grove: InterVarsity, 1980) Two of the most perceptive treatments of Barth by evangelicals are Thomas F. Torrance, *Karl Barth: Biblical and Evangelical Theologian* (Edinburgh: T. & T. Clark, 1990) and G. C. Berkouwer, *The Triumph of Grace in the Theology of Karl Barth* (Grand Rapids: Eerdmans, 1956). See also Bernard Ramm, *After Fundamentalism* (San Francisco: Harper & Row, 1983) and Donald G. Bloesch, *Jesus Is Victor! Karl Barth's Doctrine of Salvation* (Nashville: Abingdon, 1976).

Perhaps the best single volume on Barth is George Hunsinger's *How to Read Karl Barth: The Shape of His Theology* (New York: Oxford University, Press, 1991). Hunsinger argues that Barth has elements of both coherence and correspondence theories of truth, but for Barth the correspondence is not to empirical reality but to revelation itself.

58. G. C. Berkouwer, *Holy Scripture* (Grand Rapids: Eerdmans, 1975), pp. 18–19. See full discussion on pp. 12–38.

59. Ibid., p. 9. On these issues the advocates of propositionalism have misunderstood Berkouwer as grievously as they have Barth. They interpret him as abandoning the objective truth of scripture for subjective faith, failing to see that his intent is to not think in those dualistic terms at all.

60. Ibid., p. 39.

61. Ibid., p. 10.

62. Ibid., p. 166.

63. Ibid., p. 167.

64. Pinnock, *The Scripture Principle*, p. 187.

65. Ibid., p. 189.

66. Luci Shaw, "Imagination: That Other Avenue to Truth," *Christianity Today*, January 2, 1981, p. 33. The entire article is on pp. 32–33. See also Virginia Stem Owens "On Seeing Christianity in Red & Green as Well as Black & White," *Christianity Today*, September 2, 1983, pp. 38–40. Colin E. Gunton notes in this regard "that the truth of a claim about the world does not depend on whether it is expressed in literal or metaphorical terms, but upon whether language of whatever kind expresses human interaction with reality successfully (truthfully) or not." See his *The Actuality of Atonement*, p. 35.

67. Pinnock, *The Scripture Principle*, p. 191.

68. Ibid.

69. Ibid., p. 193. I discuss these in "True Affections: Biblical Narrative & Evangelical Spirituality," in Phillips and Okholm, eds., *The Nature of Confession*.

Chapter 7: The Problem of Context

1. Garrett Green, *Imagining God: Theology and the Religious Imagination* (San Francisco: Harper and Row, 1989).

2. The discussion here draws upon my previously article "How We Imagine God: Two Approaches," published in *McKendree Pastoral Review* 12:1 (May,1985).

3. Green, *Imagining God*, pp. 75–76.

4. Sallie McFague, *Metaphorical Theology: Models of God in Religious Language* (Philadelphia: Fortress, 1982), p. 38.

5. Janet Martin Soskice, *Metaphors and Religious Language* (Oxford: Clarendon Press, 1985), pp. 46–47.

6. Ibid., p. 47.

7. Ibid., p. 15.

8. Green, *Imagining God*, p. 133. Green finds such terms as "interactive" and "interanimative" misleading "insofar as they deflect attention from the single focus and unidirectional grammar of metaphoric speech." To make this clearer he develops new terminology: Richards' "tenor" is in fact the *subject*, "What the metaphor is about;" the "vehicle" is "the metaphor itself." While it is true the metaphor "interacts with" or "animates" its subject, Green's terminology emphasizes that the point of the metaphor is to enable us to depict "an otherwise inaccessible subject."

9. McFague, *Metaphorical Theology*, p. 17.

10. Ibid., p. 18. McFague rejects an incarnational Christology which she believes promotes an idolatrous identity of the human with the divine. She instead proposes a "parabolic christology" which she believes more appropriate "for the Protestant sensibility and the modern mentality."

11. Ibid., p. 108.

12. Ibid., p. 20.

13. For McFague, metaphors become literal in two ways. Because they are preserved in ritual and tradition they are especially prone to be literalized over time (*Metaphorical Theology*, p. 38). Moreover, idolatry occurs when "the fallible, human words of Scripture are understood as referring correctly and literally to God" (p. 4).

14. McFague, *Metaphorical Theology*, p. 5.

15. Ibid., pp. 19, 32.

16. Ibid., p. 3.

17. Ibid., p. 8.

18. Ibid., pp. 8–9.

19. Ibid., p. 9. I shall say more about this questionable reading of the tradition in chapter nine.

20. Ibid., p. 10.

21. Ibid., p. 9.

22. Green, *Imagining God*, pp. 121–22. Here Green adopts the "cultural-linguistic" approach of George Lindbeck.

23. Ibid., p. 99.

24. Ibid.

25. Ibid., p. 106

26. Garrett Green, "The Gender of God and the Theology of Metaphor," in Alvin F. Kimel, Jr., ed., *Speaking the Christian God: The Holy Trinity and the Challenge of Feminism*

(Grand Rapids: Eerdmans, 1992), p. 59. The essays in this volume deserve careful attention. In addition to Green's, that of Colin Gunton is especially insightful.

27. Ibid., p. 61.

28. Ibid., p. 60.

29. Ibid., p. 61.

30. For a thorough discussion of biblical imagery for God as well as a critique of the "goddess spirituality" of radical feminism, see Aida Bensancon Spencer, Donna F. G. Hailson, Catherine Clark Kroeger, and William David Spencer, *The Goddess Revival* (Grand Rapids: Baker, 1995).

31. Shelly Paul discusses three approaches to trinitarian language: the substitution approach, which replaces the male metaphors; the nonsubstitution approach which argues that Father, Son, and Holy Spirit is the revealed name of God; and a variety of mediating approaches which can lean either way. She proposes retaining the classic trinitarian formula while complementing it with other biblical images, including feminine ones. I endorse this approach. Furthermore, she is right to emphasize the Trinity as essentially a communal and relational God, characteristics which should be reflected as well in human society as the created image of God. As she says, this should especially characterize the church. See "The Doctrine of the Trinity: The Personal and Relational God" in Catherine Clark Kroeger, Mary Evans, and Elaine Storkey, eds., *Study Bible for Women: The New Testament* (Grand Rapids: Baker, 1995), pp. 570–76.

32. Elouise Rennich Fraser, "The Church's Language About God," *Priscilla Papers* 6:2–3 (Spring-Summer, 1992), p. 6. Her article is reprinted from *The Other Side*, December, 1987.

33. C. René Padilla, *Mission Between the Times: Essays on the Kingdom* (Grand Rapids: Eerdmans, 1985), p. 83. This view is endorsed as well by Orlando E. Costas in *Christ Outside the Gate: Mission Beyond Christendom* (Maryknoll, N.Y.: Orbis Books, 1982), pp. 5–12.

34. The CBMW produced the "Danvers Statement" in 1988 which provides a succinct statement of its views, as well as a lengthy book of essays edited by John Piper and Wayne Grudem entitled *Recovering Biblical Manhood and Womanhood: A Response to Evangelical Feminism* (Wheaton, Il.: Crossway, 1991). See also Mary Kassian, *The Feminist Gospel* (Wheaton, Il.: Crossway, 1992), George W. Knight III, *Role Relationship of Men and Women* (Chicago: Moody, 1985) and James B. Hurley, *Man and Woman in Biblical Perspective* (Grand Rapids: Zondervan, 1981).

Signers of the "Danvers Statement" include theologians John M. Frame, Wayne A. Grudem, H. Wayne House and Ken Sarles; biblical scholars Gleason Archer, James Borland, Weldemor Degner, George W. Knight III, Douglas J. Moo, Raymond C. Ortlund, Siegfried Schatzmann, and Larry Walker; and a number of others such as Mary Kassian, Beverly LaHaye, Rhoda H. Kelley, and John Piper. Their Board of Reference includes theologians Carl F. H. Henry, J. I. Packer, Harold O. J. Brown, Gordon R. Lewis, R. C. Sproul, John F. Walvoord; biblical scholar D. A. Carson; plus Jerry Falwell, D. James Kennedy, John MacArthur, Jr., Pat Robertson, Paige and Dorothy Patterson, and Adrian and Joyce Rogers, and others.

35. The CBE has produced a "Statement on Men, Women, and Biblical Equality" and publishes a journal, *Priscilla Papers*. It is informally linked with its British counterpart, Men, Women, and God. The two best presentations of the egalitarian

position are Rebecca Merrill Groothuis, *Women Caught in the Conflict* (Grand Rapids: Baker, 1994) and Elaine Storkey, *What's Right With Feminism* (Grand Rapids: Eerdmans, 1985). A good overview of all the issues in the debate thus far is Stanley J. Grenz with Denise Muir Kjesbo, *Women in the Church: A Biblical Theology of Women in Ministry* (Downers Grove: InterVarsity, 1995). Other important works include Faith McBurney Martin, *Call Me Blessed* (Grand Rapids: Eerdmans, 1988); Patricia Gundry, *Woman Be Free! The Clear Message of Scripture* (Grand Rapids: Zondervan, 1977); Gretchen Gaebelein Hull, *Equal to Serve* (Old Tappen: Revell, 1987); Aida Besancon Spencer, *Beyond the Curse: Women Called to Ministry* (Nashville: Thomas Nelson, 1985); and Gilbert G. Bilezikian, *Beyond Sex Roles* (Grand Rapids: Baker, 1986).

One important project by an international team of egalitarian women scholars is the *Study Bible for Women: New Testament*, edited by Catherine Clark Kroeger, Mary Evans, and Elaine Storkey (Grand Rapids: Baker, 1995).

Besides those authors mentioned above, signers of the CBE statement include theologians Roger Nicole, Gabriel Fackre, Vernon Grounds, Robert K. Johnston, Kenneth Kantzer, Howard A. Snyder, Ronald J. Sider; biblical scholars W. Ward Gasque, F. F. Bruce, Gordon Fee, David A. Hubbard, A. Berkeley and Alvera Mickelsen, David M. Scholer; and a large number of scholars and ministers including Stanley N. Gundry, Jo Anne Lyon, Myron S. Augsburger, Ray Bakke, Tony Campolo, Richard C. Halverson, Roberta Hestenes, William J. Hybels, Bruce Larson, Richard F. Lovelace, David L. McKenna, Stephen C. Mott, Richard J. Mouw, Grant R. Osborne, Cornelius Plantinga, Jr., Lewis B. Smedes, Ruth A. Tucker, Mary Stewart Van Leeuwen, Timothy Weber, and Nicholas Wolterstorff, and others.

The recovery of evangelical feminism for the contemporary church began with the publication in 1974 of *All We're Meant to Be* by Letha Scanzoni and Nancy Hardesty (first published by Word, with a third edition by Eerdmans in 1992). This led to the forming of the Evangelical Women's Caucus. However, disagreements over a range of issues, including homosexuality, led to the formation of CBE and the EWC being renamed the Ecumenical Womens Caucus. It should be noted that Hardesty and Scanzoni in their latest edition remain "convinced that the Bible, rightly interpreted, does support, indeed does demand, full equality for women." (p. 5) Theirs remains a "biblical feminism."

36. Leading theologians associated with CBE include Roger Nicole, Millard Erickson, and Kenneth Kantzer, all of whom are strict inerrantists.

37. Kantzer delivered this address to the Christians for Biblical Equality International Conference, Winter Park, Colorado, held August 15–18, 1991.

38. Christian feminists from a more theologically liberal perspective include Rosemary Radford Reuther, Letty M. Russell, and Elisabeth Schussler-Fiorenza. While they understand the Bible to reflect patriarchal bias, they have developed hermeneutical strategies to identify its central liberating theme or to uncover the egalitarian church which the patriarchal text obscures.

Post-Christian feminists like Mary Daly have abandoned the Christian faith entirely as intrinsically incompatible with dignity and equality for women.

39. Robert K. Johnston, *Evangelicals at an Impasse*, p. 59.

40. Ibid., pp. 57–58.

41. Ibid., p. 65.

42. Grenz and Kjesbo, *Women in the Church*, pp. 140–41.
43. Groothuis, *Women Caught in the Conflict*, p. 113.
44. Ibid., p. 114.
45. Ibid., p. 113.
46. Johnston, p. 74. John Christopher Thomas, a Pentecostal New Testament scholar, has developed a hermeneutic which takes account of something like a continuing actualization of scripture. Based on the Jerusalem council in Acts 15, Thomas proposes a dynamic integration of community, the Holy Spirit, and scripture. The experience of the community, attributed to the work of the Spirit, may raise inter-pretative issues which potentially revise a previous understanding of God's pur-poses. Under the guidance of the Spirit the community searches the scripture, which ultimately may be understood in a fresh way but also may finally rule out the new experience. Scripture as interpreted by the Spirit in community remains the final authority. See "Women, Pentecostals and the Bible: An Experiment in Pentecostal Hermeneutics," *Journal of Pentecostal Theology* 5 (October, 1994), pp. 41–56.
47. For discussions of the role of women in the eighteenth-century Wesleyan awakening see Earl Kent Brown, *The Women of Mr. Wesley's Methodism* (Lewiston: Edwin Mellen, 1983); Paul Wesley Chilcote, *John Wesley and the Women Preachers of Early Methodism* (Metuchen: Scarecrow, 1991); and Chilcote, *She Offered Them Christ* (Nashville: Abingdon, 1993). The contribution of the nineteenth-century evangelical awakening to women's rights is discussed in Donald W. Dayton, *Discovering an Evangelical Heritage* (New York: Harper & Row, 1976); Nancy Hardesty, *Women Called to Witness: Evangelical Feminism in the Nineteenth Century* (Nashville: Abingdon, 1984); Hardesty, *Your Daughters Shall Prophesy* (New York: Carlson, 1991); and Janette Hassey, *No Time for Silence* (Grand Rapids: Zondervan, 1986).
48. Groothuis, *Women Caught in the Conflict*, p. 109.
49. By "central truth claims" and "essentials" I mean the classic teachings on Trinity, incarnation, cross, and resurrection; these and not the Enlightenment should be the underlying assumptions for Christian doctrine. I do *not* mean to endorse the teaching of historic theologians concerning women, which owed more to their own cultural assumptions than to the message of scripture.

What I am suggesting here is that evangelical feminists read scripture and tradition from a different perspective than nonevangelicals. It is not that they tolerate alleged hierarchical and dualistic thinking; rather they simply do not see these as characterizing scripture or the heart of the Christian tradition. Rather than subject scripture to a feminist critique, they develop the explicit and implicit feminist critique which is within scripture.

These differences have late-nineteenth century roots. Liberal feminists herald the publication of Elizabeth Cady Stanton's *The Woman's Bible*, issued in two volumes in 1895 and 1898, which argues that scripture itself has a sexist bias. Evangelical feminists look back to Katherine Bushnell's *God's Word to Women*, published in 1919, which accepts the authority of scripture but raises questions of bias in translation and interpretation.
50. Storkey, *What's Right With Feminism*, pp. 133–37.
51. Ibid., p. 137.
52. Newbigin, *The Gospel in a Pluralist Society*, p. 141.
53. Thielicke, *The Evangelical Faith*, 1:26.

54. Ibid., pp. 125–26. This is similar to the point concerning "Jesus is Lord" in section one of this chapter.

55. See for example Stephen B. Bevans, *Models of Contextual Theology* (Maryknoll: Orbis, 1992). Four of his five models seem susceptible to this critique. See also Newbigin's concern in this area in *The Gospel in a Pluralist Society*, pp. 148–151.

56. Steven J. Land, *Pentecostal Spirituality*, p. 38.

57. Dean Fleming, "The Third Horizon: A Wesleyan Contribution to the Contextualization Debate," *Wesleyan Theological Journal* 30:2 (Fall, 1995), p. 152. This is a crucial point. Evangelicalism today has an ongoing debate over "marketing" the church, often by making it "seeker sensitive." Large megachurches have emerged through creatively developing forms of worship and outreach that speak to the largely unchurched baby boomers and generation X. They perceive themselves as reaching new generations with the gospel (which the more traditional churches have failed to do); critics accuse them of presenting the gospel in such a way that it affirms rather than challenges the consumerism, individualism, and materialism of Western society. In my view there is much to be said for both sides of the debate, and would hope evangelicals would live within the tension as they actively engage in evangelistic and caring outreach. Fleming's comment indicates the source of my uneasiness with David F. Wells' analysis of the current state of evangelicalism in *No Place for Truth: Or Whatever Happened to Evangelical Theology?* (Grand Rapids: Eerdmans, 1993). I certainly share his concern that evangelicals in North America are uncritically adopting the therapeutic and pragmatic norms of modern culture, and that this is accompanied by a devaluation of the role of theology in the church. I also agree that there is an objective truth which can be known and communicated. But it is one thing to insist that there is such a truth and another to act as if we can have this truth in a decontextualized form. While I would agree with Wells that theological reflection is necessary to the life of the church, our theology cannot be abstracted from culture any more than it can from language. The theological task is not to escape culture but to discern between true and false contextualization. Thus our confidence in the truth we proclaim at the same time insists on self-critical reflection and careful listening to biblically faithful perspectives from cultures other than our own.

58. See for example Lesslie Newbigin, *Foolishness to the Greeks: The Gospel and Western Culture* (Grand Rapids: Eerdmans, 1986); William A. Dryness, *How Does America Hear the Gospel?* (Grand Rapids: Eerdmans, 1984); and Alfred C. Krass, *Evangelizing Neopagan North America* (Scottdale, Pa.: Herald Press, 1982). The experiences of Newbigin and Dyrness in Asian cultures sensitized them to the ways the West has engaged in cultural accommodation of the gospel.

59. Padilla, *Mission Between the Times*, p. 88.

60. Costas, *Christ Outside the Gate*, p. 13.

61. Ibid., p. 15. While Costas begins with contextual experience in the sense that he lists it first, it is clear that it is scripture and not culture that governs the gospel message.

62. Fleming, "The Third Horizon," p. 154.

63. William A. Dyrness, *Learning About Theology From the Third World* (Grand Rapids: Zondervan, 1990), p. 32. The point here is that true contextualization permits fresh and indeed distinctively new appropriations of the gospel while remaining in faithful continuity with scripture, which is used by the Christian community to

evaluate all such appropriations. This point is argued persuasively by Arden C. Autry, "Dimensions of Hermeneutics in Pentecostal Focus," *Journal of Pentecostal Theology* 3 (1993), pp. 29–50, where he states "The 'correct' reading serves the 'creative'; and the 'creative' measures itself by the 'correct.' (p. 49). Mark J. Cartledge, an Anglican charismatic, has developed this theme further, using the terms "consistency" and "innovation," in "Empirical Theology: Towards an Evangelical-Charismatic Hermeneutic," *Journal of Pentecostal Theology* 9 (1996), pp. 115–26.

64. Ibid., 31. There may be a slight difference between Fleming's "gospel center" and Dyrness' transcultural scripture. As a practical matter for both, the redemptive story is actualized in a culture when Christians of that culture search the scriptures together.

65. Costas, *Christ Outside the Gate*, p. 16.

66. Padilla, *Mission Between the Times*, p. 93.

67. Fleming, "The Third Horizon," p. 155. Gabriel Fackre makes the same point in *The Christian Story*, 2:250.

68. Newbigin, *The Gospel in a Pluralist Society*, p. 147.

69. Padilla, *Mission Between the Times*, p. 89. See also comments in Fleming, "The Third Horizon," p. 160, and the discussion in Dyrness, *Learning About Theology From the Third World*, pp. 20–22.

70. Millard J. Erickson, *Evangelical Interpretation* (Grand Rapids: Baker, 1993), p. 125.

71. Newbigin, *Truth to Tell*, p. 34. Millard Erickson's comments in this area are perceptive: "We have sometimes proceeded as if our interpretation of a given text is the way it is, the true and perhaps the only way to look at that text. In a postmodern world ... we may discover that what we thought was the full meaning of the text was only the Western, white, middle-class, male interpretation. A truly postmodern hermeneutic will need to be fully global and fully multicultural" (*Evangelical Interpretation*, p. 125).

Chapter 8: The Love of God

1. Thomas F. Tracy, *God, Action, and Embodiment* (Grand Rapids: Eerdmans, 1984).

2. Ibid., p. 3.

3. Ibid., p. 20.

4. Ibid., p. 22.

5. Ibid., p. 3.

6. Ibid., pp. 47–66.

7. Ibid., pp. 92–107.

8. Ibid., p. 98.

9. This is another indication of the indebtedness of rational propositionalism to the categories of modernity. More exactly, what has occurred is the recasting in Cartesian terms of classical theological concepts, many of which have their roots in the Greek philosophical tradition. While not at all against the utilization of philosophical terms, I will argue that their content must be shaped according to special revelation as provided through the biblical narrative.

10. Tracy, *God*, p. 58.

11. Ibid., p. 60.

12. Ibid., pp. 111–18. Tracy examines several alternative ways of describing God as embodied, but finds them all theologically inadequate.

13. Ibid., p. 123.

14. John Wesley, *Explanatory Notes Upon the New Testament* (Grand Rapids: Baker, 1981, reprinted from an undated edition published by the Wesleyan-Methodist Book-Room, London), 1 John 4:8.

15. Colin E. Gunton, *Yesterday & Today: A Study of Continuities in Christology* (Grand Rapids: Eerdmans, 1983).

16. Ibid., p. 72.

17. Ibid., p. 86.

18. Ibid.

19. Ibid., p. 77.

20. Ibid., p. 78. ·

21. Ibid.

22. Ibid., p. 107.

23. Ibid., p. 100.

24. Among the most thorough critiques are Luke Timothy Johnson, *The Real Jesus* (San Francisco: Harper Collins, 1996); Gregory A. Boyd, *Cynic Sage or Son of God?* (Wheaton:Victor, 1995); and Michael J. Wilkins and J. P. Moreland, eds., *Jesus Under Fire* (Grand Rapids: Zondervan, 1994); the last two are written by evangelical scholars. A superb comprehensive survey of the entire range of contemporary scholarship concerning the historical Jesus is Ben Witherington III, *The Jesus Quest: The Third Search for the Jew of Nazareth* (Downers Grove: InterVarsity, 1995). Two earlier evangelical studies should also be noted: N. T. Wright, *Who Was Jesus?* (Grand Rapids: Eerdmans, 1992) and James D. G. Dunn, *The Evidence for Jesus* (Louisville: Westminster/John Knox, 1985).

25. Johnson, *The Real Jesus*, pp. 60–79.

26. Ibid., p. 85.

27. Ibid., p. 140.

28. Ibid., p. 133. But for Johnson the Christian faith does involve historical claims.

29. Ibid., p. 144.

30. Gunton, *Yesterday & Today*, p. 82.

31. Ibid., pp. 81–82. Here Gunton draws upon Dietrich Ritschl, *Memory and Hope: An Inquiry Concerning the Presence of Christ* (New York: Macmillan, 1967). Ralph Del Colle, in "Trinity and Temporality: A Pentecostal/Charismatic Perspective," likewise argues that eternity in scripture seems to mean "time as everlasting rather than timeless" (p. 101). He understands God to experience temporaliyy both through the incarnate Son and the indwelling Spirit which constitute two distinct ways of relating to created reality. See the *Journal of Pentecostal Theology* 8 (April, 1996), pp. 99–113.

32. Ibid., p. 105.

33. Donald G. Bloesch, *God the Almighty* (Downers Grove: InterVarsity, 1995), p. 86.

34. Gunton, *Yesterday & Today*, pp. 117–18. See the entire discussion on pp. 111–19.

35. Ibid., pp. 123–24. See the entire discussion on pp. 119–24. Thomas F. Torrance's position is explained in his *Space, Time & Incarnation* (Oxford: Oxford University Press, 1969).

36. Ibid., p. 125.

37. Ibid., p. 160. See the entire discussion on pp. 139–66.

38. William J. Abraham, *Divine Revelation and the Limits of Historical Criticism*, p. 53.

39. Ibid., p. 56.
40. See the discussion in Gunton, *Yesterday & Today*, pp. 94–96.
41. See the treatment of God's pathos in the prophets in Abraham J. Heschel, *The Prophets* (New York: Harper & Row, 1962), 2 vols.
42. With Jürgen Moltmann, I understand the cross as an event involving the Trinity. The Son dies upon the cross, the Father experiences the death of the Son, and the Spirit who unites in love now also unites in death. Although the *perichoresis* of the three is affirmed, the Father is not on the cross, as in the patripassionist heresy. For Moltmann's position see *The Crucified God* (New York: Harper & Row, 1974).
43. See the discussion of impassibility in Bloesch, *God the Almighty*, pp. 92–95 and Clark H. Pinnock, *et al.*, *The Openness of God* (Downers Grove: InterVarsity, 1994), pp. 118–19. I strongly identify with their carefully nuanced discussions, which avoid at the same time an unfeeling God and the God of process theology.
44. John R. W. Stott, *The Cross of Christ* (Downer's Grove: InterVarsity, 1986), p. 168. Stott's images include propitiation, redemption, justification, and reconciliation, all of which overlap the metaphors discussed by Colin Gunton.
45. Colin E. Gunton, *The Actuality of Atonement*, p. 46.
46. Ibid., p. 47.
47. Ibid., p. 76. Gunton notes that early Christians in some cases viewed "the cross as a defeat which the resurrection turned to victory." He agrees this is true in one sense, but notes as well that Jesus' going to the cross is itself a victory, a theme which John, Paul, and the author of Revelation share (p. 77). Likewise, Stott argues that "the cross was victory won, and the resurrection the victory endorsed, proclaimed, and demonstrated" (*The Cross of Christ*, p. 235). I do not at all disagree that the cross is in itself a victory, but would nonetheless insist that it can be construed as such only because Jesus was raised from the dead. Apart from the resurrection the cross would be a tragedy. Moreover, it is the resurrection which gives the life and death of Jesus its eschatological force: this life is the life of the Kingdom, this Jesus (the one who was crucified) is Lord now and forever.
48. Ibid., p. 77.
49. Ibid., pp. 74–82.
50. Ibid., p. 84.
51. Ibid., pp. 95–96. Gunton here notes an element of truth in the impassibility doctrine. God is not personally harmed by our sin and the atonement is thus not about placating God (p. 96). What is harmed is our relationship to God, one another, and God's creation; the atonement is about restoring and transforming those broken relationships.
52. Ibid., p. 113.
53. Ibid., pp. 118–19.
54. Ibid., p. 125.
55. Ibid., p. 126.
56. Ibid., pp. 62, 83, 138.
57. Stott, *The Cross of Christ*, pp. 123–24. Gunton discusses Anselmic satisfaction as an element of the justice metaphor, as setting right what human sin has disordered, an act of grace in which God does not permit humans to destroy themselves (*The Actuality of Atonement*, pp. 87–93).
58. Ibid., p. 151.

59. Gunton, *The Actuality of Atonement*, p. 165. Gunton notes that as "Jesus is our substitute, it is also right to call him our representative." As representative, Jesus "represents us as man before God in order that we too may participate in a like relationship." (pp. 166–67) Substitution and representation are correlative terms describing the one act of atonement.

60. "Wrath of God" and "love of God" are not equivalent terms, however. Wrath is not in itself a character trait of God, but rather a manifestation of God's holiness and love as God encounters sin. Love is at the very center of God's character. See the helpful discussion in Bloesch, *God the Almighty*, pp. 141–42.

61. Gunton, *The Actuality of Atonement*, p. 164.

62. Ibid., pp. 156–57.

63. Hymn 27 in *A Collection of Hymns for the Use of the People Called Methodists*, Franz Hildebrandt and Oliver A. Beckerlegge, eds. (Oxford: Clarendon Press, 1983), p. 114; Vol. 7 of *The Works of John Wesley*.

Chapter 9: The Power of God

1. The Christian tradition has on the whole not emphasized Spirit Christology, in spite of its clear biblical basis in all four gospels, and especially in Luke-Acts. The reason may well be fear of an adoptionism which denies the divinity of Jesus, a not altogether unwarranted concern given the leanings of some liberal theologies today. However, a Spirit Christology which is trinitarian in nature would be both orthodox and a helpful complement to the more familiar Logos Christology. For examples of Spirit Christologies which are compatible with evangelical orthodoxy see Clark H. Pinnock, *Flame of Love: A Theology of the Holy Spirit* (Downers Grove: InterVarsity, 1996), chapter three; Thomas A. Smail, *Reflected Glory*; and Ralph Del Colle, *Christ and the Spirit* (New York: Oxford University Press, 1994).

2. The work of the Holy Spirit in creation is an often neglected topic in theology. See Clark H. Pinnock's fine discussion in *Flame of Love*, chapter two.

3. I am here endorsing the Wesleyan concept of prevenient grace. Wesley believed the moral conscience was not a natural but a supernatural gift of God, given to all persons. This conscience provided a general sense of right and wrong; to obey it was to respond to the promptings of the Spirit. The purpose, however, was soteriological: it was to prepare the heart for the gospel. See the discussion in Randy L. Maddox, *Responsible Grace*, pp. 87–90.

4. Murray Y. Dempster, "Evangelism, Social Concern, and the Kingdom of God," in Murray Y. Dempster, Byron D. Klaus, and Douglas Peterson, eds., *Called and Empowered: Global Mission in Pentecostal Perspective* (Peabody: Hendrickson, 1991), p. 24.

5. An inaugurated eschatology is compatible with three of the four common evangelical views on the millennium: historic premillennialism, postmillennialism, and amillennialism. It is at odds with dispensational premillennialism, at least as it is traditionally conceived. For insightful analyses of the strengths and weaknesses of each position see Stanley J. Grenz, *The Millennial Maze* (Downers Grove: InterVarsity, 1992) and Millard J. Erickson, *Contemporary Options in Eschatology* (Grand Rapids: Baker, 1977). Proponents of each of the four positions respond to each other in Robert G. Clouse, ed., *The Meaning of the Millennium* (Downers Grove: InterVarsity, 1977).

6. For perceptive discussions on the relationship of Christian community to the Kingdom of God, see Stanley J. Grenz, *Revisioning Evangelical Theology*, chapter 6; and Steven J. Land, *Pentecostal Spirituality*, chapter 3.

7. Rodney Clapp, *Families at the Crossroads* (Downers Grove: InterVarsity, 1993). Some prominent advocates of "pro-family" policies have linked this with a political philosophy that views government activity as intrinsically anti-family and the free market as benign. Scripture however does not endorse any particular political or economic system. Other evangelicals can and do envision public policy which strengthens the family; moreover it can be argued (without embracing socialism) that nothing has been as destructive of the family than an unrestrained capitalism. In addition, some "pro-family" advocates promote an allegedly biblical model of the family that really has more to do with the middle-class families of nineteenth century and mid-twentieth century America. As Clapp shows, there are in fact many biblical and historical models of the family. Scripture does not so much provide a single model as it gives norms which should critique and shape all cultural models.

8. Dempster, "Evangelism, Social Concern, and the Kingdom of God," p. 24. For a thorough discussion of the relationship of evangelism to social concern in light of the Kingdom of God, see Ronald J. Sider, *One-Sided Christianity?* For a full analysis of social ethics from this perspective see Stephen Charles Mott, *Biblical Ethics and Social Change* (New York: Oxford University Press, 1982).

9. Evangelical organizations committed to combatting world hunger include World Vision International and Bread for the World. The best treatment of world hunger by an evangelical is Ronald J. Sider, *Rich Christians in an Age of Hunger*, 3rd ed. (Dallas: Word, 1990).

10. Calvin B. DeWitt, "Take Good Care: Its God's Earth," *Prism* 1:2 (December/January 1994), pp. 8–11. This same issue of *Prism* contains "An Evangelical Declaration on the Care of the Creation" (pp. 12–14), authored by DeWitt, Thomas Oden, Ronald Sider and others. The Christian Environmental Association, the Evangelical Environmental Network, and the AuSable Institute are centers of evangelical environmental activism.

11. In this comprehensive sense Ronald J. Sider calls on evangelicals to be, as the title of his book says, *Completely Pro-Life*.

12. Donald G. Bloesch, *God the Almighty*, p. 135.

13. Marguerite Shuster, *Power, Pathology, Paradox: The Dynamics of Evil and Good* (Grand Rapids: Zondervan, 1987). There are a number of postmodern themes in Shuster's proposal, including an organic and communal understanding of persons and relationship, the social (and indeed spiritual) construction of "reality," and the idea that we indwell the "reality" we create, be it illusory (demonic) or actual (divine). She does however seem to conceive of persons as intellect and will; I prefer the more holistic language of the affections.

14. I am relying on the discussion of Hiebert in Thomas H. McAlpine, *Facing the Powers* (Monrovia: MARC, 1991), pp. 59–68. This book analyzes a range of positions on "principalities and powers" and their implications for mission. Views range from considering the "powers" as social or institutional entities, to understanding them as spiritual agents, to an integration of the spiritual and societal.

15. As Jesus seems to warn the seventy in Luke 10, it is important not to get distracted from ministries of evangelism, compassion, and social concern by a

fascination with the overtly demonic. To do so would serve the purposes of the Evil One as well if not more than our ignoring or disbelieving in spiritual evil.

16. Bloesch, *God the Almighty*, p. 205.

17. This is not to deny that prayers of petition do open us to receive what God gives and prayers of intercession dispose us to become participants in God's mission. It is to insist this is so precisely because they are appeals to God in which, should it be God's will, we are beseeching God to act.

18. William C. Placher, *The Domestication of Transcendence* (Louisville: Westminster/John Knox, 1996), pp. 119–27.

19. Ibid., pp. 71–87.

20. Ibid., pp. 88–107, 146–60.

21. Ibid., pp. 6–7, 9–10. David F. Wells indicates his rejection of this modern identification of transcendence with "distance" and immanence with "nearness" in *God in the Wasteland: The Reality of Truth in a World of Fading Dreams* (Grand Rapids: Eerdmans, 1994), p. 92. I strongly applaud Wells' call for the renewal of our sense of the otherness and reality of a God who is not at our disposal. However, I fear his reaction to cultural accommodation has led to a diminished understanding of the work of the Spirit in the world. Especially problematic in my view is his reduction of God's love to one of a number of expressions of God's holiness, rather than as the governing attribute of the divine character. Our problem in the church today is not that we have overemphasized God's love but that we have domesticated it, failing to appreciate its power, depth, and mystery. It is precisely *because* God is love that God is thoroughly and unalterably opposed to sin. For Wells' discussion, see pp. 133–45.

22. It is a mistake, however, to equate all uses of the term "panentheism" with process theology. Some use the term to indicate a God who is affected by creation, but unlike process theology do not lose a clear ontological distinction between Creator and creation.

23. Clark Pinnock, *et al.*, *The Openness of God* (Downers Grove: InterVarsity, 1994). The *al.* includes Richard Rice, John Sanders, William Hasker, and David Basinger. This position is defended as well in David Basinger, *The Case for Freewill Theism: A Philosophical Assessment* (Downers Grove: InterVarsity, 1996); Richard Rice, *God's Foreknowledge and Man's Free Will* (Minneapolis: Bethany, 1985); David Basinger and Randall Basinger, eds., *Predestination and Free Will* (Downers Grove: InterVarsity, 1986); and Clark H. Pinnock, ed., *The Grace of God, the Will of Man: A Case for Arminianism* (Grand Rapids: Zondervan, 1989). As we shall see, not all who gravitate toward a more interactive view of God and humanity are Arminians. However, for a vigorous defense of classical theism in its Calvinist form, see R. K. McGreger Wright, *No Place for Sovereignty: What's Wrong with Freewill Theism* (Downers Grove: InterVarsity, 1996).

24. Pinnock, *The Openness of God*, p. 108. In endorsing a "social trinity" Pinnock is part of a larger contemporary theological development. Early in the twentieth century, Karl Barth and Karl Rahner initiated a renewal of trinitarian theology in Western Christianity. Their proposals, though creative in their own right, remained in the dominant Western tradition of an Augustinian or psychological model of the Trinity which gives priority to the oneness of God. Later in the century Western theologians such as Wolfhart Pannenberg and Jürgen Moltmann embraced models

more typical of Eastern Orthodoxy, in which priority was given to the three persons. In these models, personhood is understood as constituted by the relationships within the Trinity, and the unity of God is understood by way of a mutual indwelling (or perichoresis) of each person within the others. This dynamic and somewhat communal understanding of the inner life of God has profound implications for what it means for humanity to be created in God's image: it points away from autonomy and toward more relational ideas of personhood. Such a view of the Trinity underlies much of the argument I am advancing in the book.

25. Ibid., p. 111. In a similar manner John Wesley would speak of God's intention to restore the *imago Dei*, understood as a capacity for loving relationship with God and one another. Because love, if it is really love, must be freely given, a creation which is meant by God to realize within itself the love which is in God must necessarily have creatures who themselves possess a measure of freedom.

26. Ibid., p. 115.

27. Richard Rice, *The Openness of God*, p. 38.

28. Pinnock, *The Openness of God*, pp. 118–19. For Pinnock the immutability of God refers to God's unchanging character and faithfulness, but does not mean God is unable to make changes in response to human actions or prayers. Impassibility means God is not subject to involuntary suffering, but not that God cannot be truly affected by the world or choose to experience suffering out of love for humanity. Thus he would agree with the analysis of impassibility in chapter eight.

29. Ibid., p. 113.

30. Bloesch, *God the Almighty*, p. 255.

31. Ibid., p. 258.

32. Ibid., p. 257.

33. Ibid., p. 258.

34. Pinnock, *Flame of Love*, p. 160. This does not mean that Pinnock or Eastern Orthodoxy fail to take sin seriously. The remnant of freedom in humanity does not negate our need "to be made free from sin on every level where we are held captive." (p. 176)

35. Bloesch, *God the Almighty*, p. 101. Thus Bloesch argues that God's power is "the power of his suffering love" (p. 106) and that God's freedom includes the capacity to make "himself vulnerable to pain and suffering." (p. 210)

36. J. C. DeMoor, *Towards a Biblically Theo-logical Method* (Kampen: J. H. Kok, 1980), p. 67.

37. Ibid., p. 71.

38. Ibid., p. 129. Here DeMoor is developing themes in Berkouwer's *The Providence of God* (Grand Rapids: Eerdmans, 1952).

39. Ibid., pp. 263–64. DeMoor here develops themes in Berkouwer's *Man: The Image of God* (Grand Rapids: Eerdmans, 1962). DeMoor finds Berkouwer abandoning the philosophical conceptions of omnipotence, omniscience, etc. for definitions rooted in biblical revelation. Thus Berkouwer takes seriously God's genuine astonishment at the first humans' irrational and unaccountable disobedience (pp. 265–66). This is similar to Pinnock's claim that God knows everything that can be known but has deliberately created a world in which God does not know human decisions in advance. To say God "can be surprised by what his creatures do" does not limit God, but to say God cannot create a world in which God does not know everything in

advance is a clear limitation of God's power. (*The Openness of God*, p. 123). Helmut Thielicke calls the creation of humanity "the risk of God," for by setting over against himself a being to whom he gave freedom and power he risked the possibility that the child would become a competitor," a "rival of the Creator." See *How the World Began* (Philadelphia: Fortress, 1961), p. 60.

40. This is my language. See my discussion of grace in Wesley's theology in Henry H. Knight III, *The Presence of God in the Christian Life*. Randy L. Maddox terms this "responsible grace;" see his *Responsible Grace*.

41. Nancey Murphy, *Beyond Liberalism & Fundamentalism*, p. 144.

42. Ibid., p. 140.

43. Ibid., p. 147. Murphy shows how turn of the century evangelical Augustus H. Strong anticipates just such a postmodern position (pp. 74–76, 153).

44. William J. Abraham, *Divine Revelation and the Limits of Historical Criticism*, p. 161. This would be a form of "epistemological imperialism." See the comment of Luke Johnson cited in chapter eight.

45. Ibid.

46. Charles H. Kraft, *Christianity With Power* (Ann Arbor: Servant, 1989), pp. 11–22.

47. Ibid., pp. 23–24.

48. Ibid., p. 28.

49. Ibid., p. 39.

50. Ibid., p. 45.

51. Ibid., p. 40.

52. Ibid., p. 101.

53. Ibid., p. 88.

54. Ibid., p. 89.

55. Ibid.

56. Ibid., pp. 106–107.

57. Ibid., pp. 114–15.

58. I refer here to the problem of theodicy. Simply put, it asks if God is both good and omnipotent, why is there evil and suffering? In my view all purported solutions to the problem ultimately fail, although they may well provide some insight. But though the problem cannot be solved, it has been addressed by God in the cross of Jesus Christ. We do not know in any complete and satisfactory way why there is so much suffering in the world, but we do know that God has entered into our suffering. Whatever the explanation, God is not aloof from our experience of suffering and has loved us even unto death.

59. Henry H. Knight III, "God's Faithfulness and God's Freedom: A Comparison of Contemporary Theologies of Healing," *Journal of Pentecostal Theology* 2 (April, 1993), pp. 65–89.

60. The writings of Kenneth Hagin Sr. (as well as others in the "word of faith" movement like Kenneth Copeland) consist of numerous small books; thus far I know of no single comprehensive treatment by a participant. Thus, the overall summaries have been made by critics. For a sympathetic yet critical analysis see Bruce Barron, *The Health and Wealth Gospel* (Downers Grove: InterVarsity, 1987). A more negative critique is D. R. McConnell, *A Different Gospel* (Peabody: Hendrickson, 1988). A basic presentation of Sanford's views is found in Agnes Sanford, *The Healing Light*, rev. ed., (Plainfield: Logos, 1972). For a more general defense of this approach see William

DeArteaga, *Quenching the Spirit.*

Among the more important distinctions between Hagin and Sanford is that the former emphasizes the necessity of faith in the recipient of healing while the latter calls for faith in the one who prays for the healing of others. Both understand faith as confidence that God will heal. Another difference is that the "word of faith" movement understands God to promise prosperity as well as healing.

61. Sanford, *The Healing Light*, p. 94.

62. See Kathryn Kuhlman, with Jamie Buckingham, *A Glimpse Into Glory* (South Plainfield: Bridge, 1983) and Charles Farah Jr., *From the Pinnacle of the Temple* (Plainfield: Logos, n.d.)

63. Farah, *From the Pinnacle of the Temple*, p. 75.

64. Ibid. Farah believes we sometimes have a "word" from God as to what God's will is in a particular circumstance. In the case of a severe illness, for example, this word could either direct prayer for healing or for relinquishment to death and ultimate healing. In other instances, though, there is no word from God.

65. See Francis MacNutt, *Healing*, rev. ed. (Altamonte Springs: Creation House, 1988) and *The Power to Heal* (Notre Dame: Ave Maria, 1977); John Wimber, with Kevin Springer, *Power Healing* (San Francisco: Harper & Row, 1986); and Ken Blue, *Authority to Heal* (Downers Grove: InterVarsity, 1987). MacNutt's *Healing* is an especially careful and insightful treatment. For a general discussion of healing, with chapters on MacNutt and Wimber, see Robert Dickinson, *God Does Heal Today* (Carlisle: Paternoster, 1995).

66. An excellent discussion of Wesley's view of healing, including his own practice of both prayer and medicine, can be found in E. Brooks Holifield, *Health and Medicine in the Methodist Tradition* (New York: Crossroad, 1986), pp. 8–38.

67. For an analysis of "disciplined discernment" in the Christian community from a Pentecostal perspective, see Steven J. Land, *Pentecostal Spirituality*, pp. 161–64.

68. Thomas A. Smail, *Reflected Glory*, p. 15.

Chapter 10: The People of God

1. Steven J. Land also sees a "theo-logical" connection between these three "blessings." See *Pentecostal Spirituality*, pp. 125–31. John Wesley emphasized pardon (or justification) and holiness (or sanctification, culminating in Christian perfection), with the former the precondition of the latter. For him they were both "instantaneous" and "gradual" in the Christian life. The holiness movement saw them as two instantaneous acts of grace, and began to identify the second blessing of holiness with the baptism of the Holy Spirit. This raised the issue of how power was related to holiness; typically this was solved by understanding purity and power as the two components of holiness. Pentecostals however believed power to be an instantaneous act of grace in its own right, subsequent to the other two, and identified with the baptism of the Holy Spirit. My purpose is not to address these issues of soteriological order and subsequence but to examine the inner logic of those three loci of salvation.

2. L. Gregory Jones, *Embodying Forgiveness: A Theological Analysis* (Grand Rapids: Eerdmans, 1995), p. 5. I shall be drawing on the careful reflections in this book throughout this section.

3. Colin E. Gunton, *The Actuality of Atonement*, p. 188.

4. Jones, *Embodying Forgiveness*, pp. 39–53. Jones does not want to deny that inner healing can and does result from forgiving others. This is not the point of forgiveness, however, but one of its natural and necessary effects. The point remains the healing of broken relationships and an undertaking to live life anew under the reign of God.

5. Ibid., p. 72; see the full discussion on pp. 71–83.

6. Ibid., p. 97.

7. Gunton, *The Actuality of Atonement*, p. 191.

8. See the discussion in Jones, *Embodying Forgiveness*, pp. 102–113.

9. Within the eighteenth century awakening in England, John Wesley found antinomianism to be the greatest danger to the gospel. In its more extreme form antinomianism led to the abandonment of any moral concern; a more moderate tendency was to define salvation as forgiveness so that one might go to heaven when one died rather than as a transformed life and relationships in the present. He insisted again and again that to preach forgiveness of sins apart from holiness of heart and life was detrimental if not fatal to the Christian life.

This tendency to truncate the fullness of justification has its roots in medieval Christianity, and persisted despite periodic Roman Catholic and Protestant attempts at renewal. The nineteenth-century holiness movement had sound theological and spiritual instincts when it insisted that sanctification and not justification was the point of salvation. However, the tendency of some holiness proponents to speak of persons as "merely justified" (and therefore as "carnal Christians") shows just how much a debased understanding of forgiveness was accepted as normative on all sides. Wesley vehemently opposed any language which diminished the significance of justification. For a discussion of Wesley's response to antinomianism, see Henry H. Knight III, *The Presence of God in the Christian Life*, pp. 50–78.

10. Legalism (along with formalism) was for Wesley the chief danger to the Christian life coming from outside the evangelical awakening. He was a persistent defender of Protestant views on original sin and the atonement against mystical and deist critics.

11. The presentation here may seem at variance from that of John Wesley, who understands repentance as normally prior to justification. Several points should be noted concerning Wesley's understanding. First, repentance is in response to and enabled by convincing grace—it is a work of the Holy Spirit which puts one into an active relationship with God. Second, he understands repentance as most centrally self-knowledge before God, in which we not only know that we are sinners but come to see something of the particular patterning of sin in our lives. Thus repentance is a time of graced struggle with these patterns of behavior. It is something like what happened to the prodigal son in the far country. He came to his senses and returned to the Father, seeking to be a servant. With the experience of the Father's love he was again given the status of child, a status he had all along in the Father's heart. This leads to the third point: to engage in repentance is already to be forgiven objectively; justification for Wesley is more an experience of forgiveness which enables us to begin a new life of love. The person under conviction is thus seeking experiential confirmation of and transformation by the gospel he or she has received. Finally, the result of experienced forgiveness for Wesley is repentance—the

ongoing repentance of believers—which is essential to growth in sanctification. In all of this, repentance is seen by Wesley as a response to God's gracious initiative.

12. Gunton, *The Actuality of Atonement*, p. 190.

13. Although this understanding of worship and community is deeply rooted in the Christian tradition, it at the same time is congruent with the views of post-critics like Wittgenstein, MacIntyre, and Polanyi. The community is both shaped by the narrative and provides practices which enable participants to indwell the narrative. The narrative provides the language and vision which enable people to see themselves and the world truthfully. However, more than this must be said, and that "more" has to do with the presence and power of the Holy Spirit.

14. For a discussion of this dynamic in classes and bands see Knight, *The Presence of God in the Christian Life*, pp. 95–116. A thorough analysis of the nature and purpose of the class meetings is found in David Lowes Watson, *The Early Methodist Class Meetings* (Nashville: Discipleship Resources, 1985). Wesley was drawing upon a broader tradition. The practice of forgiveness and accountable discipleship characterized not only Anabaptist and Pietist communities but monastic communities going back to the fourth century. Wesley believed forgiveness was a practice of New Testament Christianity (James 5:16) and especially sought to embody this in the bands.

15. Land, *Pentecostal Spirituality*, p. 126.

16. Jones, *Embodying Forgiveness*, p. 61.

17. Ibid., pp. 210–19. A third kind of modern analysis of forgiveness is based on allegedly universal theories of morality developed independent of the Christian tradition.

18. "Sinners, Turn: Why Will You Die." Hymn 7 in *A Collection of Hymns for the Use of the People Called Methodists*, Hildebrandt and Beckerlegge, eds.

19. Jonathan Edwards, *A Treatise on Religious Affections* (Grand Rapids: Baker, 1982), p. 11.

20. For an analysis of how Wesley abridges Edwards' *Treatise* and uses the language of affections, see Clapper, *John Wesley on the Affections*. For a comparison of Wesley and Edwards, see Steele, *"Gracious Affections" and "True Virtue" According to Jonathan Edwards and John Wesley*.

21. Don E. Saliers, *The Soul in Paraphrase: Prayer and the Religious Affections* (New York: Seabury, 1980).

22. Robert C. Roberts, *Spirituality and Human Emotion* (Grand Rapids: Eerdmans, 1982).

23. Saliers, *The Soul in Paraphrase*, p. 11.

24. Maddox, *Responsible Grace*, p. 69.

25. Saliers, *The Soul in Paraphrase*, p. 11.

26. Robert C. Roberts, *The Strengths of a Christian* (Philadelphia: Westminster, 1984), p. 23.

27. For a discussion of the patristic understanding of the passions, see Roberta C. Bondi, *To Love as God Loves* (Philadelphia: Fortress, 1987).

28. Roberts, *Spirituality and Human Emotion*, pp. 55–56.

29. Land, *Pentecostal Spirituality*, especially chapter three.

30. Roberts, *Spirituality and Human Emotion*, p. 15.

31. For an analysis of the relation of narrative to affections which discusses in brief a number of the themes of this book, see Henry H. Knight III, "True Affections: Biblical Narrative and Evangelical Spirituality" in Phillips and Okholm, *The Nature of Confession*, pp. 193–200. See also the insightful essay by Richard B. Steele, "Narrative Theology and the Religious Affections" in Stanley Hauerwas, Nancey Murphy & Mark Nation, eds., *Theology Without Foundations: Religious Practice & the Future of Theological Truth* (Nashville: Abingdon, 1994), pp. 163–79.

32. Roberts, *The Strengths of a Christian*, p. 25. Roberts views compassion as both an emotion and a style.

33. Jones, *Embodying Forgiveness*, p. 227.

34. L. Gregory Jones emphasizes the priority of grace in enabling and requiring "a life of virtuous discipleship" in *Transformed Judgment: Toward a Trinitarian Account of the Moral Life* (Notre Dame: University of Notre Dame Press, 1990), p. 111. Such a life involves being in a relationship which he calls friendship with God. The difference in his account and my own is how I conceive of the affections.

35. Roberts, *The Strengths of a Christian*, p. 27.

36. Saliers, *The Soul in Paraphrase*, p. 18.

37. Roberts, *Spirituality and Human Emotion*, p. 21.

38. Richard J. Foster, *Celebration of Discipline: The Path to Spiritual Growth* (New York: Harper & Row, 1978); Dallas Willard, *The Spirit of the Disciplines: Understanding How God Changes Lives* (San Francisco: Harper & Row, 1988); James Earl Massey, *Spiritual Disciplines* (Grand Rapids: Zondervan, 1985); and M. Robert Mulholland, Jr., *Shaped by the Word: The Power of Scripture in Spiritual Formation* (Nashville: The Upper Room, 1985). See also James Houston, *The Transforming Friendship: A Guide to Prayer* (Oxford: Lion Publishing, 1989).

39. For a study of the means of grace in the context of Wesley's theology and practice, see Knight, *The Presence of God in the Christian Life*; a briefer discussion is in Maddox, *Responsible Grace*, chapter eight. A complete list of Wesley's means of grace is found in Knight, p. 5.

40. See the discussion of formalism in Knight, *The Presence of God in the Christian Life*, pp. 16–35.

41. Foster, *Celebration of Discipline*, p. 6. Similarly M. Robert Mulholland, Jr., says that the shaping of our lives by the Word of God "is not something we do by our own efforts ... ; it is what God does in us when we are in a loving, receptive, responsive *relationship* with God." (*Shaped by the Word*, p. 91).

42. Willard, *The Spirit of the Disciplines*, pp. 40–42, 75–93.

43. Land, *Pentecostal Spirituality*, pp. 113–15.

44. For an excellent survey of the various positions, see John Sanders, *No Other Name* (Grand Rapids: Eerdmans, 1992). Proponents of various positions debate one another in Dennis Okholm and Timothy Phillips, ed., *More Than One Way?* (Grand Rapids: Zondervan, 1996) and John Sanders, ed., *What About Those Who Have Never Heard?* (Downers Grove: InterVarsity, 1995).

45. Thus I identify with much of Clark H. Pinnock's inclusivist argument in *A Wideness in God's Mercy* (Grand Rapids: Zondervan, 1992). But for an exclusivist view, see Ronald H. Nash, *Is Jesus the Only Savior?* (Grand Rapids: Zondervan, 1994). I would agree that Jesus is the only savior (as would Pinnock) but draw different

conclusions from this than does Nash. See also Millard J. Erickson, *How Shall They Be Saved? The Destiny of Those Who Do Not Hear of Jesus* (Grand Rapids: Baker, 1996).

46. That world religions posit differing salvific ends is argued in S. Mark Heim, *Salvations: Truth and Difference in Religion* (Maryknoll: Orbis, 1995). Heim seeks to find a way between "exclusivist" and "pluralist" options. For evangelical analysis and critique of pluralism, see Alister E. McGrath, *A Passion for Truth*, chapter 5; and Lesslie Newbigin, *The Gospel in a Pluralist Society*, chapter 14.

47. There have been a number of studies of spiritual gifts (*charismata*), mostly written for wide readership. Among the best are Charles V. Bryant, *Rediscovering Our Spiritual Gifts* (Nashville: The Upper Room, 1991) and Kenneth Cain Kinghorn, *Gifts of the Spirit* (Nashville: Abingdon, 1976). Bryant discusses over thirty spiritual gifts. Occasionally Bryant and Kinghorn differ in their descriptions of gifts; compare for example their discussion of pastor/shepherd. Other books on the gifts of the Spirit from a variety of perspectives include C. Peter Wagner, *Your Spiritual Gifts Can Help Your Church Grow* (Ventura.: Regal, 1979); John Koenig, *Charismata: God's Gifts for God's People* (Philadelphia: Westminster, 1978); David Pytches, *Spiritual Gifts in the Local Church* (Minneapolis: Bethany House, 1985); and Donald Hohensee and Allen Odell, *Your Spiritual Gifts* (Wheaton.: Victor, 1992).

48. Kinghorn, *Gifts of the Spirit*, pp. 36–37.

49. Juan Sepúlveda, "Reflections on the Pentecostal Contribution to the Mission of the Church in Latin America," *Journal of Pentecostal Theology* 1 (October, 1992), pp. 102–103.

50. Ibid., p. 103.

51. The recovery of this insight has led a number of writers to see ordained ministry as detrimental to the ministry of the church, in effect establishing two categories of Christians: those who minister (the ordained and/or leaders) and the recipients of that ministry (the members). For a perspective that sharply reduces the role of ordained ministry in order to emphasize the ministry of all Christians, see Greg Ogden, *The New Reformation: Returning the Ministry to the People of God* (Grand Rapids: Zondervan, 1990); for a defense of ordained or "representative ministry" as part of the overall ministry of God's people, see Thomas C. Oden, *Pastoral Theology* (San Francisco: Harper & Row, 1983). See also Pinnock's discussion of office and charism in *Flame of Love*, pp. 140–141.

52. Pinnock, *Flame of Love*, p. 141.

53. Land, *Pentecostal Spirituality*, p. 128. See the entire discussion on pp. 123–31. Although the insistence by early Pentecostals that power rests upon the sanctified life was presented in the form of a "three-blessing" schema, as a theological principle it is very Wesleyan. On this, see Henry H. Knight III, "From Aldersgate to Azusa: Wesley and the Renewal of Pentecostal Spirituality," *Journal of Pentecostal Theology* 8 (1996), pp. 82–98. For Wesley's views on the charismatic gifts see Howard A. Snyder (with Daniel V. Runyon), *The Divided Flame: Wesleyans and the Charismatic Renewal* (Grand Rapids: Zondervan, 1986); and Maddox, *Responsible Grace*, pp. 133–36.

54. Pinnock, *Flame of Love*, p. 142.

55. Ibid., p. 145.

56. Ibid., p. 142. Rodney Clapp argues that the church should be a distinctive, sanctified and subversive culture in *A Peculiar People: The Church as Culture in a Post-Christian Society* (Downers Grove: InterVarsity, 1996).

57. Miroslav Volf, *Exclusion and Embrace: A Theological Exploration of Identity, Otherness, and Reconciliation* (Nashville: Abingdon, 1996), pp. 74–75.

58. Ibid., p. 36.

59. Vinay Samuel, "Evangelicals and Racism: The Lausanne II Press Conference," *Transformation* (January, 1990), p. 29.

60. Mark Noll, *One Nation Under God? Christian Faith & Political Action in America* (San Francisco: Harper & Row, 1988). Noll not only challenges the myth of a "Christian America" but the equally mistaken myth of an America untouched by Christian influence and biblical ways of thinking. More importantly, he draws lessons from history about the pitfalls and possibilities of Christian political involvement.

61. On racism and reconciliation in Pentecostalism, see the Roundtable Discussion in *Pneuma* 18:1 (Spring, 1996), pp. 113–40.

62. The Promise Keepers movement has been controversial in some circles because some spokespersons use complementarian rather than egalitarian language concerning the relations between husband and wife and because it necessarily excludes female clergy from its meetings. However, the movement itself has been welcomed by large numbers of men and women who tend to focus on the good it has accomplished, particularly as it undermines cultural expectations that the male sphere of interest and activity lies outside the home. The integrity of its commitment against racism has not been questioned. For a range of evangelical feminist assessments of Promise Keepers which are affirming yet critical, see *Priscilla Papers* 11:2 (Spring, 1997)

63. On Hispanic evangelicalism see Manuel Ortiz, *The Hispanic Challenge* (Downers Grove: InterVarsity, 1993) and Eldin Villafañe, *The Liberating Spirit: Toward an Hispanic American Pentecostal Social Ethic* (Grand Rapids: Eerdmans, 1993).

64. On this see John M. Perkins, *Beyond Charity: The Call to Christian Community Development* (Grand Rapids: Baker, 1993) and John M. Perkins, ed., *Restoring At-Risk Communities* (Grand Rapids: Baker, 1995). Stories of some of these churches and ministries in America can be found in John Perkins, with Jo Kadlecek, *Resurrecting Hope* (Ventura: Regal, 1995); on a global scale see Ronald J. Sider, *Cup of Water, Bread of Life* (Grand Rapids: Zondervan, 1994).

65. Spencer Perkins and Chris Rice, *More Than Equals: Racial Healing for the Sake of the Gospel* (Downers Grove: InterVarsity, 1993); Raleigh Washington and Glen Kehrein, *Breaking Down Walls: A Model for Reconciliation in an Age of Racial Strife* (Chicago: Moody, 1993).

66. Perkins and Rice, *More Than Equals*, p. 66.

67. I am indebted to my colleagues Tex Sample and Derrel Watkins for in different ways showing me how compassion is insufficient if it does not take account of how persons live—their concrete practices. Sample in this regard has pioneered in the study of blue collar practices.

68. Volf, *Exclusion and Embrace*, p. 80.

69. Jones, *Embodying Forgiveness*, p. 263.

70. Richard J. Mouw, *Uncommon Decency: Christian Civility in an Uncivil World* (Downers Grove: InterVarsity, 1992).

71. Newbigin, *The Gospel in a Pluralist Society*, p. 227.